In Scripture

PRAISE FOR *IN SCRIPTURE*

"Lori Hope Lefkovitz's *In Scripture* is a cutting-edge exploration of the Hebrew Bible as a foundational text, that is, literature that has influenced our very being, our identity. This groundbreaking book will change how you read Bible stories, relate to Biblical characters, and it will shake up how you think of your own body, gender, and sexuality in light of Biblical texts." —**Lewis Aron**, director of the New York University postdoctoral program in psychotherapy and psychoanalysis; author of *A Meeting of Minds*

"This wonderful book is challenging in the best ways: it challenges conventional notions about the Bible, gender, sexuality, and tradition. Even better, it challenges each of us to read the foundational texts of our culture more deeply and to be open to new readings and to the rethinking of our own selves that these readings will prompt. This book is also sheer pleasure, a delectable treat for those who love words; Lefkovitz is a word weaver of the highest order." —**Adele Reinhartz**, University of Ottawa

"*In Scripture* challenges everything we thought we knew about the Bible, disrupting assumptions about gender and selfhood, destabilizing our wholesome and sanitized readings of the familiar narratives. Lori Hope Lefkovitz's transgressive, reconstructive, and poetic reading renders scripture newly sacred." —**Vanessa L. Ochs**, University of Virginia

"Without any loss of scholarly rigor, Lori Hope Lefkovitz moves seamlessly from theory to folk wisdom, from humor to wonderfully imaginative and cogent readings of major texts. *In Scripture* illuminates crucial issues with remarkable subtlety and clarity." —**Ronald A. Sharp**, Vassar College

In Scripture

The First Stories
of Jewish Sexual Identities

Lori Hope Lefkovitz

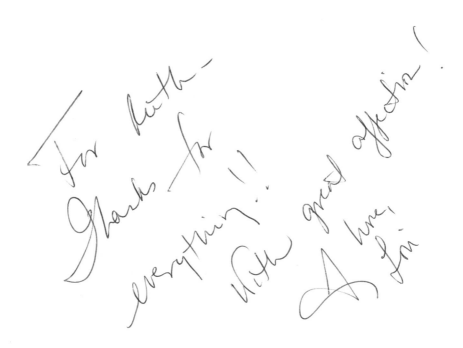

ROWMAN & LITTLEFIELD PUBLISHERS, INC.
Lanham • Boulder • New York • Toronto • Plymouth, UK

Published by Rowman & Littlefield Publishers, Inc.
A wholly owned subsidiary of The Rowman & Littlefield Publishing Group, Inc.
4501 Forbes Boulevard, Suite 200, Lanham, Maryland 20706
http://www.rowmanlittlefield.com

Estover Road, Plymouth PL6 7PY, United Kingdom

British Library Cataloguing in Publication Information Available

Library of Congress Cataloging-in-Publication Data

Lefkovitz, Lori Hope, 1956-
  In Scripture : the first stories of Jewish sexual identities / Lori Hope Lefkovitz.
    p. cm.
  Includes bibliographical references and index.
  ISBN 978-0-7425-4704-9 (cloth : alk. paper)—ISBN 978-1-4422-0306-8
(electronic)
  1. Gender identity in the Bible. 2. Masculinity in the Bible. 3. Femininity in the Bible. 4. Sex in the Bible. 5. Bible. O.T.—Criticism, interpretation, etc. I. Title.
  BS1199.G36L44 2010
  221.8'3053—dc22
                                                              2009040590

∞™ The paper used in this publication meets the minimum requirements of American National Standard for Information Sciences—Permanence of Paper for Printed Library Materials, ANSI/NISO Z39.48-1992.

Printed in the United States of America

For Leonard David Gordon
Forever

Contents

Acknowledgments

I have been presenting versions of the readings in this book for a long time in various contexts: to students and faculty at the Reconstructionist Rabbinical College (RRC) and Kenyon College, to supporters of Kolot—the Center for Jewish Women's and Gender Studies at RRC; and in other adult education settings, at academic conferences and universities, and over scholar-in-residence weekends in the Jewish community. I want to first of all thank these audiences and the students and colleagues whose energetic responses have been sustaining and whose challenging questions have been clarifying.

I am grateful to generous friends and colleagues, some of whom have had limited relationship to this manuscript, others of whom got close enough to the prose to suggest, variously, that I should tighten up or loosen up. My thanks first of all for the valuable time and attention of trusted critical readers: Julia Epstein, Jan Goldman, Adele Reinhartz, and Ronald Sharp, and for all manner of helpful conversation over the years to Rebecca Alpert, Dan Ehrenkrantz, Merle Feld, Ellen Frankel, Joel Hecker, Kathryn Hellerstein, Lewis Hyde, David Kraemer, Susan Kraemer, Laura Levitt, Mitch Marcus, Dev Noily, Vanessa Ochs, Alicia Ostriker, Michelle Reimer, Leah Steinberg, Betsy Teutsch, Patricia Vigderman, Ilene Wasserman, Paul Wolpe, and Noam Zion. The faculty community at RRC, unusual for its high level of engagement in one another's research, which we share formally and informally, has offered exemplary collegiality. Jacob Staub and Tamar Kamionkowski, the academic deans under whom I have served, encouraged this work and shared bibliography. More materially, an RRC William Fern faculty development grant supported the preparation of the manuscript, including provision for Alexis Braverman's valuable, intelligent, and cheerful assistance.

I am grateful for a Fulbright Professorship at the Hebrew University of Jerusalem during a sabbatical leave in 2003–2004, where I benefited from the hospitality of the English department under Shira Wolosky and the American studies department under Avihu Zakai, and the special friendship of Emily Budick. Alice Shalvi, my teacher and friend, graciously hosted a lecture for the faculty of the Schechter Institute, and Guy Miron, Ilana Pardes, George Savran, Linda Zisquit, and Avivah Gottlieb Zornberg were also generous colleagues. I benefited as well from the lively exchanges afforded by an associate fellowship at the Center for Advanced Judaic Studies at the University of Pennsylvania in 2004–2005 and from participation in conversations about Judaism and postmodernism hosted by Laurence Silberstein of the Berman Center at Lehigh University. Particular thanks to Ilana Blumberg, Aryeh Cohen, Robin Goldberg, and Catherine Keller who responded formally, and helpfully, to drafts of the third chapter when I presented stages of that work to the feminist research groups under Ma'yan's auspices in New York and AJCongress' auspices in Los Angeles.

I am grateful to the membership of Minyan Dorshei Derekh of the Germantown Jewish Centre for our lively weekly Torah discussions, and as a relatively new member of the Jewish feminist collective *B'not Esh*, I also want to acknowledge the privilege of being in the company of women from whose efforts my thinking has long benefited. David Sachs generously mentored me when I was a fellow at the Philadelphia Association for Psychoanalysis a decade ago, and I remain sensible to his influence and the power of his ideas. Robert Scholes, also free of direct connection to this project, was my most formative teacher, and my gratitude firmly endures. Sarah Stanton at Rowman & Littlefield has been a responsive and patient editor.

As director of Kolot, I have been privileged to work with other organizations that bring feminist learning to the Jewish community, and I thank the members of the Philadelphia Jewish Feminist Scholars Circle, as well as Eve Landau, Jill Hammer, and Rona Shapiro then of Ma'yan, Gail Reimer of the Jewish Women's Archive, Susan Weidman Schneider of *Lilith* Magazine, and Shulamit Reinharz of Brandeis University for their collaborative friendships. I am grateful to the many people who have invested in Kolot's mission to support scholarship in the field of Gender and Judaism, including Howard and Maureen Blitman, Leona Brochin, Sue Fishlowitz, Jan Goldman, David Roberts, and Margot Stein, who have been especially dedicated. Special thanks to Sally Gottesman and her family for endowing the chair that I hold. Ruth Heiges has been capable, patient, versatile, and tireless in her administration of Kolot, and

Susan Berman, Barbara Lissy, and Nancy Wimmer, partners in Kolot's development, are among those who, with Dayle Friedman, have made daily life in the office a pleasure. Most of all, Juliet Spitzer, host to learning occasions over the years, has enabled this work both through her close personal friendship, and with Phil Wachs, through continuous and sustaining support of Kolot.

Since the recent deaths of my parents, Rudy and Lola Lefkovitz, I have become aware of the extent to which my performances had been for them. Although these words echo in the hollow of their absence, I acknowledge here the incalculable contribution of their love and pride. I cherish their best gift: my lifelong confidante and devoted sister, Marcy Lefkovitz, who partners with Steven Saltzman in building such legacy as is ours, most impressively in my beloved nieces, Silvie, Charlotte, and Abigail. Janet Gordon, Sharon Gordon and Robert Dworkin have also provided the reliable emotional sustenance of close, dear family, the best benefits of long friendship, and the blessings of Lili and Jordan.

Leonard Gordon, to whom this book is dedicated, spouse for more than thirty years, has read more articulations of each chapter of this book than I would wish to admit. Everything that is the least bit worthy to which I may ever lay claim has been enabled by his efforts and improved by the gifts of his attention and keen intelligence. The perfect fruits of our partnership are Ronya Heleni and Samara Esther, to whom I am grateful—every minute and eternally—for charming my life. They have given me an infinite investment in the future and faith in its promise.

* * *

Parts of chapters of this book have been published elsewhere, in most cases considerably revised for this book, and are reprinted with permission. I acknowledge the places of their original publication: Chapter 1: "Creating the World: Structuralism and Semiotics," in *Contemporary Literary Theory*, edited by G. Douglas Atkins and Laura P. Morrow (Univ. of Massachusetts Press, 1989); "Eve in the Semiotic Garden," *The Reconstructionist*, fall 1996; Chapter 2: "Eavesdropping on Angels and Laughing at God: Theorizing a Subversive Matriarchy" in *Gender and Judaism* ed. T. M. Rudavsky (NYU Press, 1995); and "Hannah's Prayer and Reconstructionist Principles," *Reconstructionism Today* (fall 2002); Chapter 3: "Passing as a Man: Narratives of Jewish Gender Performance," in *Narrative* (January 2002) and "You Are Who You Aren't: Closets, Cabinets, and Jewish Identities," *The Reconstructionist* (fall 2001); Chapter 4: "Leah Behind the Veil: The Divided Matriarchy in Bible, Midrash, Dickens, Freud, and Woody Allen," *Hebrew University Studies in Literature and the Arts* (vol. 18, 1990) revised and reprinted in *Sister To Sister*, ed. Patricia Foster (Doubleday, 1995); Chapter 5: "The Story of Joseph: Myths of Jewish Masculinity," in

Changing: Men Issues in Gender, Sex and Politics (summer, 1987), revised as "Coats and Tales: Joseph Stories and Jewish Masculinity," in *A Mensch Among Men: Explorations in Jewish Masculinity*, ed. Harry Brod (Crossing Press, 1988); and "Delicate Beauty Goes Out: *Adam Bede's* Transgressive Heroines," in *Kenyon Review* (summer, 1987); rpt. *Nineteenth-Century Literary Criticism* (NCLC-89) ed. S. Dewsbury (The Gale Group, 2000); Chapter 6: "Miriam: A Reconstruction" *The Women's Passover Companion*, ed. Sharon Cohen Anisfeld, Tara Mohr, and Catherine Spector (Jewish Lights, 2003); Chapter 8: "Balak," *Torah Queeries* ed. Gregg Drinkwater, Joshua Lesser, and David Schneer; the introduction to my edited collection, *Textual Bodies: Changing Boundaries of Literary Representation*, SUNY Press, 1997; and Chapter 9: "Moving On: Yizkor and Life Lessons from the Book of Ruth," *Lilith Magazine* (summer, 2003).

Introduction

I was taught that we read the great books of our tradition not so much to assimilate what they say as to get them out of our system.[1] For example, our culture is saturated with images from, say, the Garden of Eden and *The Odyssey*: the forbidden fruit sometimes specified as an apple; the serpent rendered and reimagined in countless paintings; the Cyclops, a cartoon lumbering in our collective imagination along with poignant variations of Penelope weaving and a heroic sailor taking a journey that somehow is a metaphor for life. Assimilated into our bodies as palimpsest and collage, our foundation texts fill us with multiple, competing, vague, and vivid details. Reading the original stories has a consolidating effect on this internal textual swirl, bringing to consciousness a relatively coherent narrative, one that is susceptible to scrutiny, critique, and wonder. In this sense, reading the classics is a therapeutic activity, drawing sense from the disparate cultural materials of the reader's unconscious.

Reading these texts, we might be surprised by what is missing. For example, many Jewish readers of the Bible learned a legend in childhood about Abraham smashing his father's idols and are surprised to discover the story's absence from the Bible itself. Or we may impose later renderings unthinkingly, imaginatively translating the unspecified fruit into an apple or "the side of Adam" from which Eve is taken into the more familiar rib. Growing up within a culture, textual histories are forever being absorbed and revised, and so, we read texts not so much to put them in, but rather to get them out of our system. This paradoxical idea has helped me appreciate that foundation stories play a significant role in the formation of self.

1

I was also taught that the Bible is both old and young. It is young because it is closer to the beginning of things than we are—an artifact from a younger world. And it is old because it has been in the world a long time. On account of this second paradox about foundation texts—their relative freshness, as yet innocent of the texts of subsequent generations, on the one hand, and on the other hand, aged, dusty, and papered over by having lived so long in the world of ideas—I imagine the Bible as having a childlike and ancient face all at once. The two paradoxes taken together—first, that we read foundation texts less to take them in than to get them out of our system, and second, that foundation texts are at once young and old—suggest that there is a reciprocal self-formation at work in our relation to the texts that imaginatively define our beginnings.

What I am calling foundation stories have been "making" each of us since we were born, and they have been making us collectively since well before any one of us entered the world. Yet, we are constantly remaking foundation texts in our own image. Stories of (and from) our beginning insist that we are who we are because of how we began, but we necessarily read the beginning from the perspective of where we have come. Sophocles does not know Freud. But even if we reject Freud's interpretations, we cannot read about Oedipus Rex innocent of a therapeutic model of self-discovery. Irrespective of how much of Freud we have read, we will see self-deception about deep fears and wishes, primal scenes, and symbolic castration for sexual crimes. Freud's language governs our reading of Sophocles' Oedipus plays. *Oedipus*, the "Oedipus complex," and oedipal conflict are mutually created.

The Hebrew Bible has been conventionally read as the beginning of one branch of the Western textual tradition. The special rhetorical importance of any beginning derives from its power to limit the possibilities for what can follow. What we call the beginning sets the direction, and the designated end is the place from which one interprets what the journey has meant.[2] Before the beginning, anything is seemingly possible. Every speaker and writer knows that silence or a blank page is full with intimidating potential. But how the silence is broken establishes expectations for what will follow, and with each step in some direction, the possibilities for where we may go next are predicated on where we have been. In the beginning, the wealth of potential, a meaningless void, yields itself up, simultaneously, to form and meaning. Because what we designate as beginnings have this predictive importance, culture inevitably tries to go back on them, to rewrite them, to re-create the start in conformity with each new, hoped-for future. Since the biblical account of creation, there have been retellings, interpolations, interpretations, commentaries, drawings, paintings, sculptures, and advertisements that shroud the text in veils of revision. As layers accrue, it becomes difficult to read the beginning as it once was, but there is, finally, no going back on the beginning. Every backtracking acquires its significance in relation to what has already been said.

In Scripture offers interpretations of selected biblical narratives, moving from Genesis to the book of Ruth. Exercises in the application of gender theory, these readings approach the Bible's stories as foundation texts in the development of sexual identities as we know them. Because the Hebrew Bible's mythological origin stories of the Jews rest on singularly influential origin stories of "man" and "woman" and "matriarchy" and "patriarchy" (the grounding terms of masculinity and femininity), the overlapping Western and Jewish interpretive traditions have, over time, marked embodied humanity and the body's desires with some specifically Jewish ethnic shadings. I am claiming that a shifting topography of sexes, masculinities, femininities, and other cultural distinctions related to embodied sexuality have visibly evolved from early stories, including—and especially—the Bible's stories, and these have had a continuous privileged influence on the Western imagination. At the same time, even as these first stories have given definition to humanity generally, they distinguish the Hebrews, and this distinctiveness, which relates to cultural perceptions of Jewish sexuality, has been preserved, however unsystematically, through the ages.

I have tried a thought exercise that reveals what I intend when I make a claim for conventions of Jewish sexuality. I ask an audience to think of the word "masculinity" and all that the word conjures up for them. What are our cultural associations with "masculinity"? Then, "femininity": What are the connotations of the word "femininity"? I go on to ask what happens when we qualify these words with the adjective "Jewish": "Jewish masculinity"? "Jewish femininity"? For many people, the adjective "Jewish" upends the meanings of masculinity or femininity. Indeed, a growing scholarly literature supports stereotypes of Jewish difference by relating sexuality to textuality, arguing that Judaism preserved its own standard of manliness, one at odds with the ideals of popular culture.[3] Not only has Jewish sexuality been imagined to have been socially construed to be distinctive, but the Jewish body too has a history of imagined difference.

Like Jewish sexuality, the idea of a Jewish body—a much studied concept—is at once meaningless and meaningful.[4] We refer to Jewish body parts: famously, a Jewish nose, and *Lilith* magazine, a self-described feminist Jewish periodical, once devoted a good part of an issue to how Jewish women feel about their "Jewish hair."[5] It may sound nostalgic to refer to "a Jewish soul" or, richer in connotations, the Yiddish, "a *Yiddishe neshama*," but something nevertheless still comes to mind for many Jews: perhaps a soul fed on the chicken soup of *mitzvot* (the Hebrew word for "commandments"); "a *Yiddishe kopf*," which means, in Yiddish, a "Jewish head," once imputed a special kind of Jewish business sense: quick, clever, and a little devious. These associations contribute to stereotypes of Jewish bodies and (by extension, Jewish men and women) who distinguish Jews from normative humanity. But whether or not any of us individually entertains any notions of Jewish distinctiveness, it is the case that over the course of history, Jewish bodies were imagined to be identifiably *Jewish*. There have been periods of history, certain times and places, when the phrase "Jewish man" was an oxymoron, a contradiction in terms. The racial identity of the Jews, even in America, has a history related to the history of class and Jewish economic status.[6] The birth of Israel complicated these ideas, and while Israel's founding generation deliberately intended to interfere with prevailing truths about the *shtetl* Jew, consciously substituting a muscular Jew and Judaism for the frail, studious, and victimized image of the Jewish man, over time, as those ideals have been variously modified, the Israeli body and the Jewish soul have continued their ongoing, dynamic process of shape shifting.

Similarly, since those influential moments in the Garden of Eden, women have had a hard time living down the first woman's image as a sexy, curious, disobedient temptress. Sarah, Rebecca, Leah, and Rachel, those first mothers in Israel, the matriarchy, stand at the foundation of much later ideas of the Jewish mother: each heroine an anxious, eager mother, competitive, ambitious on behalf of her favorite son and on close terms with God as she negotiates her son's future. We know of course that claims about Jewish behaviors are dubious and that Jews come in all colors, shapes, and sizes. In my own extended family, we are big and small, blonde and dark, fair and ebony; we are Jews by choice and Jews by birth, multiethnic and multiracial, Eastern and Western. But myths and perceptions have been consequential. The complex terrain of the imagination shares borders with reality and has a powerful, imperialist army. How people define themselves affects how they define others, how they feel and behave, and how they are treated.

Self-knowledge is mediated by social classification systems with categories into which we are assigned, and we know ourselves from the descriptive language that is applied to us. In other words, we are proper nouns to which adjectives are attached.[7] And just as the Bible imagines that God brought the world into being through language, creating distinctions between light and dark or sea and sky that organized the whole world into meaningful proximate units, so too, we understand ourselves categorically, through language, and by comparison and contrast. We are defined by who we are and by who we are not, by the stories we tell about ourselves and the history of interpretation of those stories. Children early on assume shapes captioned by labels: "graceful," "klutsy," "kind," "sharp." Individuality, such as it is, emerges, paradoxically, through combinations of categorizations, the self located in a mobile grid: "with her father's smile"; "slower than Jane"; "fairer than his brother"; "more ambitious than Jim"; "taller than average"; "musical"; "wild." Advertising and other vehicles of popular culture teach us about the staggering, but finally, limited possibilities for living in one's roles and in one's body: "soccer mom"; "tourist"; "waiter"; "lawyer"; "American"; "Jew."

Self-constructed endlessly every minute of every day, even as we sleep, whether in silk pajamas or naked, the self experiences itself through cultural frameworks that govern how we interpret and morally assess everything from the feel of our skin to the aches of our muscles, so we know whether we are experiencing the *good* pain of exercise or the *bad* pain of aging. We watch ourselves and others—and we narrate what we see—as we live and die. No self is ever naked of culture. In this book, I am looking at a set of first stories particularly for their power to have set in motion definitions of the body, the sexual body, and the Jewish sexual body that developed over time.

My own encounters with the Hebrew Bible go back a long way, and we have met in all kinds of religious and academic contexts. Although I trained as a literary critic, I have been both a casual and serious reader of biblical criticism and the Jewish commenting tradition, enough to know that the details of almost all my interpretations are available elsewhere, whether in rabbinic Midrash, feminist polemics, or in any of the many critical studies of the Bible that fill my shelves. I have myself been writing about the Bible for a quarter of a century, and the great challenge of putting this book together has been the work of bringing the pieces into alignment with one another and with my present convictions. In doing so, I have had to face the question of this volume's particular contribution.

My students have fortified me with the best answer that I can offer. Although many of these learners are well versed in Bible texts, they still find something fresh, even startling, in these demonstrations of a relationship between biblical foundation texts and the contradictions of Jewish sexualities as we experience them in our culture and in our lives. So, while the Bible and *Hamlet* do not themselves change, what does change, ironically, are the presumably timeless truths through which we interpret the world, guaranteeing that each generation will produce its share of doctoral dissertations and new books on texts about which everything seems to have already been said. The purpose that I imagine distinguishes the readings in this book, taken together, is the project of queering or denaturalizing sex in the very place where nature and sex were first and authoritatively invented, represented, and inscribed, at least in this branch of the cultural imagination. Some ideas are familiar in academic or philosophic forums that seem radical or counter-intuitive in popular contexts, and the idea that I want to put before you here, arguably the main premise of this book, is that the body in which you live is formed as much—if not more so—by culture as by nature.[8] Everything has a history, including our material bodies.

This study of Bible stories inquires into the origins of our perceptions of the Jewish body's sexuality and, by extension, changing attitudes toward Jewish men and women. The Bible's narrative renderings of early male and female characters are first indications of what it would come to mean to have a Jewish body or to be a Jewish woman or man. *In Scripture* asks about what meanings we find "in scripture" today—what readings of these stories now seem irresistible—playing off the idea that scriptural text has become cultural inscription: that which is inscribed in sacred scripture has been written into and on the text that is the personal self.

Identity categories find narrative definition (in the Bible, in subsequent literature, and in culture more generally) in terms of one another, and in representation, these identities are endlessly self-contradicting and self-undermining. Reading through the lens of contemporary theory, I take seriously the presumption of an evolving culturally constructed reality. The Bible's first stories have a privileged status in the history of the body's construction that comes from their having been apprehended for so long as "the beginning" and, as such, layered over with subsequent rewritings and interpretations that build on and adjust the beginning to account for, or prescribe, the present. If, as I believe, identity categories— man, woman, Jew, queer—have no ontological status but rather develop meaning over time, then the exercises in reading in this book are meant to be invitations to consider how the overlapping histories of these designations have had consequences in our lived reality.[9]

In this book, I introduce some basic theoretical principles through readings of Bible stories that suggest alternative ways of talking about the relationship between textuality and sexuality, between gender and Judaism. I have developed these readings over years, often to illustrate how critical theory can contribute to Jewish feminist thought, and my frames of reference may betray my own beginnings as a student of Victorian literature and narratology. The reading strategy is unorthodox, moving both forward from the Bible to later Western stereotypes, presuming that the Bible is critically influential in our self-understanding, and backward, presuming that readings that seem inevitable today are a consequence of the institution of truths that have been put in place over the millennia between biblical times and the present. By this logic, for example, it is irresistible to see the snake in the Garden of Eden as a sign of male sexuality just as the primary families in the Abraham cycle seem to represent versions of oedipal romance. Through this reciprocal engagement of scripture and subsequent cultural reinscriptions, I mean to identify what now seems to be the biblical invention of categories of gender and ethnicity and chart reinventions that work to maintain the appearance of the naturalness of gender and ethnicity as such.

In this regard, the book's chapters are variations on a theme and together comprise a sustained response to the challenge, posed by Judith Butler at the conclusion of *Gender Trouble*, to "denaturalize gender." Butler concludes her own philosophic argument with a question: "What other local strategies for engaging the 'unnatural' might lead to the denaturalization of gender as such?" Behind that question is the explanation that immediately precedes it:

> The deconstruction of identity . . . establishes as political the very terms through which identity is articulated. . . . The internal paradox of this foundationalism is that it presumes, fixes, and constrains the very "subjects" that it hopes to represent and liberate. The task here is not to celebrate each and every new possibility *qua* possibility, but to redescribe those possibilities that *already* exist, but which exist within cultural domains designated as culturally unintelligible and impossible. . . . Cultural configurations of sex and gender might then proliferate or, rather, their present proliferation might then become articulable within the discourses that establish intelligible cultural life, confounding the very binarism of sex, and exposing its fundamental unnaturalness.[10]

Perhaps any number of gender systems might have been—or will yet be—developed from these same origin stories (analogous to what *Star Trek* referred to as "alternate timelines"), but the particular story structure that we imagine connects our historical moment to our biblical origins is the one made visible by our own historical position. We can analyze our origin stories and discover that they have had a role in fashioning us, but what we are capable of recognizing in our own origin stories is restricted by how we have come to define ourselves. This double consciousness of looking forward and backward is a strategy to challenge whatever it is that we take for granted as natural, including definitions of the sexes, sexuality, and ethnicity.

Genre matters. Readers are only in a position to interpret a text once they have made some determination as to what the text is: we read and assess an advertisement using different tools and criteria than we bring to a poem. Even then, we read with particular interests, concerns, and questions: you can read the ad for product information or cultural information; you can read the poem to illuminate the life and times of the poet or the heart of the person who directed this poem to your attention (or both and much more). The Bible, not so much a book as a library, an edited collection of layers of texts compiled over long centuries, is a mix of genres, including myths, historical memories and fantasies, legal traditions, poetry, and really, who-knows-what, thoughtfully redacted. It is often read "as" literature, implying that it *is* something else, but honoring the coherence to which we have ascribed it, partly by virtue of its existence for so long between two covers. This study of the biblical authorization of gender as we know it—and reciprocally, of how gender as we know it governs our reading of Bible—accepts, for these purposes, the Bible's self-presentation as a fanciful history of the present (albeit, creatively redacted and full with important interruptions) into which humanity is first inscribed and purposefully refined.

In the biblical origin story, nature begins in Eden, the place where culture is born. "Knowledge and Nakedness: Eve in the Garden of Signs" considers the first three chapters of Genesis as "a cosmic semiotic event" in which a linguistic classification system is put in place that organizes reality and establishes some of the grounding Western assumptions about sex and gender. In the Hebrew Bible's creation myth, the *tohu vavohu* or "hurly burly" that precedes world creation is a dark, wet place, the womb of cognitive chaos that precedes God calling the world into being by naming the series of oppositions that establishes a fundamental but arbitrary classification system. Genesis 3 first contradicts our experience that people emerge from female bodies. Then, although the female is said to tempt the man to disobedience, Eve is first tempted by a walking, talking serpent—a "snake" that, as punishment for successful temptation, loses his erection. Here are early textual moments that suggest gender trouble in Paradise. Does female sexuality tempt man out of Edenic peace, or does this myth imply that disembodied male sexuality, an entity with a mind and voice of its own, is responsible for the first temptation? In the first chapters of Genesis, we have the inscription of man and woman in the world as opposites defined hierarchically by their sex. But a close look at a series of sexual reversals will expose ambiguity, ambivalence, and instability.

In the following chapter, I import categories of analysis from French feminist theory to begin to theorize the field of Jewish feminism. I wonder what we might say about Judaism if our primary categories were, for example, "fluids" and "voices" rather than "Torah, God, and Israel." Considering a moment of enigmatic laughter in the story of Sarah, the first matriarch, and the incoherent muttering of Hannah (mother of the great prophet Samuel), I suggest that the Jewish woman's body, her fluids and her voices, provide bases already inscribed in the Jewish textual tradition for an alternative account of woman's presence in text and world.

Through this attention to laughter and muttering, water and blood, I explore a pattern of biblical mothers whose barrenness is associated with verbal ambiguity and textual disruption. Sarah's laughter and Hannah's incoherent grief are textually subversive, as is the defining fact of their identity as barren mothers: a mother cannot, by definition, be barren. But just as the first males bring forth the first life—first God, then Adam—so whenever a hero is born into the narrative, God's power is necessary to remove the curse of barrenness. The relative authority of mother and father proves as unstable as the sexual instability just below the surface of the creation stories that establish male and female in the first place. These barren mothers typically have domestic authority over their sons by virtue of an arrangement with God that limits patriarchal prerogatives: God asserts "listen to Sarah" when she privileges Isaac over Ishmael; Rebecca manipulates the preferment of her favorite son Jacob to the detriment of Isaac's beloved Esau. This image of mothers who enforce the privileging of younger, gentler, domestic sons persists late into the twentieth century in the stereotypes of the overpowering Jewish mother and the intellectual, poorly athletic, dependent, dutiful Jewish mama's boy. These stereotypes linger.

In Chapter 3, "Passing as a Man: Patriarchal Gender Performances," I consider multiple constructions of specifically Jewish masculinity in the Bible and the commenting tradition over time. Again, based on the premises that identity is performative, that Jewish, sexual, ethnic, and racial identities have no stable definition, and that identity performance is central to the myths of the Hebrew matriarchy and patriarchy in both the Bible and later elaborations, in this chapter I begin to analyze origin stories of Jewish gender identity and enactments of masculinity. I ask what exactly is going on when, in Genesis 27, Jacob inherits the patriarchy and narrative future by donning animal skins and masquerading as his twin, the hunter, Esau. Using elements of queer theory, especially analyses of "camp," and postcolonial theory, in particular Homi K. Bhabha's description of "colonial mimicry," I suggest that the mother's ambitions for her son compromise both the son's and the father's autonomy as each becomes a patriarch by pretending to be the man whom he imagines (or fears) he is not. These readings raise epistemological questions about self-deception and the meaning of "knowing" even one's most intimate relations.

In Chapter 4, "Leah Behind the Veil: Sex with Sisters from the Bible through Woody Allen," I specify the features of a ubiquitous, semipornographic narrative pattern in which the hero sleeps with his wife's sister. The biblical Jacob's marriage to sisters allows us to see how other popular plots, including biographies of Charles Dickens and Freud and Woody Allen's *Hannah and Her Sisters*, collectively offer the reassurance that women, no matter how close, principally envy one another, and that this envy can be exploited to ensure patriarchal mastery over women, who will apparently always choose male seed over loyalty to one another.

These stories of homosocial bonding and asymmetrical triangles of desire are, it seems to me, variations on the Leah-Rachel story that emerge with particular force at historical moments of women's collective political activism, and the hero in this story is typically represented as suffering from a relatively weak masculinity.

Just as Jacob mimics masculinity, his son Joseph mimics political power. Chapter 5, "Coats and Tales: Joseph and Myths of Jewish Masculinity," includes readings of several transfigurations of the Joseph story in the Hebrew Bible, Midrash, and the Koran, focusing on the different renderings of Joseph's striped coat. I contrast Hebrew scripture's tolerance for ethical ambiguity with the Koran's preference for clear divine justice and suggest that the unambiguous beauty of the biblical Joseph became encoded as effeminate and impotent in correspondence with changing characterizations of the Jewish man in Western culture. Joseph's distinctive beauty and chastity map onto his outsider national identity as a powerful Hebrew in Egypt.

Using a concept developed by Ilana Pardes, who discovers what she calls "counter-traditions" in early layers of biblical narrative, in Chapter 6, "Miriam's Fluid Identity," I isolate the four references to the heroine Miriam (a childhood miracle, where she saves the baby Moses in the Nile; her leading the women in a victory dance at the Red Sea; God "spitting" at her and giving her leprosy when she claims a place of power; and the drought that accompanies her death) and conclude that these episodes, as well as the reaction of the people, suggest the possibility that the Bible's Miriam (whose name contains the word for "sea") is a late incarnation of a stronger character in the prehistory of the text, one whose powers are associated with water.

Chapter 7, "Bedrooms and Battlefields," describes how a negative image of the male Jew's masculinity and sexual vulnerability developed in tandem with the figure of the "Jewess" as sexually overpowering, insatiable, and fatal. Here, I focus on Judges 4 and 5, and observe that Jael is typical of a class of biblical heroines who enact a heightened and false femininity, luring the strong male enemy into her tent and penetrating him (in Jael's case, with a tent pin) when the reader and the man have every reason to expect that it is she who will be penetrated. Delilah, Jael, Tamar, Esther, and Judith are heroines (often closeted or masquerading) who together suggest a biblical rule that persists in popular culture, namely, that the bedroom is the battlefield where men always lose. In the context of the readings of masculinity that precede this chapter, I conclude my case that gender and sexual reversals are so pervasive in biblical narratives as to ultimately confound the stability of the categories themselves.

With few exceptions, Hebrew scripture inscribes the female body as barren mother (the matriarchs, Samson's mother, Hannah), seductress

(Eve, Tamar, Delilah, Jael), or rape victim (Dinah, Tamar, the unnamed woman in Judges 17–21). As mother and seductress, she plays a disempowering role in relation to her sons and lovers. And though mother and harlot are famous opposites, what these figures share is their controlling power over the men in their stories, the fault line along which the opposition collapses. The long prevalent stereotypes of the Jewish mother (self-sacrificing) and the Jewish American princess (selfish) also seem to be opposites, but they descend from the older fictions of Hebrew women who control men. The Jewish American princess grows up to be a Jewish mother.

In Chapter 8, "Other Boundary Crossings: Of Talking Beasts and Bodies Fragmented," I discuss a set of stories in which the sexed body is a site of representation and describe how, beginning with the rape of Dinah, individual bodies figure the body politic. The story of Balak (a fable with a talking donkey and sword-yielding angel in Numbers 22–25) like Judges 19 (a strange allegory about an anonymous judge who twice traverses tribal Israel to recover his concubine from her father's home only for her to suffer rape and death) defy the conventions of biblical realism. I use the concept of "carnival," with its upside-down strategies and a structuralist methodology to elaborate on the ever-more complicated disruptions of those oppositions that give the illusion of stable identities in a realistic world. The characters in these stories disrupt bourgeois notions of a stable self. Because the judge cuts the woman's body into twelve fragments that become telegrams to the tribes, signifying the fragmentation of the people Israel, I argue that this story reconfigures national identity, anticipating the unifying vision of the books of Samuel and Kings.

A more culturally sophisticated classification system than that of the first chapters of Genesis, Judges 19 undermines its own social oppositions and reversals: night and day; wife and harlot; safety and danger; excess and restraint; licit and illicit relations; family and strangers; hospitality and violation; and finally, masculinity and femininity are among the oppositions that are rendered unstable in these unstable times. It is a story about thresholds and transgressions, and they are geographic and political. This judge has no name because he is everyman, and the unruly body wishes to violate him because it is lawless; the system has failed, making way for the book of Samuel and the rule of kings.

The final chapter, "Oy! Was That a Close Call: Ruth and the Fundamental Jewish Story," begins with the story of the near-sacrifice of Isaac as a prelude to a discussion of the book of Ruth as encoding the near-miss and the triumph of faith over fear as the basic myth of Jewish identity in contemporary times. I situate the story of Ruth in the context of other stories of barrenness, on the one hand, and seduction, on the other, asking what

the implications of these stories in their totality have been for the conception of Jewish masculinity and femininity over the generations.

The main metaphors in this story are food and sex. Ruth begins with
famine in Bethlehem, "The House of Bread," and barren women, and it
ends with plenitude, a successful seduction in fields of waving barley and
an unusually promising baby. As in other stories discussed here, again
the individual body, the land of Israel, and the body politic symbolically stand in for each other—alternately barren and fertile, depleted and
blessed—and it is the individual who perseveres to satisfy life's hungers
who moves us forward on the road to ultimate redemption. Echoes of
Adam and Eve, Rachel and Leah, Judah and Tamar, and the book of Job,
as well as Deuteronomic and Levitical laws of redemption and levirate
marriage reverberate until the text swells to the conclusion that although
elusive meaning is life fragile, and our fates unpredictable, the small individual persevering in the impulse to satisfy life hungers plays the most
crucial role—unknowable even to the self—in the vast plan of history.

In Scripture: The First Stories of Jewish Sexual Identities establishes a particular set of connections between Bible stories and us today. Story readers
habitually find themselves in any text: we identify with characters, make
connections with our own experiences; we discover role models for life,
or language to reconsider or reframe our judgments and self-assessments.
The varied contexts in which many of us read the Bible—inside and outside of the academy and worship places—make the project of self-location
in the Bible's stories less casual than what we do as a matter of course
when we read a classic novel or popular romance. The Bible is an ancient
book, generically mixed up, and as a sacred text, its authority over readers
is typically strong or weak—rarely neutral. Like most formidable entities,
it invites strong acceptance and strong resistance. Addressing myself to
the question of what the Bible demands we should be, it is my hope that
the readings in this book both honor the Bible's power and exploit its vul-
nerabilities, celebrating its sustained literary authority while dislodging
assumptions about sex, gender, and ethnicity that have come to seem natural, in part because of the Bible's unique authority in our cultural history.

1

Knowledge and Nakedness: Eve in the Garden of Signs

GARDEN OVERLOOK

The first signs of gender trouble appear in Paradise, that endlessly reproduced garden of delights, whose cultural fruits include a proliferation of images of manhood and womanhood, each an effort to recharacterize the prototype of man and woman, Adam and Eve.[1] Origin story of our own present, leading to millennia of accounting woman responsible for the world's troubles (dissenting readers conclude that blaming Eve is a misreading of the text), the narrative invents man and woman and attempts to fix Adam and Eve's sexual identities and roles.[2] But the effort to define the sexes finds internal resistance in the text itself, as each complexity in the story compromises its own conclusions. In the biblical place that "man" and "woman" come to life, they will not come to definition, and as we will see in subsequent chapters, the distinguishing qualities of matriarchy and patriarchy—grounding terms of masculinity and femininity—are similarly unstable.

Which sex creates life? The codifiers of the text would have presumed that life emerged from the bodies of women, but in this origin story, the Creator God is designated masculine, and the first woman is born from the body of a man. Which sex tempts which? Eve does give the fruit to Adam, but she is first sweet talked with promises of power by an erect snake an anthropomorphization whose punishment for the success of his seduction is loss of erection and God's promise that he would thereafter be permanently vulnerable to woman's heel. This beast, disembodied and disowned male sexuality, absolves Adam of responsibility (because he was thinking with his snake?). Later artistic renderings of the snake will variously depict a male or female anthropomorphic beast, just as Lilith— introduced by later myths into the garden story as Adam's rejecting first wife—becomes transmogrified into Samael, a male antagonist to God in Jewish mystical literature, making both the snake and Lilith alternately male and female, of unsettled sexuality.

The site of sexuality dissociated from its body is a common old story, as for example, "Pandora's box," from which all the ills of the world fly, though Pandora is perfection itself. A further regress: what is the allure of the luscious, juicy, tempting fruit that is so irresistible that to taste it the first mythic humans would violate the command of God? And a final pair of reversals: in the story, the snake exploits Eve's vulnerability, but in the punishment, it is he who becomes vulnerable to her heel. Similarly, in the story, Adam yearns for Eve, first requiring her in his unfulfilled life and then eating the fruit that she offers, but the punishment, a mirror reflection, asserts that woman will yearn toward man, but he will rule her. The primacy, culpability, and characteristic natures of the sexes will not settle.

We will also see the origins of a long-standing cultural equation in the three equivalent consequences of eating the forbidden fruit: death, knowledge, and sexual self-consciousness. Desire (for fruit, for sex) and libido (the drive for knowledge and the ambition to eat and to mate) manifest as both death wish ("you will die") and pleasure principle ("the fruit is beautiful and delicious"). As this influential story installs the two-sexed system into the origins of humanity, it already embeds the tension between competing drives. From the equivalence of death, knowledge, and sex emerge the fundamental mysteries and paradoxes of human existence as we have constructed them in Western, particularly psychoanalytic, thought.

ACCOUNTING FOR AND PRESCRIBING THE PRESENT

The power of first stories, like that of scientific constructions of human origins, is that they tell us not only how things came to be as they are, but why they must be as they are; they at once account for and regulate the present. Though we may have multiple, fanciful accounts of human beginnings, the stories of Adam and Eve and Prometheus and Pandora, fantastic though they may be, enshrine and perpetuate abiding beliefs about humanity and sexuality in the West. Where myth and science agree, we discover bedrock prejudices about reality and nature.

Creationism and the theory of evolution actually share a set of assumptions about life's origins and human purpose. First among them is that a chain of cause and effect links who we are to the "nature" of earlier incarnations of humanity. Whether descended from Adam or ape, humans inherit identity, and humanity's beginnings account for facts of life in the present. Each narrative also emphasizes reproduction as a goal of life, and each accordingly presumes a division of all creation into male and female halves, driven into each other's sexual embrace for the purpose of filling the Earth. Whether a loving God set life in motion or an amoral Nature operating according to her laws, the result is the same, science and religion alike addressing the mysteries of the universe in agreement that there are two sexes obedient to the demand to fruitfully multiply, "populate the Earth" or "propagate the species." These two influential, competing master narratives have forged a consensus around the origins and the purposes of life.

Moreover, beginning from the shared premise of two sexes fundamentally driven to propagate, the logic of religion and science both lead to the conclusion that other human aspirations are variations, harnessing, or channeling of libido. Yet, sexual (animal) drives and cultural (human/divine) aspirations are also imagined to be opposed to each other, humanity struggling between "baser" urges and "higher" values, a struggle that reflects the tension between God's demand that humanity populate the Earth and humanity's having been created in the image of the One, nonprocreating God.[3]

Biologists, such as Anne Fausto-Sterling, philosophers, and theorists, chief among them Judith Butler, have invited us to entertain other possibilities, suggesting, for example, that humanity is composed of multiple sexes, or, alternatively, that sexual distinction is as arbitrary as other social and cultural conventions.[4] Two sexes, like the idea of a continuum between masculinity and femininity, can be thought of as culturally installed, not unlike the code of traffic signals. Just as green could have come to mean "slow," red "go," and other colors—in the conventions of this alternative universe—assigned more nuanced directional meanings, so we might walk Christopher Street in Manhattan or the Castro in San Francisco, watch the drag balls of *Paris Is Burning*, encounter out-of-the-closet transsexuals and intersex and wrap our brains around the possibility of sex as a convention, a three-dimensional array that defies the simplistic categories long taken for granted. At the very least, stylized sexing, boyish girls, and girlish boys perform sexual identity and alert us to a dizzying array of human possibility that begs for a sex and gender system with more boxes and more flexible borders. As for reproduction, it may be the business of some, but by no means all, creatures. For those who do breed, with more and less felt urgency, well, even then, reproduction is the work of a percentage of any modern lifespan, and not necessarily the defining business of whatever it is that "being" means. Why must two propagating sexes define humanity? We have come to (or returned to) a time when it is possible to imagine otherwise.

Imagining otherwise, we can read the first several chapters of Genesis as a parable of meanings, a story that describes the installation of a cosmic sign system (a variation on the designation of the Bible by Northrop Frye, following William Blake, as "the Great Code"), culminating in the inscription of human sexuality as we have come to know it.[5] Such a reading—that is, one based on a critique of identity—will necessarily discover the beginning of gender trouble in the place where sex begins, in Eden.

SORTING THIS FROM THAT: CREATION AS CLASSIFICATION

Although Genesis begins with the phrase, "in the beginning," the text cannot actually imagine a moment before which there was no before. Before creation, there was *"tohu vavohu,"* "hurly burly," an incomprehensible jumble, sometimes translated as "formless void": unshaped prelinguistic, cognitive chaos. The beginning refers, rather, to the birth of meaning.

Creation occurs in language. The hero, a Creator God, names things, and in so doing, they come into being, and they are good. These acts of naming serve, more precisely, to organize the chaos by making distinctions, as God's voice reaches into the chaos, the *tohu vavohu*, and separates out the light from the darkness, the heaven from the earth, the earth from the water, and so on. Creation occurs in language, is a matter of naming—of making distinctions—and more specifically, creation is a matter of articulating opposites. Or: taxonomy creates reality.

Psychoanalytically, life is a series of punctuated separations, beginning with birth and ending with death. Like the world, each of us emerges from a dark, wet place into a sensory confusion, the hurly burly of meaningless void. Language organizes our chaos too, as the all-powerful parent, through speech, distinguishes light from dark, wet from dry, day from night, sun from moon, and often, Mama from Papa, organizing each small reality according to the classification system of the language and cultural systems into which one happens to be born. With language acquisition, reality comes into being. The sensory chaos, the cacophony, the swirl of color and light is organized as the world's pieces are named, and the brain slowly filters out the irrelevant—because unnamed—sounds, sights, and other inputs that are superfluous because they have made no linguistic claim on our attention. A matter of communal consensus, vocabulary creates life in detail, distinguishing the cat from the mat, this from that, the walk from the run, or skip, or hop. An alternative linguistic consensus would yield a modified reality.

The familiar oppositions of the first chapter of Genesis (light and dark, heaven and earth) organize primal chaos as God creates a system of classification that makes sense of the nonsense by mapping the world. These oppositions, after all these many years, seem natural; they roll off the tongue. But there is actually nothing inevitable about the opposites here named, and each acquires its value only in relation to its designated opposite. Dry earth below, for example, first opposes a watery heaven above and later stands distinct from the Earth's ocean waters. Earth need not have been opposed to heaven: hell, had it been a relevant category in the mind of this author, might have been created to oppose heaven. And although Hebrew has only a single designation for the two English words heaven and sky, the different pairings of heaven and earth, earth and sky, and heaven and hell suggest the possibility of different underlying assumptions about life and the world. Like organizing the mess in a teenager's room, the trick is to identify what can plausibly go with what, and where to make it all fit: sweaters, here; books, there; color-coded or season-coded, in height order or alphabetized, we impose a system that eventually seems natural enough. When anomalies assert themselves, we may adjust or cram, rarely appreciating that each anomaly exposes the randomness, and inadequacy, of the system itself. Dusk and dawn, cloudy skies, moonlit nights, dampness, indeed all of experience, challenge the rigidity of the oppositions day and night, light and dark, or wet and dry. At many moments, looking out the window, it is hard to say for sure whether it is precisely light or dark. But in the creation story, each instance of separation locates meaning—locates existence itself—where difference is asserted. A tenet of the science of semiotics is "meaning is located where difference is perceived."

Just as meaning is located where difference is perceived, so too, where there is difference there is hierarchy. But where we locate difference is, finally, arbitrary. In each case of an opposing pair, we meet a meaningful distinction because we know which half of the pair is superior and which inferior: light is preferred to dark, heaven to earth, sun to moon, and so on for each named and created thing. Night and moonlight may be better for romance than sun and day, and one can imagine circumstances when it is better to be wet than dry, but by and large, living in a shared culture, we take oppositions for granted and also know—absent any context at all—which half of any pair is favored.[6]

Near the end of this process, the most important act of creation occurs. Against the creation of animal life is produced humanity: "male and female created He them." Here, no significant distinction (and therefore no hierarchy) is established between the sexes because humanity is given only one name. In Genesis 2:4, the redactor goes back on the beginning,

and the reader of the Bible is presented with a second, and according
to source criticism, actually an earlier, version of the creation story. In
this story—which the habituated filmgoer or reader of modern stories is
likely to interpret as a flashback, a more detailed close-up of the making
of humanity—the map gets infinitely smaller as we are removed from
the cosmos and placed on a pinpoint on Earth: the Garden of Eden, a
microcosm of the world. From this utopia, human history will emanate.
Just as the Bible begins with grand oppositions, the garden story adds two
more oppositions that are central and meaningful hereafter: the opposition between man and woman and, more deeply, between knowledge
and nakedness. The Freudian account of the psyche, deeply ingrained in
our culture, obeys these Edenic divisions, as all knowledge is represented
as a variation of sexual knowledge, and all production a channeling of
libidinal drives.

In this story, man—not humanity (male and female)—is formed. As a
sculptor removes a meaningful shape out of clay, Adam is distinguished
from the earth with which he shares a name (*"Adam," "earthling,"* from
the Hebrew *"adamah," "earth"*) and placed in Eden. Here, man is primary.[7] What follows is a history of the present, as the story dictates to
its readers how to organize their lives in a post-Edenic state. Here too
are intimations of the extended hierarchy that eventually was elaborated
into "the Great Chain of Being": vegetable life, animal life, woman, man,
angels, God, each, in turn, serving the other.[8] Man's fate is to toil cursed
ground and earn the family's keep. Woman's fate is pain in childbirth and
to yearn toward a husband who will lord over her. The story's conclusion,
with its simple, clear, gender-based social organization, seems to follow
from the gender divisions and roles in the story itself. A closer reading
belies that clarity, however, revealing that the gender trouble in Paradise
is not so much between the sexes—the basis for a long-standing social
quarrel—as trouble distinguishing between sex roles. Which is which and
which does what: Who creates life? Which sex tempts which? Who yearns
toward whom?

In this second beginning—though the earlier story of creation—Adam
is given the divine prerogative of naming as God parades the animals
before Adam and invites Adam to identify them. Adam will thereby master his world as God owns the cosmos that he named. As Adam creates
his universe on Earth, he looks for a companion but finds none suitable.
God puts Adam to sleep and significantly, in a strikingly counterfactual
moment, he removes the first woman from the body of the man. In naming Eve, Adam asserts his ownership through the prerogative of naming.
Whenever we name others, we also locate ourselves. (A life-and-death
corollary of this rule is that rebellion is principally seizing the power to
name.[9])

God and Adam, who are male, are the first sources of life, both as creators of life and those who name the world into meaning. Valued and divine as creation is in the Bible's beginning, however, at the myth's conclusion, Eve—whose name means "life," underscoring her identity as life-giver—receives her procreative function as a punishment for disobedience. In another reversal of value signs, childbearing is identified not as a blessing but as Eve's curse. The first makers and consumers of this myth understood life as emerging from the bodies of women, but subscribed to an origin story that first divided the social world into men and women, identified a male Creator God and a primary male from whom the first woman was removed, and then cursed women with childbirth. Beneath the story lies a fear or envy of female sexuality, and a series of reversals, beginning with the birth of the first woman from the side of a man, betrays, and attempts to allay that fear.

THE ORIGINS OF THE FATAL FEMALE: DEATH = KNOWLEDGE = SEX

The Eden story creates a seamless equivalency among the multiple consequences of eating the fruit of the forbidden tree, establishing a subtle chain of cultural associations among death, knowledge, and sex. God admonishes Adam not to eat from the tree in the center of the garden. At that moment, the reader knows that Adam will do so, because where there is an admonition, there will follow a transgression, or there would be no story. Three apparently separate consequences threaten to follow from this transgression. First, God declares that this eating will result in *death*. The snake comes and promises Eve that eating will bring, not death, but divine knowledge: the first people will know what God knows. When Adam and Eve do eat of the tree, they apparently neither die nor do they acquire any immediate special knowledge. They do not dramatically collapse like Disney's Snow White when she bites the hag's shiny apple, nor do they suddenly come to an understanding of the cosmos, astronomy, physics, or specialized agricultural formulae, like the scarecrow in *The Wizard of Oz*, who, upon receiving his diploma, can confidently, in a new professorial voice, recite Einstein's theory of relativity. The only knowledge that Adam and Eve acquire is knowledge of their own nakedness, an awareness of their sexuality (and perhaps of their own insufficiency).

Nonetheless, the reader does not conclude that either God or the snake lied. Instead, we experience the actual consequences of the transgression as somehow resolvable into Adam's and Eve's awareness of sexuality, as if death and godlike knowledge, respectively promised by God and the snake, are bound up in the nakedness of the first humans. We unconsciously reconcile these apparently different consequences—as interpreters of Bible and writers of Midrash (rabbinic narrative commentaries) have long done, explaining, for example, that even though Adam and Eve did not die with their first bite, eating does bring death into the world. We reflexively reinterpret the story as including the origin of mortality as the human condition.

In assimilating these consequences into one another, the text establishes what has become a long-standing, quiet, cultural equivalence among death, sexuality, and knowledge. The story itself enforces this equivalence linguistically in the descriptions of the snake as "clever" or "subtle" (in Hebrew: *'arum*) and of Adam and Eve as "naked" (in Hebrew: *'arummim*). This pun—or the linguistic association of nakedness and subtlety or slyness—connects knowledge and sexuality in a way that participates in the reversals that characterize this story. Adam and Eve are unselfconsciously naked (*'arummim*) until they are encouraged by the subtle (*'arum*) snake to indulge, after which they "wise up" to their nakedness, conscious perhaps of their own affiliation with the snake, as naked innocence (*'arummim*) resolves into the subtlety (*'arum*) that allows for disobedience.

The equation among death, knowledge, and sex is culturally familiar, sustained in linguistic details across languages. "To know in the biblical sense" means to have sexual intercourse because the verb "to know" (as in: "Abraham knew Sarah") euphemistically, or perhaps simply literally indicates that they did what was necessary for procreation. In the Bible, when one character "knows" another, the assertion is typically followed by the promise of an impending birth. In Elizabethan English, "to die" is a euphemism for sexual climax, the rough equivalent of the French *"un petit mort,"* "a little death," which also refers to climax. Perhaps this language was biologically predictive—or primitive biology led to these linguistic choices—insofar as semen was imagined to contain the life force, and male sexual emissions were a kind of slow suicide. (On this account, only men must "die" during intercourse.) Also by this logic, in the heterosexual sex act, man lost his life fluid and the receptacle, the woman, was imagined to be energized by sex, an empowering that begins in Eden, and as we will see later, persists and is elaborated in subsequent biblical stories of sexual seduction, such as that of Samson and Delilah. Sex, though irresistible, means death for men—a sapping of the life fluid—and empowerment for women, the vessel for his seed. Belied by the hard fact of women's frequently dying in childbirth, this origin story establishes two sexes, the male primary, and it establishes that for men, knowledge and sex are both deadly consequences of a woman's relationship with the (his?) snake.

THE SNAKE AND THE BOX

From a literary point of view, any creature in the garden might have asserted itself as the first tempter. John Milton's epic commentary (a Christian midrashic poem), *Paradise Lost*, introduces Satan into the garden story, arguably making a hero of that fascinating fallen angel who appears nowhere in the original text but whom we may have to willfully exorcise from our consciousness when we read the Hebrew Bible. In *Paradise Lost*, following Christian and some rabbinic traditions, it is Satan who enters the body of the snake. First, however, in the Miltonic fantasy of an Eden populated with talking creatures of all varieties, Lucifer manifests toad-like, whispering in Eve's ear while she sleeps, to infiltrate her unconscious.[10] This toad metaphor effectively suggests that any creature might have been responsible for tempting Adam and Eve, but the interpretive tradition that has long read this story has belabored the fact of the tempter being a serpent. Milton, like the author of the Zohar (a thirteenth-century mystical commentary to the Bible), allows us to imagine that the snake's seduction was not simply verbal. Seduction, which in the story is accomplished by words, typically carries the implication of sex, an implication literalized in interpretations that imagine the serpent to have insinuated itself into Eve's body, depositing, in the language of the Zohar, "its filth" in Eve.[11] These interpretive traditions imagine sex before the sin of disobedience, in the temptation itself, between the woman and "the snake."

Culture has come to blame Eve for the first sin of disobedience.[12] The story rests on a displacement, however, since it is the snake who initiates the temptation, sensually, directing Eve's attention to the beauty and promise of the forbidden fruit. The desirability of forbidden fruit—pretty, sweet, juicy, and delicious—resonates with descriptions of feminine sexuality, extending the code of the sensual beyond the erect snake to the fruit, in another regress and reversal, as male and female desire for each other functions in a rapid relay of signification in the garden story. Even as female sexuality is said to tempt man and ruins his Edenic peace, driving him out to labor (the man's punishment for disobedience), the story displays some unease about which sex does the sexual tempting. By now, the snake as tempter has more than a little inevitability about it. We do not have to invoke Freud to recognize the snake as a classic phallic symbol, and to name it as such has an embarrassing obviousness. Children may be led to imagine a snake that lost its legs as punishment for its crime, but more logically, and in the tradition of art, the snake stands on its tail. Eve is tempted by an erect snake. And when the deed is done, this loquacious, excitable beast will be punished with the loss of its erection, humbled into slithering away, with God's declaring the snake to be woman's enemy and vulnerable to her "heel." Again, the male cultural unconscious betrays awe at the snake's persuasive power even as it manifests fear for the vulnerability of future snakes when exposed to women's regret and anger.[13]

Female sexuality brings the greatest threat to obedience to God and to personal peace and Edenic tranquillity (at least from the story's male perspective, in this two-sexed garden). She tempts and she brings trouble, the disquieting knowledge of the body in its nakedness. At the same time, not far below the story's surface or consciousness, male sexuality is at fault, and worse, is uncontrollable because disassociated and disembodied, appearing as it does in the form of an externalized erect snake, which, in woman's presence, is charmed upright (as if out of the basket). Before the woman tempts the man, the seductive, talking phallus tempts the woman. And Adam, thus magically deprived of reason, avows neither relationship with the snake nor any capability to control it.[14] Adam sacrifices innocence, out of a double consciousness that deprives the man of ownership of his own seductive capacities, a split consciousness that we will see again in Genesis in the twinning of Jacob and Esau, the smooth man of the tent and the hunter, who compete to inherit the patriarchy.

After the series of oppositions in the first two chapters of Genesis (sky/ earth; land/sea; day/night; sun/moon), the second and third chapters make the most important cultural distinction of all. Man opposes woman; innocence then opposes experience, and woman destroys innocence and gives it a second opposite term: guilt. In the chain of signification, experience is equivalent to guilt.[15] Among the many things that Adam has named, that is, in the whole world of man's possessions, woman (and not so much Eve as the fact of female sexuality) is a threat to male piety. It is a culturally familiar condition: women held responsible for male desire. Later generations of Jewish readers who imagine Paradise as the all-male world of the schoolroom might suppose that had the world not had women to tempt men from virtue and study, nothing would invite their thoughts to stray or lure their bodies from their benches. It is a moral we know well: Man must master woman, not so much because she sinned, but again, more deeply, because if female sexuality is not kept under control, woman has the power to continually destroy man's peace. This message is reinforced with a vengeance in biblical stories of seduction (discussed in Chapter 7). In cultural mythologies, for each oppressed population, we imagine that if released, they would be overpowering, often sexually. In this version of Hegel's master-slave dialectic, women must be controlled, as slaves had to be controlled, because of their dangerous sexuality. The story's relentless logic argues that women's apparent beauty and innocence are particularly threatening because of their capacity to undermine male reason, a message implicit in words like charming, spellbinding, and alluring, part of an extended descriptive vocabulary that characterizes female desirability as entailing a deprivation of one's better judgment.

This two-sex system is encoded elsewhere at the mythic foundations of Western thought. In Greek myth, Prometheus ("Forethought") creates humanity—as the story's later introduction of Pandora implies, in male form—as a kind of plaything, one which the gods generally scorn, until the scorn turns to contempt when Prometheus takes his game too far, defying Zeus's prohibition and stealing a spark of the gods' fire for mankind. Fire threatens to make humanity altogether too much like the gods. Analogous to the forbidden fruit of Eden, fire (a metaphor for knowledge, warmth, light, and technology) gives humanity divine potential. Knowing that the gods will wish to punish him, Prometheus warns his brother (and narrative double) Epimetheus ("Afterthought") to accept no gifts from the gods.

The gods devise a package that proves irresistible. Each god contributes his or her best gift: love, beauty, grace, and every appealing attribute is given to this new creature, Pandora ("All-gifts"), named for the full complement of gifts bestowed on the first woman. She herself is perfection, but she comes with a box, which she is ordered not to open, a box that contains the world's troubles, as well as the small saving addition of "hope." Epimetheus transgresses (again, following the narrative rule

Michelangelo Buonarroti (1475–1564), Original Sin. Ceiling frescoes after restoration. In Michelangelo's triangulated sexual encounter, the snake's sexual identity is ambiguous. Notice, too, the position of Eve's head as she has apparently transferred her attention from one "snake" to another. Erich Lessing / Art Resource, New York.

"where there is an admonition, there will be a transgression") and accepts Pandora, and Pandora, too, predictably disobeys, opening her box and releasing trouble, and hope, into the world. Like the serpent, "the box" is a disembodied part, a metonym, slang still current in the English language. Humanity's aspiration to have the knowledge of the gods—forbidden fruit/fire—is tied to the inability to resist the temptation of female sexuality and her inability to keep her box closed.

Paradoxically, the divine knowledge to which man aspires is of a piece with his attraction to the woman, whose presence interferes with the homosocial relationship between man and his god. This story too betrays the fear of female sexuality in our cultural unconscious: all might have been peaceful between man and his creator-god were it not for that box and the troubles it cannot manage to contain. But in that box too, and the procreative possibilities for which it stands—babies emerge from the selfsame box—resides hope, the potential for eternal life, after a fashion, among mortals. Like Eve, Pandora is about the dangerous temptation of female sexuality and its association with birth and death, mortality, and the cycle of life that are accounted for in these creation myths. Our most powerful origin stories connect sin and morality and sex and immortality, in a confusing chiastic structure—life, love, irreverence, and death inextricably bound up in one another.

If Genesis 1–2:3 is an allegory of birth and acculturation, the story of the garden is most familiar to critics as an allegory of adolescence. Although adolescence is a late invention, the triumph of psychoanalytic thought in our culture makes seeing the Garden of Eden as a tale of puberty unavoidable. The innocent Adam and Eve, content in an Edenic first home where everything comes easily and where their needs are effortlessly met, are admonished by a seemingly all-powerful parent to resist forbidden knowledge, even as God knows that eventually they will feel internally compelled to disobey. And compelled they are: first Eve is tempted by the promise of the seductive snake who tells her that by tasting forbidden fruit she can be like her awesome parent and enjoy parental knowledge, power, and freedom. And just as male sexuality tempts Eve, she easily seduces Adam, who does not want to be left behind. Once the children have shown signs of sexual self-consciousness, God, the Father, has no choice but to conclude, with a sigh, that these are children no more. The consequences are clear: it is time to expel them from this Edenic childhood home so that they can build a home of their own, facing the real conditions of life outside the garden of childhood. He will labor a resistant earth, and she will labor to bring forth babies. But the divine parent's banishment is regretful and nostalgic, and God, true to his emerging character as a parental hero in the rest of the Bible, says, in effect, "Don't be strangers. I'm here for you. Leave, but please stay in touch, and be good."[16]

Because this allegory, like many interpretations of the garden story, makes Adam and Eve roughly equivalent, it minimizes the distinctive characterization of the separate natures of man and woman and the extent to which those differences are inscribed on the body. Over time, as we will see, women's nature attaches ever more energetically to her sexuality. In subsequent biblical narratives, and much of Western literature, woman-hood is also increasingly split—and variously evaluated—between the two sexual roles of mother and seductress, both of which are contained, prototypically, in Eve, who is both first seducer and first mother. Even early readers of the garden myth, however, retrofit the story with a second female presence, in the introduction of Adam's first wife, Lilith, shifting the emphasis of Eve's identity to primal mother and characterizing Lilith as sexual predator.

LILITH: THE FIRST WOMAN SPLIT

Source critics were, of course, not the first to notice that there are two creation stories and that woman, in particular, seems to have been created twice. In the first chapter of Genesis, humanity is created male and female, and in the second, Adam's partner is removed from his side. Lilith thus becomes identified as the first wife. By inserting Lilith's story into this gap in the text, the midrashic tradition in effect doubles the biblical oppositions, creating two, opposed prototypes for womanhood. Eve, who in the Bible is active and disobedient, becomes, relative to Lilith, her own opposite. As traditions developed, Eve, by comparison with the rebellious first wife, is domesticated, characterized as pliant, maternal, nurturing, passive, and long-suffering. Lilith, by contrast, is disobedient, vengeful, aggressive, and destructive of babies and domestic peace. In the combination of these two figures we have the basic contradictions and stereotypes of womanhood, as these persist through the dichotomies of virgin or ma-donna, on the one hand, and harlot, on the other. The virgin and mother (managed and sometimes opposing social roles) are classically combined in Christianity in the Virgin Mother, a type that descends from the "barren mother" of Hebrew scripture.

In the earliest Jewish attestation of Lilith, *The Alphabet of Ben Sira* (circa tenth century), Lilith, who was created coequal with Adam, initially rebels by refusing to assume the bottom sexual position. Using the (until now, male) power of naming with magical results, Lilith invokes God's "ineffable name" to flee Eden, and when God, at Adam's request, sends three angels to reclaim her for the man, God threatens that if she does not return she will be doomed to a demonic life, regularly losing thousands of nascent demon babies. In what strikes me as the one of the funniest declarations of early narrative, Lilith prefers this punishment to returning to a life subordinate to Adam. The story belies God's ultimate authority—he lacks the power to persuade Lilith—and belies the perfection of Paradise for both sexes. Lilith prefers exile.

An earlier Midrash recorded in *Genesis Rabbah* also briefly recognizes a first wife, though one not called Lilith, and explains that Adam found her repulsive ("full of discharge and blood") because they were effectively born together in each other's sight. God has another try, and having learned from his mistake, first puts Adam to sleep, sending the narrative message that sexual desire requires mystery (and childbirth requires anesthesia). As these traditions developed, Lilith is sometimes identified with the snake, pictured in art as a beautiful, naked woman from the waist up, with a serpentine bottom half;[17] in Kabbalistic stories, she is sometimes identified as the female partner of Samael, God's negative counterpart (in a symmetry that makes Lilith the negative of the *Shechina*, God's feminine manifestation). In these traditions, Lilith regrets her exile and is desperate to reenter human community—like angels and other demons, all of whom envy humanity—and man's sinful fantasies gain her entrance into human beds, where she steals sperm from which to fashion her demon babies. She is held responsible for masturbation, nocturnal emissions, and infant mortality, and remembering that sperm was imagined to contain full potential people (*homunculi*), Lilith is on the spot to collect these tragic, unrealized souls.

If the reigning emotions in Eden are all varieties of desire—lust and envy—with an unsettled quality as to which sex acts first and most destructively on the lust and envy that God wishes humanity to control, the Lilith traditions remain within the code of sexual desire and replicate the sexual confusion and misdirection of the Eden narrative, complicating the already fragmented characterization of Eve with her photographic negative in a prior woman. But the very traditions that identify Lilith with the prior woman also sometimes identify her with the snake, alternately putting Lilith in sexual relation with Eve and Adam, confounding the two-sexed heterosexual system built in Eden.[18]

In other stories, Lilith is collapsed into Samael—as God and the Shechina are also two manifestations or names for the One God—exemplified in one memorable tale, in which a man is seduced by the beautifully transmogrified Lilith (she is described as having long red hair, a representation preserved in later paintings) only to wake up to find her having returned to her natural shape as the horrifyingly hideous Samael. Again, these elaborations on Genesis, which are intended to define man and woman and yoke woman's sexuality to sin, cannot manage to fix the sexes in place. No sooner does Lilith manifest as beautiful sexual manipulator than she is revealed to be male. Whether female sexuality controls man or is controlled by him is a persistent confusion.

The reclamation of Lilith by Jewish feminists—the title of the Jewish feminist magazine, a popular subject of the first wave of Jewish feminist essays and of "modern Midrash" and poetry—worked variously to appropriate and transvalue her demonized strengths and to recuperate Lilith's relationship with Eve by integrating the dichotomization of womanhood.[19] As I will discuss at greater length in the chapter on Leah and Rachel, women are rarely seen in productive relationship with one another in biblical narrative, and Judith Plaskow's revision in the story "Epilogue: The Coming of Lilith" implicitly addresses the tendency of foundation myths to represent women principally in relation to their husbands, sons, and lovers. In Plaskow's epilogue, which reads like an allegory of generational conflict early in the women's movement, Eve catches a glimpse of Lilith (someone who is like her) but about whom Eve has heard terrible things from Adam. Some girl talk convinces Eve that Lilith has been unfairly maligned, and when they become friends, Adam and God are both "expectant and a little afraid."

As in many Lilith poems, Eve is the housewife (who senses "greater capacities within herself"), and Lilith, who knows the advantages of liberation, is also a little lonely. As constructed in Genesis, Eve and Adam, who eat fruit and launch civilization together, are partners and antagonists in a story that struggles and fails to settle their sexual definitions; over time, Eve's sexuality was reconstrued to make her into both Adam's opposite and the figure of primal mother, opposed to what would become throughout the Bible the other "type" of woman, the predator-seducer. The early feminist fantasy of a collaboration between the two types represented by Eve and Lilith, with hints of an excluding relationship, besides whatever sociological or other realities it exposes, also exposes the energy and the ease with which these traditions manage the boxes in which the sexes had for so long been fixed. These boxes try—and continuously fail—to control both the definitions of the sexes and the channels of desire. Within those traditions that link Lilith with the seductive serpent, Lilith titillates Eve.

In one of Enid Dame's Lilith poems, "Lilith's Talent," Lilith mothers "energy," the "unpredictable spark into a world that needs it," but which men, afraid, "insist" on calling demons. In another ("Lilith"), Dame represents Lilith as "storming out of Eden into history." A witch in the Middle Ages, today she works in New Jersey, takes art lessons, and lives with a cabdriver. At the same time, she recognizes that although she could not live with Adam ("patient," "hairy," and "safe" but who "consulted God like an almanac" that always proved her wrong), she sometimes cries

Collier, John (1850–1934), Lilith. The identification of Lilith and the snake confuses the sexual identities of seducer and seduced. Reproduced by kind permission of Sefton MBC Leisure Services Department, Arts and Cultural Services, Atkinson Art Gallery.

"in the bathroom / remembering Eden / and the man and the god / I couldn't live with." Here, Lilith is the type of the mild female rebel who resists social role assignment—differently manifested at different historical moments—who got what she wanted, but not without consequence. The enviable naughty girl misses safety and the house and garden that she sacrificed for her freedom. I linger on these recent poetic responses to the Lilith born in the midrashic and mystical literature only to point out how continuous a tradition of stereotypes evolved from introducing Lilith into Eden. Even in her feminist incarnations, Lilith functions as a foil that subdues Eve's sexuality, enabling Eve to more appropriately assume her out-of-Eden functions as wife and mother.[20] Eve, no less than Lilith, resists control.

Although Lilith is a later addition to the myth, we should remember that in the narrative sequence, she precedes Eve and is effectively gone before Eve is created. Rabbinic Midrash imagines that after Lilith is banished from Eden, God labors with extra caution to create Eve free of the vices inherent in his first failed attempt to produce a fit companion for Adam. Nonetheless, Eve is first to sin, and religious interpretations of the Bible have rationalized a long history of the denigration of women by focusing on Eve's having eaten the fruit and offered it to Adam. More important, however, is that Eve's bad behavior is somehow related to the imagined distinctiveness of her body. A classic rabbinic commentary, for example, relates Eve's having been drawn from Adam's side rather than from some other part of the body to God's intention to make the first woman "chaste." The text, as paraphrased by Louis Ginzberg in *The Legends of the Jews*, has God saying:

> "I will not make her from the head of man lest she carry her head high in arrogant pride; not from the eye, lest she be an eavesdropper; not from the neck, lest she be insolent; not from the mouth, lest she be a tattler; not from the heart, lest she be inclined to envy; not from the hand, lest she be a meddler; not from the foot, lest she be a gadabout. I will form her from a chaste portion of the body."

Ginzberg continues:

> and to every limb and organ as He formed it, God said, "Be chaste! Be chaste!" Nevertheless, in spite of the great caution used, woman has all the faults God tried to obviate. The daughters of Zion walked with stretched forth necks and wanton eyes; Sarah was an eavesdropper in her own tent, when the angel spoke with Abraham; Miriam was a talebearer, accusing Moses; Rachel was envious of her sister Leah; Eve put out her hand to take the forbidden fruit, and Dinah was a gadabout.[21]

Each biblical heroine in this list is identified by faults implicit or explicit in her stories, but more importantly, the fault of each woman is ascribed to the fact of her being a woman, a descendant of Eve (as if, somehow, women descend from women and men from men). Still more important, each fault is defined as a failure of chastity linked to an unchaste part of the body: whether hand, mouth, neck, foot, or heart. Although these body parts are human, their nature in women is marked by wantonness. Finally, what is stunning about this rabbinic fantasy of God's creation of Eve is the ease with which God is represented as helpless against women's ability to subvert his will. What must these rabbis have thought of God, if desperate as he seems to have been to make woman chaste, she continually thwarts his best efforts?

More likely, however, this fantasy says less about rabbinic assessments of God's power than about the rabbis' unconscious conviction that women are beyond control, despite heroic attempts. What we will see repeatedly in subsequent chapters is a construction of female sexuality in biblical narrative in which woman, whether in her role as mother or in her role as seductress, possesses extraordinary power, even in relation to God. Variously, in different stories, this subversive power defies God's efforts to know her mind, puts her in victorious conspiracy with God against the will of men, or enables her to defeat men physically much stronger than she. How Eve, first mother and first seducer, is figured in her story generates the proliferation of images of decisive female power, the locus of which is in her sexuality. Though God himself demanded of each female part that it be chaste, generations of heroines proved that womanhood, by a definition outside of her Creator's control, is incompatible with that effort.

Biblical heroines divide generally between mothers and seducers. The following chapter looks in particular at the power of biblical "barren mothers"—an oxymoron that captures the paradox of women's powerless power—and in subsequent chapters, I will consider the paradox of seductresses who lack sexual desire as well as the relationship of these self-contradictory characterizations of womanhood to the construction of Jewish masculinity. In the book's final chapter, closure brings us to Ruth, who is in some ways a redemptive reprise of Eve, another character who is defined both by her identity as a first mother (in Ruth's case, of the messianic line) and ultimate (in her case, pious) seductress.

2

Sarah's Laughter: Matriarchal Incoherence and the Vexed Sign of Woman

OVERVIEW

Sarah, the first matriarch, is associated with laughter. In a posture that can serve as a metaphor for the position of women in history, the ancient heroine eavesdrops on Abraham and the angels at the tent flap to learn about her own future. When an angel reveals that she will become a mother in her old age, Sarah's response is an ambiguous laughter. Even God is perplexed. He asks Abraham: "Why did Sarah laugh?" and when Sarah, afraid, denies having laughed, God, like Freud after him, indicates that although he evidently sees what women do, he is at a loss for an explanation.[1] God replies, without apparent judgment, "but you did laugh" (Genesis 18:13–15)

It is a rich sign, this laughter, full of interpretive possibility: laughter of delight, of terror, of skepticism (the usual interpretation), of bemusement, of bitterness, of mirth, of sexual pleasure, of who-knows-what. Just as the creation story may be read as a cosmic semiotic event that organizes the categories of our reality, so Sarah's laughter gives us a legacy of semiotic possibility, an invitation to revisit Eve in the garden of meanings and recognize that "Woman" itself is, like all identity categories, a vexed construct susceptible of radical reimagining.

In the Garden of Eden, the site of perfection, God creates two sexes, male and female, each with apparently distinct natures and life roles. As I hope I have shown, when these first people enter into the complexity of narrative, they themselves become complicated, and sexual confusion proliferates. The fact and meaning of male and female is unsystematically undermined, first by the details of the Bible story itself, second by elaborations on the Eden story over time in literature and art, and third by the interpretive tradition. Just as the Bible takes two sexes for granted, it also assumes the naturalness of the nuclear family. With an emphasis on the origin myths of Jewish motherhood, this chapter discusses how the Bible establishes and disrupts the concept of the nuclear family and the gender roles of parents and children.[2]

If we approach the biblical invention and representation of motherhood obliquely, through the stories' "fluids and voices," we notice that laughter, muttering, and blood flow from women as boundary-spilling excesses interfere with the Bible's attempts to delimit female roles. Looking at the barren mother stories of Sarah and Hannah with attention to voices and fluids—a shift away from the more usual categories of analyses of Jewish theology (such as God, Israel, and Torah)—exposes confusions in the elaborations of gender and power in the Bible.[3] Within the Bible's dichotomized universe, these heroines subvert the neatness of social categories. The distinctive voices and fluids of women characters reveal "Woman," as a category, to embody the paradox of being at once within the category of "Human" and outside the parameters of a hypothetical normative humanity. Moreover, this paradox is incorporated into the son, who becomes a progenitor of Jewish masculinity, ultimately, masculinity with a difference. As early as Eve, woman deviates from an unrealized ideal of womanhood that ultimately calls into question the very possibility of gender norms.

Sarah laughs. Hannah, mother of the prophet Samuel, prays so grievously and incoherently that the priest, Eli, rebukes her for drunkenness (1 Samuel 1–2:10). These details are part of biblical type scenes that have been called "annunciations," stories in which heretofore "barren women" have an encounter that predicts their fertility.[4] Not only do these "barren mothers" vocalize enigmatically; they are themselves enigmas. Since a mother, by definition, cannot be barren, the class of biblical "barren mothers" is literally a contradiction in terms. Moreover, as mothers, these heroines persist in violating the boundaries of gender roles and social norms: in special relationship with God, they have an overriding authority in the family and in determining the political future (roles that belong, in theory, to the father) and are often instrumental in subverting patriarchal authority by overturning rules of primogeniture. Maternal incoherence—here, anticipatory laughter or whimpering—functions like static on the screen, disturbing the superficial, conventional picture of a mother-father-son(s) (rarely daughters) family arrangement. Sarah and Hannah are exemplary barren mothers.[5]

ORIGINAL FAMILIES: BORN OF THE BARREN MOTHER

As a history of the world, the Bible begins with creation and the first family, followed by genealogies that lead to Noah. But as the generations multiply, there is a growing conflict between the linearity of narrative and the three-dimensional, exponential character of populating the Earth. Increasingly, it becomes impossible to give everyone a story, diminishing the Bible's capacity to thoroughly fulfill its implicit promise to be the sacred history of God's creation. The problem is solved first in the generation of Noah by destroying creation and beginning over, after which the Bible promises instead to become the story of the seed of Abraham, a limiting gesture to the line that leads to the people Israel, whose story this book becomes. From the competition for God's favor in the story of Cain and Abel through the patriarchs, Genesis includes sequential stories of sibling rivalry, as sons compete for their place in the narrative future to become the next father of the triumphant line. In every case, the competition between brothers displaces a competition between wives or parents, in which, invariably, the beloved matriarch wins the future through the son of her choosing.

When a biblical hero has a birth story, his mother is barren, necessitating the Creator God's reentry into human history. Just as the first males bring forth the first life—first God, then Adam—so whenever a hero is born into the narrative, God must remove the mother's curse of barrenness. Ironically, both childbearing, which is Eve's punishment, and infertility are represented as curses. An unintended consequence of God's intervention is the double diminishment of the patriarch, who is inadequate to bring this pregnancy into being. Although the mother is represented as barren, God impregnates where the husband has failed. Inasmuch as barrenness is also a possible punishment for infidelity, it is also susceptible to being a sign of a man's shame.[6] Second, God and mother establish a bond around this pregnancy that gives the mother an unusual influence over her son's future, which, in the cases of Samson and Samuel, she promises to dedicate to God's service. (The virgin birth and sacrifice of Jesus are a culminating and exaggerated variation of these patterns in Christian scripture.)

The relative authority of mother and father proves as unstable as the sexual instability that lies just below the surface of the creation stories that establish "male" and "female" in the first place. God the Father not only supplants the human father but God bonds with the wife: God tells Abraham to "listen to Sarah" when she privileges Isaac over Ishmael; Rebecca manipulates the preferment of her favorite son Jacob to the detriment of Isaac's beloved Esau, apparently on the basis of God's prophecy when

the boys were in utero (Genesis 25:23); Hannah with independent authority surrenders her son Samuel to temple service; Samson's anonymous
mother, who is also barren, takes the Nazirite vow of abstinence from
wine and haircuts on behalf of her unborn son. Her husband, Manoah,
is represented as an ineffectual, even foolish, character. The empowerment and self-confidence that coincides with pregnancy for these heroines anticipates the Freudian representation of the pregnant woman as
"having" the phallus that is equivalent to male authority. Pregnancy, in
Freud's theory, is the consolation for the fantasy of castration (penis envy
replaced by longing for a baby), with the son/fetus being the equivalent
of a maternal penis.[7] These biblical foundation stories establish the precedent for the Freudian characterization of female desire and satisfaction:
envious longing for a child followed by the presumption of authority
with pregnancy.

In three ways, then, maternal distinction is assimilated into the main,
These stories also deliberately associate the hero's prelinguistic self-
formation with "the maternal," which (like the Lacanian imaginary)
entails the first separations and losses born of entering into language
and the symbolic order of the father.[8] Weaning is dramatically marked
in both the stories of Isaac and Samuel: Abraham has a weaning party
for Isaac, and Samuel is delivered into temple apprenticeship when he is
weaned. This transition to independence from the maternal body brings
the significant sons into the narrative world of men, but not before their
mothers, in an excluding conspiracy with God, have set the direction
for their adult leadership roles. Moreover, the mother's unconventional,
nonverbal self-expression is assimilated into the identity of the son: just as
Isaac (whose name means "he will laugh") carries laughter in his name,
so Samuel's name, which means "God heard," is the permanent reminder
of his mother's extraordinary capacity to reach God's hearing. In a mirror
inheritance from his mother, Samuel grows up with a special capacity to
hear the voice of God, and the tradition will honor Hannah's effective, but
misunderstood prayer strategy by codifying it as the standard for Jewish
prayer (quietly and with moving lips).[9]

In three ways, then, maternal distinction is assimilated into the main,
male tradition: first, naming the sons in honor of the maternal passion
for them ("he will laugh" and "God has heard" respectively); second, ap-
propriating Hannah's unorthodox prayer style by making it the rule for
both men and women, and finally, in liturgically assimilating the corpus
of biblical women's poetry (including Hannah's prayer and the songs
of Miriam and Deborah). Perhaps sensitive to the subversive power of
women's voices, Jewish tradition suppresses these exuberances. Rabbinic Judaism makes special efforts to manage both the voices and fluids
of women (for example, with menstrual regulations and prohibitions
against women's public singing).

Born of passionate barren mothers and with rare textual attention to the transition of their weaning, Isaac and Samuel are also deliberately associated with blood. Just as laughter is ambiguous and overdetermined, so too blood—the sign of the woman (menstruation) and the sign of the Jew (circumcision)—carries gender ambiguity that makes blood a focus of Jewish legislation. Menstrual blood, paschal blood—the sign on the doorposts that saves the Israelites from the angel of death—blood of circumcision, and blood of the sacrifices are all mutually implicated, ambiguous signs of both holiness and impurity, staining the ultimate liminal place, the border between life and death, and the entrance to the physical body.[10] Isaac's body is marked by the sign of the covenant with the blood of the first circumcision, a cut to sexual flesh that is a permanent reminder of male vulnerability. Later, Isaac's near sacrifice at the hands of his father exaggerates that vulnerability. With his weaning, Samuel enters temple service, the site of cultic sacrifice, the place of holy blood. These heroes, associated with maternal laughing, crying, milk and blood, are prototypical mama's boys.

This image of mothers who enforce the privileging of their sons—often younger, gentler, and more domestic boys—persists late into the twentieth century in the stereotypes of the overpowering Jewish mother and the intellectual, poorly athletic, dependent, dutiful Jewish mama's boy. These lingering stereotypes of empowered and castrating Jewish mothers who conspire with God, and Jewish husbands and sons whose masculinity is compromised relative to other men—stereotypes that are ingrained through repeated patterns of representation from the Bible through Philip Roth's *Portnoy's Complaint*—are one ethnic variation on the ideological and sociological installation of the normative nuclear family. The stereotype of the silenced Jewish family man is evidenced in a joke so classic that a version of it finds its way into *The Norton Anthology of American Jewish Literature*.[11] It is the one about the Jewish boy who comes home and announces proudly that he got the part of the Jewish husband in the school play, at which the mother screams that he must "go back to the teacher and demand a speaking part!" This joke, ostensibly at the expense of the Jewish husband, manages to slander wife, mother, and son as well. If the Jewish husband is henpecked, like Bontshe Shvayg and Gimpel the Fool (stock Jewish characters who are quiet and accepting in the face of every indignity), the implication is that the Jewish man's silence is best explained by the Jewish wife and mother, whose shrewish voice fills all the available space.[12] The son is doubly silenced by the joke: first, by the example of the father whom he is presumably destined to become when he himself becomes a Jewish husband (a worse fate perhaps than playing the role in a school drama), and second by his controlling, interfering mother who deflates his boast by scripting a response to his teacher. The implication too is that the Jewish mother, and not the Jewish father, sets the bar for Jewish masculinity.

The "biblical family," like the "oedipal family" in Sophocles' plays, distinguishes itself by dysfunctions that presume an unrepresented "normal family" from which the matriarchs and patriarchs deviate. Psychoanalytic descriptions of "normative" and "healthy" environments for childrearing emerge from this presumption of the inevitability of the nuclear family composed of two parents and children. The stories of primal families are stories of atypical families and generate the need for an analytic vocabulary of dysfunction to describe such extraordinary circumstances as competition between co-wives, the near sacrifice of sons, and bitterness between spouses and brothers. These first family stories suggest paradigms of psychological struggles within the nuclear family model, as particular deviations from an implicit norm. In our example, the stories presume paternal authority and maternal fertility and passivity as the rule but repeatedly represent infertile and assertive mothers and fathers rendered circumstantially submissive.

In the elaboration of separate spheres for men and women—especially within the family—Midrash and Bible scholarship, from the anthropology of Carol Meyers to the personal psychodynamic explorations of Peter Pitzele, builds on the biblical foundation of the family.[13] Against a background of family norms, deviations from these roles become productive of particular neuroses. The patterns of these Bible stories ultimately yield sons with the "Jewish neuroses," popularized, mocked, and also valorized by Woody Allen, or sexual neuroses, including impotence and homosexuality, which are presumed to derive from the dynamics of one's family of origin. (I return to this construct of Jewish masculinity in the following chapter on Jacob and Esau.) Moreover, woman, here in her role as mother and elsewhere in her role as lover, is, like Eve, ambivalently represented in the system. She is at once relatively powerless and dependent (on God, husband, and son) and overempowered, fierce in her pursuit of her maternal and political interests.

EAVESDROPPING ON ANGELS AND LAUGHING AT GOD: THEORIZING A SUBVERSIVE MATRIARCHY

Sarah's behavior borders on heresy. She eavesdrops on angels and laughs at God. At best rude, eavesdropping is more usually manipulative, an effort to discover what one is not meant to know, and in political contexts, the activity may of course be treasonous and dangerous. Eavesdropping on angels conjures up a Lucifer who illicitly acquires divine knowledge and whose response is brazen, inappropriate, and disrespectful: seditious laughter. Laughing is always potentially ambiguous: it may be mirthful, skeptical, contained, or hysterical; ironic, nervous, delighted, humored, or mean. But when the object of laughter is God, surely this laughter is loud and demonic, at best profoundly embittered, at worst, frankly evil.

But when Sarah eavesdrops on Abraham's conversation with God's messengers who came to declare her fate, and even when she laughs, the reader does not disapprove, and the text too is comfortable with her behavior. Denied direct access to power—sacred or otherwise—Sarah presents an image of women who position themselves to "overhear" the plans of gods and men as a survival strategy. To the extent that men "live" within institutions and women "survive" them, we see a distinction built into the etymology of "sur-vival" itself, "over" living, or living "over," like "overhearing" as opposed to simply living and hearing. Because woman is positioned at the boundary between inside and outside, what is insidious behavior for men can be normative for women.[14]

As a foundation text, the Bible installs the family and gender roles within the family through repeated narrative patterns. Within these patterns, fluids and vocalizations challenge bodily limits with failures of containment. Sarah's motherhood is replete with bodily details: Sarah names her menopause; she is aware of her body's being beyond childbearing years, and in referring to her husband's old age, she hints at his limitations as well. In these episodes, both Abraham and Sarah "laugh," a verb used elsewhere in the Bible to refer unambiguously to sexual play. This linguistic echo suggests that their laughter may be the laughter of *jouissance*, shuddering and orgasmic, and productive of the boy whose name hopes for more of the same.[15]

When Isaac is born, "Abraham was a hundred years old. . . . Sarah said, 'God has brought me laughter [alternatively: "playing"]'" (Genesis 21:5–6). Here, laughter or sport is linked to Abraham and Sarah's old age, and with the new baby named for laughter, they confound the picture of new parents as young parents. I am reminded of the quip attributed to George Bernard Shaw that "we do not stop playing because we grow old; we grow old because we stop playing." This story's repetitions around words with multiple meanings that derive from the shared root letters for "play," "sexual sport," and "laughter" shake up not only family roles but also the construction of the body along the axis of age.

Perhaps uncomfortable with the picture of an elderly new mother, Midrash keeps this wife preternaturally young and beautiful, explicitly because she had not endured the ravages of pregnancy and childbirth.[16] Another effect of Sarah's youthful appearance is to honor the classic split between the sexual woman and the maternal woman: in the rivalries between Hagar and Sarah, Rachel and Leah, and Hannah and Penina, the infertile co-wife retains her sexual desirability to a greater extent than the less attractive, fertile mother. The commentaries make much of Sarah's youthfulness in her old age: according to the text, Sarah died at "one hundred years and twenty years and seven years," a phrasing interpreted by the rabbis to mean that at one hundred, she was as sinless as a seven year old and as beautiful as a twenty year old. She is called "Yiskah" (a name derived from "looking") because people "used to gaze at her beauty."[17] At once old, barren, envious, and desperate with longing *and* beautiful, fertile, playful, privileged, beloved, and authoritative, the barren mother multiply confounds and reinvents a woman's body and her roles.

Other commentators, unhappy with the implication that God does not understand Sarah's motivations, translate instead of "Sarah laughed," "Sarah mocked" or "derided." God's question is then rhetorical, a reproach in the syntax of a question: "Why do you mock, Woman, am I, God, not capable of anything?" The answer is implicit in the question.[18] It is through this word again, the root letters of which give us "to laugh," "to mock," and "to sport," complete with an ambiguous rendering of "play," that we are asked to understand Sarah's banishment of Ishmael and Hagar. Sarah sees the older brother "playing with" (some translations render it "mocking") the younger. But this verb "to play" or "to mock" (*mitzachek* in its biblical rendering) also comes from the same root as Isaac's name; so in playing (with) Isaac, Ishmael "isaacs Isaac."[19] Midrashim speculate about what Ishmael did. Were the boys playing pretend, and did Ishmael play the part of the favored younger child, forcing Sarah to banish her son's would-be usurper?

This activity reverberates in Isaac's life. As an adult, Isaac will be caught attempting to pass his wife off as his sister (a story-type repeated from his parents' youth) when he is seen "sporting with" ("isaacing") his wife (as sister), Rebecca. Accordingly, importing this rendering back to his youthful experience, a less innocent reading is that in "isaacing Isaac," Ishmael plays dirty, plays with Isaac sexually, and Sarah responds with appropriate necessity to banish the boy. It is indeterminate of course, but that finally is the point. Sarah's laughter, and Isaac as heir to her laughter, yields only ambiguity, and in so doing it participates in the mystery of God's working in his history book.[20]

Abraham, the first patriarch, gives us monotheism, faith, and duty. We remember Abraham, above all, as the knife-wielding father ready to sacrifice the son named for laughing. One might notice here that Sarah's bequest can be construed as the opposite of duty, something more anarchic and illogical than the obedience made emblematic by Søren Kierkegaard's philosophic elevation of Abraham's leap of faith. Her narrative, by contrast, displays a consciousness of her own and her husband's sexual bodies, with its oblique reference to menarche, intercourse, and male potency, all coded as liminal or doubtful because associated with the sexual bodies of the aged.

CO-WIVES: FROM TENSION TO TALK THERAPY

Eve and the Lilith tradition inaugurate a long history of division between the figures of mother and lover (madonna and whore). The woman who experiences long years of infertility is the wife who retains her youthful beauty, does not have to be shared with sons, and remains the focus of her husband's attentions. In the rivalries between Hagar and Sarah, Rachel and Leah, and Penina and Hannah, the text builds and rebuilds triangles of envy: one woman envies the other's being loved, while her rival envies her fertility; the patriarch (who has both women) wonders why his love is not enough to satisfy the infertile wife. These stories settle all competitions in favor of the barren wife.

Sarah's infertility is a source of tension in her relationship with Hagar, mother of Abraham's son Ishmael. Although Abraham and God both affirm Sarah's authority over Hagar, Sarah reacts aggressively to Hagar's taunting. In the next generation, Rebecca, who communicates with God when her sons are struggling in utero, helps Jacob outsmart his father and brother. A generation later, Rachel's desperation for a child and envy of her less loved, fertile sister provoke her husband, Jacob, who wonders what *he* is supposed to do ("Am I God?" he asks) and why his love is not enough to satisfy her. God, however, answers Rachel's plea with Joseph, whose heroism will occupy the final chapters of Genesis. In a reprise of these patterns, Hannah, too, is not satisfied with the double portions that are proof of her husband's love and preference for her over the taunting co-wife, Penina.

In the representation of Hannah's and Penina's competition over childbearing, in Hannah's self-evaluation being dependent on her fertility, and in her ambitions for a son are time-honored biblical patterns with persistent consequences. Typically in the Bible we do not see women in relationship with one another, and when they are, the dominant discernible emotion is envy. They default to competition for the man who triangulates between them. From Hannah and Penina through countless contemporary films, including Hannah's namesake in Woody Allen's *Hannah and Her Sisters* (which I look at closely in Chapter 4), the representation of a man choosing between women who, at least in the case of sisters, might be expected to be more devoted to one another than to him is an age-old literary consolation in a culture that fears women's intimacy. This text's privileging of fertility (the woman's self-evaluation depends entirely on her being a mother) is also a time-honored priority with devastating consequences for generations of infertile women.

Although Sarah's laughter and Hannah's prayers are suspect and subject to interrogation by the angel and the priest, respectively, the text vindicates the heroine. The pattern of suspicion and vindication heightens the reader's appreciation for the heroine distinguished by the privilege of freedoms commensurate with her earlier desperation.[21] Hannah and the priest, Eli, do not at first understand each other. Neither is there reason to hope that the temple official will doubt his judgment. Hannah is a childless woman, and both facts—her childlessness and her being a woman—reduce her status and, potentially, her credibility. Like Sarah, Hannah might be described in today's vocabulary as lacking self-esteem. Eli, in a role at the high end of the social spectrum, rebukes Hannah because he misreads her behavior as a symptom of inebriation. Remarkably, Hannah and Eli come to mutual understanding in the service of the divine plan for the people's future. Ultimately, Eli assures Hannah that her prayers will be answered.

Rereading the text from our own historical position, we see the start of a tradition that distrusts women's seriousness of purpose. We also see the consequences to her of humiliation and a counterforce that enables her to transcend the circumstances of her life and the constrictions of her sex. Twice in the story Hannah is represented as being in so much distress that she does not eat. After she talks with the priest and successfully articulates her own needs and the depth of her feelings, and after she is able to imagine, from his response, a more hopeful future, Hannah eats. Soon after, she conceives.

The efficacy of Hannah's prayer and her conversation with the priest function as a kind of therapeutic practice, prayer as talk therapy. Similarly, while anorexia nervosa is a diagnosis late in the history of ideas, a disease of the modern era to which high-achieving girls, afraid of the contradictory demands of adult womanhood, are particularly susceptible, at this juncture it is hard not to notice that Hannah exhibits symptoms of a like disorder. Although assured of being specially loved, Sarah and Hannah live in competitive situations and are ambitious. They struggle with mixed messages about their worth and the basis of female value. These circumstances lead to classic symptoms of anxiety or hysteria: for today's readers, these disorders, however unconsciously, offer us plausible explanations for Sarah's laughter and Hannah's anguished cries.[22] Also in anachronistic vocabulary, we might say that Hannah's anxiety and depression inhibit her eating, and self-starvation inhibits ovulation and menstruation. The story relates that Hannah unburdens herself emotionally, finds support from a male authority, eats, and then miraculously conceives.

Eli and Hannah's clarifying exchange can be read as an effort to partner in discovering God's will in the difficult-to-deal-with fact of Hannah's childlessness. Sarah's laughter, Hannah's mumbling, and God's choices challenge readability, revealing the basic insecurity of life. Part of the optimism of Hannah's story's rests in the assumption that communication can actually effect a change of heart: Eli reverses his negative opinion of Hannah and promises her the hoped for reward for her pious prayers. It is actually no small thing for the priest to adjust his view.[23]

A GLOSS ON LAUGHTER:
MOTHERS, WITCHES, AND HYSTERICS

Writing about Rabelais in a discussion of "the history of laughter," Mikhail Bakhtin explains:

> Laughter liberates not only from external censorship but first of all from the great interior censor; it liberates from the fear that developed in man during thousands of years: fear of the sacred, prohibitions, of the past, of power. It unveils the material bodily principle in its true meaning. Laughter opened men's eyes on that which is new, on the future.[24]

Although Bakhtin's analysis locates this kind of laughter, and this function for laughter, at a relatively late historical date, Sarah's laughter conforms to this description. Well before the feudal fear to which Bakhtin alludes, Sarah's laughter at the prospect of having successful intercourse and bearing a child in old age intimates at the power of laughter to mitigate fear of the sacred. Sarah's laughter as an old woman on the verge of pregnancy is also bound up with "material bodily principles" (maybe even, by some readings, "the grotesque") while "pointing in the direction of the future" (Isaac: "he will laugh").

I am making much of Sarah's laughter. By way of justification, I want to borrow the argument from French feminist thought that woman's laughter signifies something over and above human laughter, and a woman's laughter can no longer be read innocent of its many associations. It is laughter, not reason, that Kathleen Norris requests in her poem "A Prayer to Eve." She begins: "Mother of fictions / and of irony, / help us to laugh." A resonant sentence from Hélène Cixous's famous essay of 1975 "The Laugh of the Medusa" asks us to look again at the Medusa: "You have only to look at the Medusa straight on to see her. And she is not deadly. She's beautiful and she's laughing." Carol P. Christ, in her "reflections on a journey to the Goddess," which is the subtitle of her book *Laughter of Aphrodite*, writes self-reflexively about "Gavriel's laughter" entering her bones. The reference is to Elie Wiesel's *Gates of the Forest*, which begins with mythic laughter rising above the corpses of angels who had entered into mortal struggle. In this laughter, as in the laughter of Aphrodite that she hears on a personal journey in Lesbos, Christ finds a "mediator of transformation."[25] Not mirth, this laughter distances Christ from pain.

Fluids and voices, like otherwise neutral human body parts, are always potentially gendered. The rabbinic Midrash in which God creates the first woman from a chaste part of the body, avoiding the hands, feet, neck, and a list of human parts from which Eve was not created lest she be wanton—among the faults that God tried but failed to obviate in woman—reflects the presumption that even body parts common to the sexes are differently construed when they attach to woman. Granting themselves a similar presumption, Cixous and Catherine Clément invite us to celebrate, by reevaluating, the extra-human qualities of features of woman. For example, the distinctively human activity of laughter, peculiarly understood when associated with women, links laughing women to witches and hysterics, within the category of "the monstrous." Clément writes with pleasure that laughter "breaks up, breaks out, splashes over," "petrifying and shattering constraint."[26] Invoking Mary Douglas's analysis of forbidden foods, Clément sees women's laughter, by analogy, as a category violation, like lobster (a walking fish) and also like other uncontained, ambiguous human products that are at once life-sustaining, deadly, and uncontainable.

With reference to this laughter, Clément quotes Mary Douglas's *Purity and Danger*:

> Each culture . . . attributes a power to some image or another of the body, according to the situation of which the body is the mirror. . . . The things that defile are always wrong one way or another, they are not in their place or else they have crossed a line they never should have crossed and from this shift a danger for someone results.[27]

Douglas identifies that which defiles as that which is outside of recognized category boundaries: obvious examples in Judaism include bodily emissions. Blood should be inside; when it is outside, it defiles and is impure. If bugs crawl and fish swim, a fish that crawls (like a lobster) is unkosher, a category violation. Clément glosses Douglas by invoking Lacanian psychoanalytic theory: "To break up, to touch the masculine integrity of the body image, is to return to a stage that is scarcely constituted in human development; it is to return to the disordered Imaginary of before the mirror stage, of before the rigid and defensive constitution of subjective armor." Clément explains that "[a]n entire fantastic world, made of bits and pieces, opens up beyond the limit, as soon as the line is crossed. For the witch (the hysteric), breaking apart can be paradise, but for another it is hell."[28]

Woman's laughter (her heaven, his hell), Clément implies, is a category violation in our culture. The monstrous laughter associated with hysterics and witches brings Clément, through Douglas, to the Lacanian imaginary, that is, to the prelinguistic connection to the mother, or, as I want to have it, to matriarchy itself, before the entry of the child into the Law, before the child is taken over by the father, law, reason, and logic. Abraham's celebration at Isaac's weaning is evidence that ancient ritual since lost to us marked this psychological transition from the chaotic prelinguistic maternal imaginary to the more settled state of paternal law. Here, weaning represents not traumatic loss (as Melanie Klein suggests) but a positive movement to cultural containment. This appreciation of weaning as the happy independence of son from mother finds expression in the metaphor for contentment in Psalm 131:2: "But I have taught myself to be contented like a weaned child with its mother; like a weaned child am I in my mind."

These constructions of woman's laughter, blood, and milk as dangerously, unnaturally, even inhumanly uncontained remind me of a piece of graffiti from a fraternity bathroom: "Never trust anything that bleeds for seven days and does not die." Why is this advice as funny as it is disturbing? Because all of us, even women, function within a system in which unstopped bleeding means death. Forgetting the very humanity of women who menstruate for seven days and do not die, this injunction against trusting women (who are implicitly not human, witches) startles us into an awareness that women stand outside looking in, in the most surprising places, even in the most natural places and even in women's own consciousness. Hence the angel and the priest approach the hero's mother with curiosity and suspicion. Woman's laughter or tears, like woman's blood, is gender specific and unpredictable—not simply human.

Cixous begins "Laugh of Medusa" by promising to speak about women's writing and enjoining woman to "write herself" because women have been driven from writing "as violently as from their own bodies— for the same reasons, by the same law, with the same fatal goal." Implicitly, woman claims writing by reclaiming her body. With dangerous, compelling enthusiasm, Cixous promises: "Now, I-woman am going to blow up the Law; an explosion henceforth possible and ineluctable; let it be done, right now, in language." A feminist reading practice of biblical gender roles attends to "laughter," "milk," and "blood," in keeping with Cixous's ultimate reminder that woman "writes with white ink."[29] The voices and fluids, the sounds and sensations of being human, are relentlessly marked by gender.

Laughing, crying, singing, water, milk, and blood have sexual and gender significance. Biblical literature offers early representations of associations that have become integrated into the Western mythology of the feminine. Future brides, such as Rebecca and Tsipporah, are located by wells, and Miriam is especially associated with water. I think too of mother's milk, the celebration at Isaac's weaning, Yael's gift of milk to Sisera before she murdered him, and blood's monthly presence, the Levitical purity laws, the blood of childbirth, circumcision, and sacrifice, and the absence of blood lamented by Sarah when she doubts that she can conceive after her time. Whether the connotations are positive or negative in a particular context, certain fluids and articulations of voice have accrued meanings that contribute to something like a code of woman's mystery and power in our cultural heritage.

HUMAN VERSUS WOMAN: UNDOING BY OVERDOING

From such classic statements as the essays in Susannah Heschel's *On Being a Jewish Feminist* through Plaskow's most recent work, Jewish feminist research frequently begins by positioning woman in her alterity or her absence. Whatever the field of investigation—biblical narrative, rabbinic Midrash, *halakha*, myth, ritual, *shtetl* life, or contemporary life—women have been located as the so-called Other within the male normative discourse that names her, defines her, legislates for her, and restricts her. Scholars notice that woman's body is energetically defined by its difference, and in so doing, participates in a process that ties woman to man by the energy of opposition. For example, in her essay "*Mizvot* Built into the Body: *Tkhines* for *Niddah*, Pregnancy, and Childbirth," Chava Weissler begins by reminding us that "[o]ne of the important insights of feminist theory is the alterity, the otherness of women. Men are the rule, women the exception. . . . The female body, like the female person, is the exception."[30] Reading biblical women as represented in tension with the normative, embodying an empowering Derridean *différence* (mysterious, ambiguous, multivalent, and acting outside of verbal language) instead exposes incoherence in both the categories of "woman" and "Jewish man."

This attention to subversive features of the biblical matriarchs risks the appearance of essentializing woman (an objection leveled at the French feminist theory cited earlier). On the one side is the image of overempowered mothers and seducers, dangerous and controlling; on the other side are feminine ideals, Victorian-style paragons of womanhood elevated to the pedestal that becomes her prison.[31] Diana Fuss cautions against oversimplified rejections of essentialism, and I appreciate that theorists such as Cixous, Clément, and Luce Irigaray have long exaggerated female difference (as in the leisurely descriptions of women's laughter and its effects that I quote liberally in this chapter) for the purpose, in Irigaray's words, of "undoing by overdoing."[32] My own exaggerated attention here to Sarah's laughter and Hannah's muttering is my attempt at "undoing by overdoing." Patti Lather describes this kind of feminist reading practice as the difference between Newtonian linearity and quantum physics. She writes: "Feminism displaces the articulation of postmodernism from the site of the fathers and opens up the possibility of a heteroglot articulation premised on multiplicities and particularities."[33] As early as the biblical matriarchs, woman is conceptually incoherent. Denise Riley is reassuring: "That 'women' is indeterminate and impossible is no cause for lament. It is what makes feminism."[34]

Riley, who echoes Desdemona's question to Iago in the title of her book "*Am I That Name?": Feminism and the Category of Women in History*, and Lather in *Getting Smart* both demonstrate that the history of feminism is a dialectical history of efforts to define woman in her historical, sociological, and even biological specificity (justifying women's community and women's political organization) and simultaneously to expose unjust definitions of woman as different from person. Attempts to absolutely define woman are ultimately and inevitably falsified. Riley cautions: "For 'women' are always differently re-membered, and the gulf between them and the generally human will be more or less thornily intractable."[35] Underlining such details as eavesdropping, laughter, and muttering as subversions of ordinary speech, and oblique reference to life fluids, maternal blood and milk is my way of drawing attention to the disruptions of gender roles in the two-sexed family system of the Bible's first stories.

Sarah at the tent suggests an alternative discursive possibility to woman as Other. Instead we see woman as outsider looking in, with powers and privileges that accrue from a distance. To return to this allegory: Sarah laughs. Whether she laughed because she finds the idea of conceiving a child in old age ludicrous, or whether she laughed with delighted surprise, or whether she laughed with bitterness—having longed all of her life for a child, in old age God's promise comes so very late—the text does not say. Although God asks Abraham (guy to guy) why Sarah laughed. The first matriarch represents woman as eavesdropping and laughing, and it represents God in relation to her as deferential to her psychic complexity, as if God (and for "God" one may read "Man" or "History") speaks with clarity, and woman responds with ambiguity. God inquires, receives no satisfying response, and the text shrugs. Later God gives Sarah authority over Isaac's future, as well as authority over the bondswoman Hagar and her son Ishmael. "Listen to Sarah," (Genesis 21:12). God tells Abraham, whom the rabbinic tradition by and large imagines is too naive to understand accurately Hagar and their son.

The other matriarchs are similarly devious and subversive, and they too are approved of by the God of Hebrew scriptures. As we will see more fully in the next chapter, Rebecca eavesdrops on Isaac and Esau, after which she tells Jacob how to steal the blessing of the firstborn. When Jacob says that he is afraid, Rebecca answers with evident self-confidence and in stereotypically maternal fashion, "I'll accept the blame." Rachel steals; Leah tricks Jacob in the marriage bed. Women are often represented as subverting male intentions in the very process of fulfilling God's mysterious plans. The matriarchs, like tricksters, thus fulfill a sacred function precisely by breaking the rules.[36]

Family rules and family roles, especially in relationship to power and inheritance, are made visible by these narrative challenges to them. By making the matriarchs barren and subversive, rule-breakers of body and character, the text locates the matriarchs in carnival time.[37] At once insiders and outsiders, like Sarah at the tent flap, these heroines who laugh and wail, who are authorized by God himself to subvert male regulations, allow the reader to unconsciously entertain the possibility of a social world turned upside down. More subtle, the universe of the Bible's first families is not so much inverted as distorted, on the level of small details of family roles and carnal expressions and possibilities. Like laughter and liquid, gender resists containment into the neat categories of familial roles.

3

Passing as a Man: Patriarchal Gender Performances

Identity performance recurs in the myths of the Hebrew patriarchs and matriarchs. Situating the story of Jacob pretending to be Esau in Genesis 27 in its context among other biblical tales of masquerade and also at the beginning of cultural myths of Jewish gender identity, I read this small episode as an instance of Jacob acquiring the narrative future by success-fully passing as a man. By the middle of the nineteenth century, many details of this story had come to be marked by gender: the donning of animal skins (an artificial assumption of virility); the particular pretense of Esau hunting game for fresh meat (by contrast with Jacob serving up his mother's stew made from a domesticated animal); Jacob's distinc-tive voice (which is susceptible to the interpretation of compromised masculinity); and the patriarch Isaac's blindness (according to Freud, a literary figure for castration or impotence[1]). Like Jacob, other politically motivated Hebrew characters in biblical narrative also assume roles in power using strategies that later become suggestive of passing as well as suggestive of what Homi K. Bhabhacalls "colonial mimicry" (Joseph and Moses passing, for example, as high-stationed Egyptians).[2] These enact-ments of both masculinity and authority, and changing attitudes toward these heroes, contribute to changing ideals of manliness. Evolving over time, the term "man," without positive content of its own (in Judith But-ler's words, an "ontologically consolidated phantasm"[3]), acquires a set of related negative definitions: man means "not woman," "not queer," and "not Jew." Man is defined by negation.

Playing with a definition of identity that goes something like "you are who you aren't," I understand the biblical episode of Jacob masquerading as Esau as one origin story of Jewish gender ambiguity and performative masculinity. Jacob, the son who is allied with his mother, dresses in animal skins to pass as Esau, and so, to pass as the kind of man who can inherit the patriarchy. Reading backward from our own cultural moment—by which time the categories of "Jew" and "woman" have an overlapping history—the deception that earns Jacob the title of patriarch reads as a story of his ability to fool his old, blind father into believing that he possesses the requisite virility, signified by a metaphoric assumption of animality, to be a patriarch. In what follows, I attempt a redescription of the multiplicity of gender identity based on biblical passing narratives, narratives that at once depend on and confound sets of alternating oppositions among the identity categories "man," "Jew," "woman," and "queer."

YOU ARE WHO YOU AREN'T: THE STORY

What exactly is going on when Jacob puts on hairy animal skins and pretends to be Esau? In Genesis 27, Jacob, who will become the last of the three patriarchs, receives his father Isaac's best blessing by successfully passing himself off as his older twin Esau. It is a campy sort of masquerade: Jacob covers his neck and arms in animal skins so that when touched by his old, blind father, he will feel like his hirsute brother. Their mother, Rebecca, who has been eavesdropping on her husband and elder son, knows that Isaac has sent Esau to hunt and prepare fresh game so that he may bless Esau sated from this meal, and it is Rebecca who then dresses Jacob in Esau's finest clothing so that Jacob will carry Esau's scent. Jacob himself expresses some reluctance to go through with this plan, afraid that his father may detect the truth. But Rebecca, acting with a conviction that suggests divine sanction, urges Jacob on. She seems ambitious on Jacob's behalf and her response would, in later generations, sound stereotypical of the Jewish mother whose controlling behavior at once promotes her sons and infantilizes them: she says, in effect, "Don't worry, I'll take the blame."

Although the disguised Jacob identifies himself as his brother, Isaac does register some suspicion. When Jacob presents a maternal stew made from a domesticated beast as if it were the hunted game, Isaac says he is surprised by how quickly Esau has returned from his hunt. Jacob then implicates God in the deception, crediting God for having given him luck in the fields. Before conferring the best blessing on Jacob, Isaac once more signals his own suspicion by remarking that his son feels and smells like Esau but has the voice of Jacob.

Jacob's victory belongs at least in part to his mother, at whose behest he performs, with her pulling the strings. Although both Isaac and Rebecca are said to disapprove of Esau's marriages to local Hittite women, Isaac apparently remains prepared to confer the better blessing on Esau, his first-born son. Indeed, the whole of the myth may serve to explain Jacob's running away to marry not one but two of Rebecca's nieces. Jacob is so identified with the maternal that these marriages keep him as close to her as is legally possible without violating incest laws. (How the doubling of wives functions to mitigate Jacob's weakened virility is the subject of the next chapter.)

Considered from a psychodynamic point of view, this story is, in Erich Auerbach's memorable phrase, "fraught with background"[4] about family dynamics and alliances and family secrets. Not only do we see the father and mother divided from each other, each apparently favoring a different son, but also the mother here may be understood to painfully betray both her husband and her elder son. The text's relative silence about the divisions and betrayals in this family of four, and the reader's acceptance of them, directs us to read for psychological rather than social realism. The text's realism is further compromised by the deception itself. Some suspension of disbelief is required for us to accept a parent's mistaking animal skins for the arms of his best-loved child. But again, since these unrealistic details are not experienced as parody, the reader adjusts expectations to read for the psychological insights characteristic of myth.

DOPPELGÄNGER: THE TWIN WITHIN

This foundation myth of patriarchy contributes to a stereotype, significantly later, of compromised Jewish masculinity. It is easily read as that version of the Freudian family romance that has become both a caricature of the Jewish family and the Freudian formula for the production of homosexual men: a manipulative mother, a blind (read castrated) father, and the son whose confused identity emerges out of this family dynamic.[5] And one can read this story, like other stories of the Hebrew patriarchy, as a victory of the more feminine domestic son over his more masculine rival brethren. The son who inherits the narrative future is younger, and this relative youth in their families (Isaac, Jacob, Joseph, Moses, David, Solomon) is represented through greater attachment to or dependence on the mother, greater vulnerability, and comparative smallness; the younger son is also less hairy and less wild and therefore has features that would in later generations—the nineteenth century in particular—be identified as feminine, contributing to the anti-Semitic characterization of the Jews as a feminized people. An alternative psychological reading suggests itself: the sons of the patriarchs, the competing brothers, represent a split self-projection of a father anxious about his masculinity and the legitimacy of his own authority. Within the powerful patriarch is the insecure boy who feels like a fraud. The older boy, who is supposed to inherit according to the rules of primogeniture, is represented as unbridled masculinity, and the younger, whose role it is to reverse the rule of primogeniture, represents the threat of the more maternally allied aspects of the patriarch himself.

If the brothers divide gendered traits between them, then Jacob's putting on of animal skins is a kind of cross-dressing. Allied with the maternal and in the feminized position in the family romance, Jacob goes to his father in drag. But he presumably is a man—and in so performing, he acts like his father Isaac before him and like his son Joseph after him—Jacob is a man in drag enacting masculinity. The patriarchy itself is thus built on the foundation of radically destabilized identity categories.

As we have seen, by this point in the biblical text Rebecca's subversive eavesdropping has already been established as characteristic of the matriarchs, prefigured in her mother-in-law Sarah's eavesdropping on the angels and Abraham in Genesis 18. And the victory of the smaller, younger, and gentler boy is similarly prefigured in Isaac having inherited before his older half-brother Ishmael. The matriarchs, working conspiratorially with God, manipulate the patriarchs and acquire power through the more domestic son whom the mother prefers. The relationship between God and mother disempowers the human patriarch as the biblical patriarchal narratives represent God as the ultimate father of history in a way that compromises the sexual potency and domestic authority of human fathers. Another contrast between the divine and human father underscores the instability of patriarchal identity. God—Yahweh—carries the name "I am that I am"; Y-H-V-H derives from the verb "to be." God is what he is, while Jacob has to be who he is not in order to inherit the patriarchy.[6] Although patriarchy has since come to signify the grounding origin of masculinity, the stories that establish the binary terms matriarchy and patriarchy themselves represent an always already feminized, insecure, and undermined patriarchy.

Each of the first two biblical patriarchs, Abraham and Isaac, fantasizes a masculine patriarchy in the person of the first-born son who is beloved precisely because he is different from the father. In Abraham's case, he is commanded by Yahweh, the Father God, however, to "listen to Sarah" when she wants to banish Ishmael. Later, Ishmael is further relegated to the place of psychic fantasy when Abraham is commanded by God to take his son, his "only son" to be sacrificed (Genesis 22:2). This "only" son is, of course, Isaac, and Abraham is famous for his act of surrender. Because of the divine alliance with the matriarchs, the surrender is also articulated along a gendered binary, and the human father is twice the loser in adulterous and oedipal triangles: first, to God and wife and second, to wife and the younger son who is oedipal victor.[7] The fantasy of independent masculinity is then self-incorporated in the younger son who becomes a patriarch as his brother/double/twin fades out of the narrative future. For both Isaac and Jacob, life defeats the boy's effort to grow to independent manhood (independence from women must remain a wish), as it is the domesticated child who succeeds only through what may be experienced as the shameful, and even shaming, ruses of his mother.

Jacob's wearing animal skins echoes, oddly, his father Isaac's having been nearly sacrificed when, miraculously, a ram appears to replace him on the altar.[8] Isaac bound like an animal represents the father-son rivalry and the traumatizing moment when the child is made acutely aware of his vulnerability beneath the all-powerful father. Because Isaac is relatively unelaborated in the Bible, it is perhaps not surprising that commentators (Rashi, following *Genesis Rabbah*) link Isaac's close call to his later blindness.[9] Insofar as blinding represents unmanning (in literature, punishment for sexual crimes: Oedipus, Samson, Charlotte Brontë's Rochester), Jacob's passing, in the code of the animal, poignantly references the human-animal substitution of a generation earlier, importing the danger of that moment to the risk of this son's transition to adult power.

Just as Jacob's animal skins echo backward, so too Ishmael's having played with Isaac predicts Jacob's playing at being Esau. As we have seen, Abraham and Isaac lose Ishmael when Sarah insists on banishing her bondwoman and son because she sees Ishmael "playing with Isaac" (Genesis 21:9). Some interpreters add simply that this was wild, ungentle play. But because Isaac's name in Hebrew derives from the verb that means "laugh, play, or mock," if we preserve the Hebrew word play, Ishmael can be said to "isaac Isaac." Among the alternative rabbinic, midrashic interpretations of this activity are that Ishmael's play is homoerotic, and Sarah is therefore justified in protecting her young son; another reading is that in "isaacing Isaac," Ishmael is pretending to be Isaac, dramatically enacting Isaac's role as future patriarch.[10] Jacob's successful identity masquerade vis-à-vis his brother retrospectively validates Sarah's decision, proving that she has good reason for concern that the rehearsal that she catches might ultimately lead to a performance that could threaten her son's position as inheritor. On the other hand, if we see the brothers as representing the split self-projection of an internally divided and anxious father, then the competing readings of Ishmael's "playing with" and "playing at being" Isaac are reconcilable as a representation of mirror-stage narcissism, autoeroticism, and homoeroticism. By controlling her son(s)' self-playing, Sarah further extends maternal authority over the kind of man who will be inheritor.

In the case of the twins of the next generation, the mother's choosing one over the other commands more interpretation (both being equally hers), and these interpretations waver between uniting and splitting the brothers' identity. Some readings of Jacob's masquerade as Esau offer the suggestion that Jacob does actually become Esau when he tries on the role.[11] This interpretation is consistent with the medieval belief that clothes literally make the man. A woman who dares dress as a knight and strap a sword around her middle might awaken to find herself literally transformed.[12]

The ambiguity of Jacob's identity with respect to Esau is also reflected in the history of interpretation of their twinning. Some commentators, such as the first-century Alexandrian Jewish exegete Philo, read these twins as complete opposites (in *Questions in Genesis*, Philo says they are opposite in all ways except their arms, which explains Isaac's mistake in remarking that "these are the arms of Esau"); others, such as the medieval commentator Rashi, read them as such closely similar twins that they were indistinguishable until the age of thirteen.[13] According to the latter view, they began life identical, including their voices; thus, the distinctiveness of Jacob's voice is so subtle that it is not surprising that Isaac doubts his hearing. Josephus makes a word play of Esau's "redness" (*edom*) interpreting "*edmon*" to mean that Esau is the more "manly." And Avivah Gottlieb Zornberg reads Jacob as literally acquiring and assimilating the Esau persona of wild complexity (and sexuality) into his own smooth identity as a step in earning the blessing and making himself fit to be patriarch.[14]

One effect of the narrative masquerade is to integrate sons who are split halves of the father: independent (masculine) ego-ideal and mother-dependent (feminine) child. Retrojecting the twinning of (opposite) sons into the story of Ishmael and Isaac, and reading that twinning as opposing forces within the father (the patriarchy), leads to the implication that the game of "isaacing Isaac" may be perceived to be autoerotic and narcissistic. Just as God asks his children not to eat of the forbidden fruit that will awaken their sexuality, the episode of Sarah banishing the older boy to protect the younger reflects a maternal impulse to keep her son a child as she polices his (self-)play. In the story of Isaac and Ishmael, the free, undisciplined (masculine) boy is banished, leaving the domesticated man who is fit for company and women. This man is thereby made feminine—or better, brought under maternal control—to become marriageable. Significantly and paradoxically, masculinity is compromised by civilizing, through the very gestures that take the son from what Freud would later codify as a stage of narcissistic homoeroticism to the presumption of heterosexuality.[15] Once blind and old himself, Isaac has his own fantasy of masculine authority in his thwarted wish to prefer Esau. It is in Jacob's effort to fulfill that fantasy that the patriarchy's femininity takes on the political character of gender masquerade or drag. The next generation—which twins the brothers and adds the masquerade—duplicates this process in a way that deepens the confusion of gender categories: Jacob, under total maternal control, first plays at being a man like Esau, then is forced to separate from home, marry two women, father twelve sons, and become the ultimate patriarch.

THE SELF IN THEORY

The competition between Jacob and Esau creates a dynamic by which the patriarch "is who he is not," and the perceived similarities and differences between these twins contribute to the mixed conceptualizations of Jewish masculinity. Conundrums of gender are bound up with the conceptual difficulties of identity more generally. The concept of "the self"—like the terms "man" and "woman"—begs questions of continuity in time and space.[16] Identity presumes stability; indeed, "identity" means sameness. But, is a self continuous with who he or she is, was, or will be? How do tricks of memory, traumas, brain changes, or a cold affect who we are in relation to ourselves? Similarly, what is the relationship between our habitual uses of the terms "man" and "woman" (as if they have some kind of universal applicability) and the range of manifestations of male and female performances in different times and places?

Jacob and Esau are early instances of a kind of literary doubling in which siblings are made meaningfully similar and different and thus present opportunities to explore different narrative trajectories through their fates as doubled characters.[17] Because self-definition emerges out of a process of compare and contrast, even identical twins are known by a magnification of perceived difference, differences that, however slight, become self-defining.[18] Gender binarism participates in this system, and readers often experience gender characteristics as being among the variables that distinguish even same-sex siblings, with one perceived to be more masculine or feminine than the other.

Jacob's performance as his brother is, on the one hand, a foundation story for a continuous history of self-enactments, including medieval carnival, Renaissance cross-dressing comedies, and contemporary drag—cultural effects that are happy expressions of the conventionality of gender. On the other hand, Jacob's acquiring the place of narrative privilege by pretending to be the man who he isn't is also a foundation story for a history of sometimes deadly rereadings of Jewish men as occupying a middle gender, not-quite-men. (Jewish gender ambiguity parallels the history of Jewish racial ambiguity.) The Jewish male's inhabitance, and sometimes acceptance, of this middle place (as Jay Geller has shown with respect to Freud) ultimately threatens the stability of both the category of maleness and male bonding.[19]

Shakespearean comedy expresses, popularly, gender as a matter of performance. In keeping with Renaissance conventions, an audience might be invited to imagine, for example, that cross-dressed heroines can successfully masquerade as their own brothers—and be love objects for women who would have loved their brothers—thus creating delightful romantic triangles. But more fun still, since these heroines were played by boys, gender performance is both part of the story and part of the actor's work. Boys played women who were, in turn, pretending to be men until they were exposed, in the end, as women (though not exposed as women played by men). Although such comedies might have sensitized Renaissance audiences to gender enactments as performance, they also make the point that life and theater are more similar than not, a lesson famously articulated in *As You Like It*: "All the world's a stage / And all the men and women merely players." In its time, one might have appreciated the point that among the things we play at is being men and women.

At the same time, by contrast with cultural expressions of gender and ethnic identity as a mere pretense, science was codifying the distinctive nature of the male Jewish body. Important physicians in seventeenth-century Spain documented the "fact" that Jewish men menstruate. In addition to spreading the plague, Jewish men "leaked impure blood." This impure menstrual blood and the impure blood of racial impurity were mutually informing, and as John L. Beusterien shows, the language of impurity migrated from medical into legal discourse. Beusterien cites a 1632 treatise on Jewish maladies by Doctor Juan de Quiones, an official of the court of King Philip IV, that explains that Jewish males "every month . . . suffer from a blood flow *as if they were women*."[20] According to John M. Efron, despite significant medical studies that documented that Jews in nineteenth-century Germany were extraordinarily healthy (statistics showed that Jews lived longer, had lower infant mortality and death rates than Christians, and suffered less from alcoholism and the most common diseases of the day, including deadly childhood diseases such as measles and scarlet fever), "the modern era has seen the construction of an enduring Jewish type—the sickly Jew." Efron explains that the concept of gender is critical to solving the riddle of how the statistical evidence that showed the Jews to be "a healthy vigorous people" didn't interfere with both medical and popular culture's view of the diaspora Jew as "unmanly": "frail, timid, weak, and sickly." In the range of literature that he examines, Efron finds the Jew to be "the opposite of his idealized Gentile neighbor":

> While the latter was lithe, well-proportioned, athletic, calm, and self-possessed, medical science portrayed the Jew as corpulent, having a sweet-tooth, misshapen, decidedly unathletic, nervous, even hysterical. What is remarkable about this composite picture of the Jewish male is how closely the description resembles the common image of women at the fin-de-siècle. They too were supposedly given to hysteria, were physically vulnerable, and were too delicate for the great outdoors. These were not the traits ordinarily associated with European males. They were, however, peculiarities that the medical establishment identified as being shared by Jews and women alike.[21]

The traits of "adaptability" and "mimicry" were, significantly, considered to be survival skills of both women and Jews, in Jewish self-descriptions as well as in anti-Semitic representations.

Finally, by the nineteenth century it was understood that Jewish men even committed different kinds of crimes than did Gentile men: Jews were more susceptible to cheating and other "white-collar" crimes.[22] Jacob both mimicked Esau and twice "cheated" him; in this regard too, Jacob represents a prototype of modern ideas of the Jewish (feminine) man.

JEWISH CAMP

In his introduction to *The Politics and Poetics of Camp*, Moe Meyer suggests that "[w]hat 'queer' signals is an ontological challenge that displaces bourgeois notions of the Self as unique, abiding, and continuous while substituting instead a concept of the Self as performative, improvisational, discontinuous, and processually constituted by repetitive and stylized acts." An allegory for self-transformation, Jacob's successful masquerade as Esau works like queer parody insofar as it displaces abiding notions of the self. Meyer observes that "[c]amp, or queer parody, has become an activist strategy."[23] Ironically, Meyer's celebratory description of queer parody is strikingly similar to Otto Weininger's disparaging description of Jewish men in his 1903 best-selling treatise *Sex and Character*: "The congruity between Jews and women further reveals itself in the extreme adaptability of the Jews . . . in fact the mode in which, like women, because they are nothing, they can become everything."[24] Ann Pellegrini, pointing to the work of Daniel Boyarin, Jay Geller, Sander L. Gilman (and I would add Howard Eilberg-Schwartz) notices the contemporary interest in tracing "the persistence and impact of a certain homology: 'Jew-as-woman,'" and Pellegrini directs our attention to Weininger's significance in joining the "Jewish question" and "the woman question." Pellegrini concludes that because Weininger represents the "eternal Jew" through the "eternal feminine," he "articulates the 'racial' difference of 'the' Jews through the 'sexual' difference 'man/woman.' In this interarticulation, Jewishness becomes as much a category of gender as of race." This homology has the disquieting effect of queer parody. Jewish men—at once as "adaptable as women" and positioned as women (Isaac, Jacob)—expose gender itself as an effect, as imitation, and as performance. Jewish masculinity aligns with a developing concept of "queer" in the post-Freudian cultural imagination.

The "eternal feminine" of the Jew is of course a historically limited "feminine" with a corresponding masculinity that belongs peculiarly to the period from Charles Darwin through the 1970s. In placing the Jew in the position of the feminine, Eilberg-Schwartz's *God's Phallus* and Boyarin's *Unheroic Conduct* both invite us to imagine a post-Romantic Western femininity. For Eilberg-Schwartz, the Jew-as-woman (in particular as soul-mate to the masculine Divine) implies an unconscious and anxious homoeroticism; for Boyarin, the Jew-as-woman means having values that go against the grain, a Jewish alternative value system that, as in Carol Gilligan's *In a Different Voice*, privileges qualities that we have come to associate with the female values of Jane Austen's drawing rooms. Even these theories occasionally assume a continuous definition of what makes a man and of what defines masculinity, suppressing the variability of ideal masculinity among cultures and over time. Eighteenth-century high culture in Europe defined masculinity as heightened feelings (the cult of sensibility), in a culture in which the well turned-out male aristocrat wore powdered wig, high heels, frilly blouses, and spoke and carried himself in ways that were later characterized as feminine. It was only when the Great Chain of Being was challenged by the theory of evolution in the nineteenth century that man was redefined as a species of animal rather than a lesser variation of angel. Accordingly, idealized masculinity became increasingly beastly and predatory: it took on the appearance of the hairy hunter Esau. The famous anti-Semitic categorization of Jewish men as being as smooth and manipulative as Jacob, "like women," flourishes in this period of redefinition of masculinity. (At the same time, a competing stereotype of the Jewish man as bent, old, and bearded—in the style of Shylock and Fagin, male equivalents of the witch—also flourished.)

When social Darwinism redefined "man" as an "animal," it became increasingly desirable to be beastly: hairy, strong, wild, naturally selected for victory in the new marketplace. And it is against this background that Isaac, Jacob, Joseph, and ultimately Woody Allen (as explained in the next chapter) become suspect men, and "Jewish man" becomes an oxymoron, a contradiction in terms. Even so, this different, feminine man retained some desirability, evolving into the stereotype of the hardworking, gentle Jewish husband and father. Similarly, Christianity complemented the all-powerful patriarchal God with the more feminine male divine son, Jesus. When the nineteenth-century Darwinian revolution challenged biblical authority, Christian secular culture identified masculinity as animal. Jews and women were left behind in an old paradigm of aristocratic gentility, and the "man as beast" replaced the ideal masculine figure of eighteenth-century Europe.

Queerness as oppositional stance presents itself as a political threat that has implications for how we might understand nineteenth-century anxiety about (male) Jewishness as a variant on womanliness. Citing Thomas A. King's contribution to his volume, Meyer writes that "the history of queer practices . . . has valuable implications for marginal social identities in general. . . . Queer sexualities become, then, a series of improvised performances whose threat lies in the denial of any social identity derived from participation in those performances."[25] The threat that the Jew became in modern European culture may also derive in part from the perception that Jewish men too enact a "series of improvised performances" (Weininger's characterization of their feminine "extreme adaptability") and are without a stable self. Jacob's donning of animal skins is, in this regard, another carnival practice of upside-down identity. His performance conforms as well to Mikhail Bakhtin's description of carnival practices that have both conservative and subversive functions: such gender disruptions reenforce what are considered to be meaningful gender differences even as such reversals subversively undermine the inevitability of these identity categories.[26]

COLONIAL MIMICRY: "ALMOST, BUT NOT QUITE"

Jacob mimics Esau to become a patriarch. In so doing, he pretends to be the first-born son whom his father loves and the grown man of stature fit to be patriarch. It is an imitation on the axes of both gender and power. Bhabha describes how masquerade or mimicry has a political effect with a psychological overlay in his discussions of colonial "mimicry" of the colonizer class. Bhabha's analysis of colonial mimicry as mocking approximations of authority is analogous to Jacob's mimicry of Esau in ways that can further clarify the disturbing effects of enactments of Jewish masculinity. Bhabha writes that mimicry is "almost but not quite" (the scent and feel, perhaps, but not the voice); mimicry is a "double articulation": "a complex strategy of reform, regulation, and discipline which 'appropriates' the Other as it visualizes power. Mimicry is also the sign of the inappropriate, however, a difference or recalcitrance which . . . poses an immanent threat to both 'normalized' knowledges and disciplinary powers."[27] Jacob mimics masculinity and power as his son Joseph and later Moses will also mimic Egyptian nobility (discussed in Chapter 5). In these Jewish stories, drag and passing are overlapping strategies of miming power that leave a gap within the self, the very space that enables self-deception. Bhabha's insight that mimicry is like a presumed original but with a telling—and annoying—difference clarifies how the perception of such difference inspires disgust (and self-disgust), perhaps of the sort that can explain Weininger's (self) loathing. In this way, the construction of the Jewish man imitating "gentile" masculinity signifies a particular kind of homelessness. The mimicry and identity masquerade in stories about the Jewish patriarchy stand at the beginning of a tradition in which the Jewish man is conceived of as alienated: not at home either in the world or in his own body.

In the unconscious of post-Romantic Western culture, the Jew works as a fun-house mirror that always reveals the instability of both gender and sexual identity. The Jew is a frightening reminder that the categories by which culture confidently asserts the knowability and naturalness of gender and sexuality have no reliable boundaries. And it is the potential hiddenness, the potential the Jew has to pass into privilege, a potential once associated with the light-skinned black that exaggerates the anxiety. Sander Gilman reminds us that the identifying sign of circumcision is a site of castration (disempowering; woman-making) and needs to be hidden because it inspires both anti-Semitism and Jewish self-hatred.[28] Moreover, the language of the Jews is a similar sign of ambivalence because it can serve both as mask of the successfully hidden Jew and reveal, by its difference, Jewishness. (Jews are thought to have private languages and to speak differently; for Weininger, they speak like women.) Thus, those whose speech is "too Jewish" (Jackie Mason is Gilman's example) and those who efface their Jewishness (hidden Jews) are a source of distress to Jews and non-Jews alike.

In "Imitation and Gender Insubordination," Judith Butler writes that "[d]rag constitutes the mundane way in which genders are appropriated, theatricalized, worn, and done; it implies that all gendering is a kind of impersonation and approximation." If we go further with Butler that "compulsory heterosexual identities, those ontologically consolidated phantasms of 'man' and 'woman,' are theatrically produced effects that posture as grounds, origins, the normative measure of the real,"[29] then both Jacob's passing as Esau and heroines of the Hebrew Bible who pass as harlots (whose masquerades result in masculine-style political and military victories) participate in a legacy of gender confusions. As I will discuss more fully in Chapter 7, femininity as drag is amply attested in biblical stories: Tamar (Genesis 38), Yael (Judges 4), Delilah (Judges

16), Judith (Apocrypha), Esther, and perhaps even Ruth (in the biblical books that carry these heroines' names) all acquire political power—in some cases deadly political power—by enacting a heightened, and false, femininity that conforms to Joan Riviere's turn-of-the century description of femininity as masquerade or drag.[30] Based on this paradigm, the acquisitive Jewish woman in popular twentieth-century stereotypes, the Jewish American princess, is also imagined to masquerade, enacting an exaggerated, costumed self. "Passing as a woman," she too acquires subversive political power analogous to the patriarchal power that Isaac, Jacob, Joseph (and later Moses) acquire when they "pass as men." The consolidated figures of the Jewish man and woman in particular underscore uncertainty: this apparent man may be Jew or queer; this apparently inconsequential woman may be deadly. In so passing, Jews remind us of the falseness and fragility of political power. In the presence of the Jew and the queer, we feel the anxiety of the Hegelian master, who knows that his mastery depends on the slave being coerced into staying in role.

Jacob's passing as a man, like Isaac's textual defeat over Ishmael, leaves traces of anxiety and guilt. The anxiety is contained and the guilt is assuaged through misogynistic textual gestures in the repetitive representations of mothers and wives. From the beginning of biblical narrative and Eve's sin through the controlling matriarchs and a string of female bedroom deceivers, the blame for disruption of power and gender hierarchy in the family is displaced onto women. Jacob's acquisition of two wives, and Leah masquerading as Rachel, is then another compensatory gesture that serves to console Jacob about his own masculinity. The doubling of wives in sisters and the consequent deprivation of intimacy between the women works to give the appearance of restabilized gender roles, covering over the unstable gendering of men at the foundation of the patriarchy.

Interestingly, in one rabbinic Midrash Leah succeeds in deceiving Jacob as to her identity in bed because her sister Rachel is under the bed throwing her voice and thus throwing off Jacob.[31] The kinky incestuousness of this Midrash—three in the bedroom—follows naturally from other moments of passing in the Genesis narratives. Both Abraham and Isaac, for political reasons and in what seem to be lifesaving lies, pass their wives off as their sisters. Again these episodes carry ambiguous import with respect to passing because in both cases the patriarchs are caught by those in power and chided for their deception. In Isaac's case, he is caught because he is seen "playing with" (isaacing) Rebecca (the same formulation as Ishmael playing with Isaac), and Pharaoh thereby understands that this is no sister.

Many biblical passing narratives are explicitly political, and in these the political and sexual often overlap. My discussion of Jacob's favorite son Joseph, also a younger son, a chaste, boastful dreamer who flaunts the garment of favoritism, looks at how details of his life story lead some medieval commentators to characterize Joseph as queer: a drag queen, a cross-dresser.[32] He also becomes an Egyptian (encoded as feminine in Greek and much Western literature) and rises to a position somewhat equivalent to our secretary of state. When his brothers come to plead for food, he is so changed as to be unrecognizable to them. It is a threshold moment: they appear and request food. Had they never appeared Joseph could presumably have lived out his years without ever recovering the identity of his youth. As it is, Joseph could have given them food and sent them away. Alternatively, he could have punished them for their cruelty and turned them away empty handed. Theoretically, he could have chosen not to out himself as a Hebrew. But the comfort of the text lies in the clear implication that he has no choice. The story takes for granted that Joseph is destined to someday reclaim his place as a leader among his brothers, and the narrative trajectory requires his eventual unmasking. In psychoanalytic terms, we have no choice but to repeatedly enact our stories. Identity is repetition compulsion.

The requirement to unmask one's Hebrew identity recurs in Hebrew scriptures. Queen Esther is queen of the realm when her people of origin come under a death sentence. She is told that she can reveal her Jewish identity to the king as part of the plan to save her people or someone else will have to save the Jews. *Performing* as sex object, she chooses in this guise to out herself as a Jew, though again the text implies that she has no choice. In this story, too, there is a threshold moment when Esther can (and yet clearly cannot) choose to keep her identity closeted. Most hidden of all, Moses raised in Pharaoh's court is a particularly reluctant spokesman for the Hebrews, but he is also compelled to "be himself," that is to be true to some birth identity that demands that he lead the people out of Egypt. Joseph and Moses, who both spend part of their lives passing as Egyptians, bracket the Egypt story. (The Hebrew word for Hebrew is *'ivri*, which means, literally, "cross-over" or "passer.")

If Joseph as Egyptian secretary has a secret, is passing, then any secretary could be passing, could be Jewish or queer, or (to extend the range of biblical examples) could get you in trouble by being somebody's wife (though she claims to be a sister). In the film *Europa, Europa*,[33] the hero's passing as a non-Jew (first German then Russian) is threatened continually by the circumcised penis that never leaves the viewer's consciousness because it could, at any moment, betray his identity, and in the filmic narrative, the homosexual interest he attracts is thereby represented as doubly life-threatening. The Holocaust story is full of episodes of passing, leaving open the question of how many born Jews passed permanently into non-Jewishness. Those who spoke German and who possessed the language skills to be effective mimics stood a better chance of successful passing. Jacob is a figure for an imaginative Western story of Jews passing as men and, therefore, as gentiles, in which the circumcised penis, a sign of compromised masculinity, poses a great risk.[34]

Until our own time, there is evidence of this cultural anxiety about who is and who is not a Jew. "Who is a Jew?" is a political question that continues to preoccupy Jews and non-Jews in relation to such matters as marriage and Israeli citizenship. The persistence of anxiety about the possibility of permanently passing out of Jewish identity was apparent in 1997, when the press revealed that former Secretary of State Madeleine Albright is the daughter of born Jews who lost their own parents because of their deadly Jewish identity. This bit of personal news in Albright's life, a woman no longer young and who had been born, raised, and lived out her years as a Christian, nevertheless provoked a remarkably strong public reaction by Jews and non-Jews alike. Why? Psychology teaches that more important than the content of a reaction is the strength of a reaction; interpreters are advised to "measure the affect." The Albright narrative rewrites the biblical stories of sexual and power politics and passing as exemplified by Joseph and Queen Esther, both of whom are compelled by the plots in which they figure to pass back and thereby reassure us of the clarity of identity; and finally, her story suggests that some family secrets (perhaps even your own) are never exposed and may pass on out of the world. The Albright family's having not passed back and Albright herself having not bothered to carefully read and interpret her family history as yet another identity story of life-saving Jewish passing seem so transgressive because that secretary's secrets, like Isaac standing before his misrecognized son, invite a terrifying question: how can one know the identity of even one's most intimate relations? You might not be who you seem or claim to be.

In these stories, the principal location of self-defining difference is ultimately *within* the self. Although it has been oft remarked that Jacob comes to the patriarchal position through trickery, it is rarely commented on that the ruse is bizarrely odd and unbelievable. This brings me back to an earlier question: how could even an old, blind patriarch mistake animal hair for the human arms of his child? Perhaps the best way to read this episode is as a gender performance in which no one is really fooled. There is, of course, ample evidence that Isaac is not entirely fooled. He twice questions the identity of his son, and before giving Jacob Esau's blessing, Isaac observes that his son feels and smells like Esau but has the voice of Jacob. It is a game of I-know-that-you-know-that-I-know. Isaac's effort to identify his son directs our attention to the sensual basis of all efforts to know someone else.[35] If the favorite son can be smelled, touched, and listened to and still be misrecognized, indeed how can we know even those with whom we are most intimate? This moment, like the Albright family story, raises the fundamental epistemological question: what does it mean to know? Alternatively, how does the self split for purposes of self-deception? (Self-deception requires two selves: the knowing deceiver and the naïve other.)

Passing is about thresholds, and thresholds are places marked by anxiety. In the Exodus narrative, the threshold is marked by blood so that the angel of death will know the unknowable, that here is a Jew who should therefore escape death. In Judges 19, the dead body of a rape victim lies draped over the threshold. Passing is the opposite of failing; a rite of passage is a success, the crossing of a boundary. "To pass" is to get away with pretending to be who you are not.

But we are who we are not. Was Esther not herself when she was seducing the king? Were Moses and Joseph not themselves as court Jews? Harry Brod makes this important point in his analysis of Superman as a Jewish story (in Rudavsky).[36] Invented by two Jewish boys during the Depression, Superman and Clark Kent (Esau and Jacob?) are one man. Actually, Superman, the resident alien, is the real person; Clark Kent, the disguise. Lois Lane loves Superman. Clark Kent loves Lois Lane. But there is a gap in the narrative logic: if Superman is Clark Kent then Lois Lane and Clark Kent love each other. But they don't. And why does Superman (presumably the real self) require Lois to love the Clark Kent (the Jacob or the Jewish) persona?

Oscar Wilde said: "Give a man a mask and he will tell you the truth," intending that a false self offers protection for honesty. Perhaps, instead, the mask *is* the honest truth, as costumes betray self images and as "jests" can be dead serious. In the Bible, it is one mask after another. From Adam and Eve's hiding among the trees, through wives calling themselves sisters, Leah's pretending to be Rachel, or Tamar pretending to be a cultic prostitute, if we pull the thematic thread of deception and life-saving lies from biblical narrative through contemporary stereotypes of Jews in popular culture, we discover stories of sexual and political passing running continuously throughout the fabric of the myth of Jewishness in both the textual tradition and the representation of Jews in history. Bringing Butler's discussion of drag and theories of camp to the subject of Jewish ethnicity suggests that Jewishness is always already sexualized and without positive content, a projective anxiety of heterosexual gentility about psychic reality, identity, and the meaningful content of subjectivity.

Passing is also a kind of failing. Yet another definition of passing is death, and this passing away—the ultimate failure of identity boundaries—may be the primary source of the anxieties that concern us in these stories about knowing who is who, as best we can, through the fragile categories established by cultural consensus. Insisting on the stability of categories of sex/gender and race/ethnicity provides elaborate defenses against death's easy and absolute erasure of identity boundaries. The enactments and concealments of both queerness and Jewishness, like Jacob's inheritance of the patriarchy by pretending to be who he was not, situate us on the razor's edge that is life itself, reminding us that however high the stakes for which games of identity performance are played, the final role, the final identity, makes all of humanity's self-defining boundaries useless defenses. The return of Adam's descendants to earth (*adamah*) erases all distinguishing boundaries invented in the elaborations of humanity.

4

Leah Behind the Veil: Sex with Sisters from the Bible through Woody Allen

THE *NEBISH* BECOMES A PATRIARCH

Woody Allen's 1986 film *Hannah and Her Sisters* represents itself and was received by reviewers as a film about attractive, urban, contemporary American women: a comic, touching inquiry into the lives and relationships of three sisters. This chapter is an archaeology of a plot that begins with the biblical Jacob's marriage to sisters and leads to a reading of *Hannah and Her Sisters* as a male fantasy in which the insecure hero overcomes his inferiority complex and becomes potent by triumphantly sleeping with his wife's sister. This fantasy repeats itself within Allen's film, and it works to empower the hero by undermining the relationship among sisters who, by all rights and by the logic of the story, should be more loyal to one another than to the men who succeed (both with little effort and with no averse consequences) in seducing them. A remarkably popular narrative pattern, this is an old story. The biblical Jacob's marriage to sisters initiates a narrative strategy that substantiates the heterosexuality of the hero type raised by a controlling mother and conveys the unlikely appeal of the mild intellectual artist—a staple of American (Jewish) comedy—who is hardworking and successful, an underdog victor in work and in bed.

As we have seen, patriarchal masculinity is compromised at its foundation, as younger brothers come into their positions of authority in ways that leave them vulnerable to self-doubt. Jacob's weakness derives from his alliance with his mother rather than his father and his dishonestly inheriting the biblical narrative future; he becomes the third patriarch by twice outmaneuvering his (elder) twin brother Esau, ultimately, by pretending to be Esau. Acting on his mother's urging, Jacob fulfills Rebecca's and God's intention that he reverse the rule of primogeniture in a ruse that undermines both his father's paternal authority and, one might suppose, his own sense of worthiness. Given this history, Jacob would be a good candidate for the disorder that psychologists later called the "imposter syndrome," an anxiety prevalent in women who hold high-powered positions more usually held by men.[1] At the close of this episode of masquerade, masculinity has been weakened all around, and Jacob flees home, also on his mother's orders and in fear of his brother, who could be expected to exact vengeance.

On the threshold of manhood, Jacob is sent away to acquire endogamous wives. Rebecca directs him to her brother Laban, presumably so that he may marry from among her nieces. Although the midrashic tradition vilifies Esau, the biblical text itself offers no explanation for his unworthiness to inherit the patriarchy except in the hint that his parents are dismayed by his marriage to Hittite women. Since the patriarchy is inherited from father to son and the matriarchy is transmitted from mother-in-law to daughter-in-law, the reader may register, if only unconsciously, Rebecca's strengthening of her own position by arranging for the next generation to doubly descend from her family. Jacob's flight to Rebecca's family is thus overdetermined: he flees from his brother's wrath; he goes to find a matrilineal wife; and he takes the journey away from (and ultimately back to) home that is part of the pattern of the hero's development in Genesis.

Superficially, the stories of the first biblical families, like the oedipal romance in its prevailing interpretation, represent the son's struggle to be a man in competitions among fathers, sons, and brothers. As I hope I have shown, however, the gendered family roles (for mother, father, and sons) are at once fixed by repetition and destabilized by the narrative details that persist in undermining the father's masculine authority, the mother's passivity, and the son's confidence in his virility. Absent in these representations of the first Hebrew families are daughters and sisters. When the sisters Leah and Rachel enter the family picture, they do so to become Jacob's co-wives, in competition both for their shared husband and over the production of sons.

Rachel and Leah's rivalry functions to fortify Jacob's patriarchal position. In these, the central episodes of Jacob's life, Jacob makes the transition from the childhood competition with Esau to becoming the ultimate patriarch, father of the twelve sons from whom the tribes of Israel will descend. Before amassing wealth, wrestling with angels, reconciling with his brother, and returning home enriched in every possible way, the text establishes Jacob by arranging for him to marry sisters. Their rivalry positions him at the center of a domestic world, more important to each of the women than they are to each other.

The plot of sisters shared by one man has enjoyed an enduring popularity, and the Victorians, in particular, loved this sin. Charles Dickens and Sigmund Freud were each imagined to have had an affair with his wife's sister. Thomas Mann's *Joseph and His Brothers* devotes a long chapter (titled "The Sisters") to the relationship between Jacob's wives. This time-honored plotline returned in a cluster of classic films of the 1980s and 1990s including *sex, lies and videotape, Like Water for Chocolate,* and *La Belle Epoque.* During the suffragette and women's liberation movements, this story that worked in the Bible to fortify an insecure hero resurfaced as a kind of social consolation. It is a fantasy in many variations with a calming effect on a culture that may be anxious about patriarchal potency and the political threat posed by women's organizing. Woody Allen's 1986 movie anticipated the public scandal years later when in 1993, he became intimately involved with the adopted daughter of Mia Farrow, Allen's own long-time partner. The successful seduction of a wife's sister or daughter responds to a subconscious resentment of women's intimacy with one another. This story says, "relax; women are easily seduced away from one another; they compete for you and envy each other, and you may have them both, at no cost."

The fantasy of illicitly having a sister-in-law derives its force from the potentially pornographic doubling of the woman, a wife and her sister. The appeal of this fantasy is, however, political. In such stories, sisters are deprived of intimacy with one another as they enter the bed of a shared man. Reassuring the relatively weak male, his potency shows up in the female belly, perversely, in a woman's conception of her brother-in-law's child. The ostensible theme of these stories is betrayal—that variety of deception that assumes intimacy—and while uncle betrays nephew, wife betrays husband, mother betrays son, and husbands betray wives, sisters are not represented as betraying one another because, in one way or another, they are deprived of the requisite intimacy. If this plot betrays a fear of women's intimacies, then among the reassurances that the plot provides is that what woman most requires is male seed. The womb occupies a central place. The feared attachment between women (exemplified in what psychology and the metaphor of sisterhood alike tell us is an especially intimate female relationship: that of sister to sister) is rendered unfulfilling and fruitless.[2] In stories in which a husband desires his wife's sister, from scripture through multiple biographies of Dickens and Freud, the regard in which the sisters hold one another is elided. In these narratives, when the sisters become mothers envy is the only expressed emotion between them.

If the Bible promises that sisters would choose a man over each other to satisfy their need for sons, the myth of Procne and Philomela (told in Ovid's *Metamorphoses*) expresses the anxiety that requires this reassurance, namely, the deep fear that a woman would kill her son for the sake of her sister. The sisters Procne and Philomela triumph over Tereus's cruel efforts to keep them apart in a story that offers the lesson that a fierce loyalty lends unnatural power to the conspiracies of sisterhood. In a gesture by which sister love is made at once greater than mother love and infinitely brutal, Procne punishes her husband Tereus for raping and silencing her sister by killing his son and serving the cooked child to Tereus for supper.

On the coin's other side, foundation stories reward girls without a mother or sisters. It is an old wisdom about Cinderella: the girl who deserves to be princess is a free agent, independent of the selfish bond between stepmother and sisters. As the Brothers Grimm tell this story, in its less sanitized version, the wicked stepmother encourages her daughters to amputate parts of their feet (a toe, a heel) that each may squeeze into the "fur" slipper. (In early versions, until the French *ver* was mistaken for *verre*, the slipper is fur.) The foot-fetishizing Prince, who evidently has dim memory of his beloved's face, is in each case deceived until his attention is drawn to the bloody fur. So, the mother, like generations of Chinese women who dutifully bound their daughters' feet to make them marriageable, initiates her daughters into women's rites of passage, into woman's blood and self-mutilation. In both Chinese lore and Freudian explanations of foot fetishism, the foot substitutes for genitalia. The unnatural (step) sister with no mother of her own and a tiny foot that does not bleed (is she still a child?) is rewarded for her isolation among sisters by becoming Princess. All of these stories betray a fear of sisterhood.

RACHEL AND LEAH IN THE BIBLE

In a classic deception, the bride's identity is somehow concealed, and Jacob, the third and last of the biblical patriarchs, marries Leah in Rachel's stead. He wakes up the next morning to find that he consummated his marriage with the wrong woman (Genesis 29:25). The story goes that Jacob has been deceived by his father-in-law, Laban, who substituted his elder daughter for his younger. Jacob had labored for Laban for seven years to earn the beautiful Rachel only to find himself married to her "weak-eyed" sister. He labors for seven more years to acquire Rachel as well.

Why did Laban substitute Leah for Rachel? The narrative's explanation is sociologically reasonable: unbeknownst to Jacob, the local custom was to marry elder daughters first; Rachel could not be married until Leah was married. Another explanation is offered on the level of characterization: because Jacob is required to labor for an additional seven years to earn the woman he wanted in the first place, the greedy Laban deceived his nephew for the extra years' labor. The larger narrative context provides the third and most compelling explanation. In the preceding chapters, Jacob, younger twin to Esau, twice "cheats" his brother of the birthright due Esau by rules of primogeniture. Just as Jacob deceived his blind father by disguising himself as Esau and answering to Esau's name to gain the coveted blessing for the first born, so, in an act of narrative justice, will Jacob be deceived in reverse fashion, getting the elder sister for the younger.

Laban's and Jacob's negotiations over Rachel and Leah represent a variation of homosocial bonding described by Eve Kosofsky Sedgwick in *Between Men*. Citing Gayle Rubin's anthropological work, Sedgwick observes that "patriarchal heterosexuality can best be discussed in terms of one or another form of the traffic in women: it is the use of women as exchangeable, perhaps symbolic property for the primary purpose of cementing the bonds of men with men."[3] With Laban, as with Esau, the men's betrayals of one another ultimately do end in reconciliation.

Structurally, the story of the sisters, Rachel and Leah, seems to double for that of the brothers, Jacob and Esau, with the gender markers reversed. In the first chapter of *Between Men*, "Gender Asymmetry and Erotic Triangles," Sedgwick responds to René Girard's suggestion, following Freud, that the erotic triangle replicates the oedipal triangle, an adult working through of the young boy's conflict of envying the father for possession of the mother. Freud and Girard posit, but do not explore, a symmetrical triangle for women. Sedgwick rightly doubts this symmetry. As early as the first rivalries in Genesis, the biblical text does represent oedipal resolution and overcoming envy between brothers (repeated in the Joseph episodes) and the absence of such transcendence in the case of sisters.

The Jacob narratives as well as later stories of a hero and sisters imagine no potential for female bonding in the negotiation over a man. This romantic triangle—two women and one man—does not create social bonds between the women because the relationship between the sisters remains unexamined, and the story permits what is not permitted by the oedipal or by the more usual adult triangle. Jacob gets both women, whose rivalry thus finds no resolution. Although Jacob's marriage to sisters is presented not as wish fulfillment, but rather as a deception in which Jacob is cast in the role of victim, nevertheless, this victim is aggrandized by Laban's trick both in the fathering of sons by sisters and in the fact that he is more important to his women than the sisters are to each other, a position which guarantees his desirability in the mind of the reader.

Since it is Jacob's act of deceiving his father that, through poetic justice, earns him the deception later worked against him by his uncle Laban, we experience this generational power struggle as the familiar Freudian father-son competition. This story conceals, however, a persistent textual anxiety about maternal and feminine power. Just as it is significant that Rebecca motivates Jacob's triumph over Esau, so too it is significant that it is Laban, Rebecca's brother, who tricks Jacob. The maternal exerts a persistent subterranean pressure on events.[4]

Parallel to the reconciliation of Jacob and Esau, the story that puts closure on the Leah-Rachel substitution is another story of envy between them and failure of reconciliation. In that story, however, it is Jacob who becomes the object of barter in the women's struggle for maternity. Leah's fertility and the handmaids' bearing Jacob sons reduce Rachel to an envy that angers her husband. One day Leah's eldest son Reuven brings his mother mandrakes (because of their shape, believed to enhance fertility). Rachel covets the gift, and Leah agrees to give her sister the mandrakes in exchange for the privilege of having Jacob in her bed that night. Leah greets Jacob that evening with the explanation that she bought him for the night, and Leah, afforded that which the root represents, conceives. Although Jacob is commodified by the women's exchange, the sisters' competition adds steady increase to Jacob's prosperity. Their rivalry comes to closure only with Rachel's premature death.

MIDRASHIC REVERSALS:
FROM THE MIDDLE AGES TO THE PRESENT

Rosa Felsenburg Kaplan's beautiful poem "Sisters" imagines Leah brushing Rachel's hair, protecting her fragile sister, and carefully choosing her words so as to spare Rachel's feelings.[5] Kaplan's fantasy of sisterly intimacy, among many contemporary Jewish women's poems that explore varieties of emotional connection between the sisters, is consistent with the classical Midrash's stunningly complete reversal of the biblical representation of the matriarchs' relationship. Wanting to eliminate those ambiguities that make Esau sympathetic and the patriarch and matriarchs unsympathetic, the Midrash, with exaggerated symmetry, imagines that Leah and Rachel are twins of equal beauty who were to have been married to their twin cousins, Leah to Esau, Rachel to Jacob.[6]

Leah learns, however, that Esau is unmitigated evil, and in answer to her pious prayers, God spares her this wicked husband. Esau's bad character also excuses his mother's manipulations, such that the Midrash represents Rebecca as a prophetess who did not so much betray her husband, Isaac, but rather deceived him in order to save him from sin. (Deception, unlike betrayal, can be for the victim's own good.) Leah is idealized; she prayed and wept hard (hence, according to Midrash her distinctive "weak eyes," or beautiful "soft eyes"), and her prayers and her piety actually earn her priority of place.[7] The Midrash makes the parallel between Jacob and Leah explicit. When asked by Jacob why she answered to her sister's name in the marriage bed, she replies, "Because I learned from you, who answered to your brother's name."[8]

The Bible does not invite us to consider what Leah was thinking when she was placed at the altar in her sister's stead. Did the sisters agree to the deception? Did Leah deceive Rachel? In the Bible, Laban is the deceiver and Jacob the deceived, and the women have neither agency nor connection. Among the silences required by this deception—and deception depends upon silences—Leah and Jacob must have spent a very quiet first night together. In establishing Leah's good character, the Midrash remedies this silence as well. A legend in the Babylonian Talmud imagines that Jacob, suspecting the possibility of treachery, gave Rachel signs so that he would be sure that he had the right sister. Rachel is said to have shared the signs with Leah so that she would not be embarrassed, and yet another commentary imagines that Rachel hid under the marital bed and threw her voice so that Jacob would believe he was in bed with her.[9] Moreover, just as some early commentators wonder whether Jacob and Esau were fraternal or identical twins, the midrashic twinning of Rachel and Leah extends the possibility of identical twins to the sisters. Esau's redness and hairiness and Leah's weak eyes can be relegated to small defining differences. Isaac's confusion between his sons and Jacob's confusion between his brides thus becomes more plausible.

The Midrash's purpose is to elevate Leah's status. She conceives first because God wants to assuage the gossip that Leah betrayed her sister, and Leah's fertility signifies divine favor. Rachel envies only her sister's piety. Leah is so devoted to Rachel that a Midrash reports that Leah bore a final daughter, Dinah, even though she had conceived a son. Out of love for Rachel, Leah (knowing that Jacob was ordained to have twelve sons) prayed that the child in her womb be transformed into a daughter so that Rachel could bear the last male child.[10] Finally, even the biblical reconciliation between the brothers is discounted by a Midrash that explains that Esau was motivated by greed.[11]

These midrashic revisions, by recovering the relationship between the sisters, create a new triangle. Midrash extends the feud between Jacob and Esau. Esau, angry that he loses his betrothed to Jacob, covets Leah. Ironically, in its effort to further divide the brothers, Midrash creates the classic homosocial bond as Sedgwick defines it. Hence the story ends with a business transaction between the brothers. The triangle presented in Midrash neutralizes the biblical triangle; Leah, of course, does not share the brothers as Jacob shares the sisters. A consequence of the Midrash's determination to glorify Jacob and vilify Esau is bonding the sisters to each other. Ironically, Leah, the less loved, is made more lovable; a competition between the brothers over a woman (Leah) is invented and resolved in the hero's favor with a negotiation, securing a homosocial bond over the body of a woman.

RACHEL AND LEAH ACCORDING TO THOMAS MANN

Thomas Mann's early twentieth-century elaboration of the Leah-Rachel relationship is a good indicator of modern assumptions about the possibilities for sororal intimacy. The sixth chapter of *Joseph and His Brothers* is devoted to "The Sisters" and begins with a cautious representation of sisterly love. Rachel at once disapproves of Jacob in her heart for his utter rejection of her beloved sister Leah at the same time that Rachel "could not quite put out of her heart all feminine satisfaction in his preference."[12] Although Rachel is a virtuous woman, her feelings about Leah are tainted. Leah is comparably ambivalent: Leah visits Rachel before the wedding, and in a symbolic foreshadowing, she tries on Rachel's veil. The scene appears to be tender and intimate, but when the narrator reports that "they caressed each other with tears," he adds, "Why did they weep? They alone knew—though I might go so far as to say that they had different reasons."[13]

As elaborate as Mann's presentation is, he neglects entirely the mystery of Leah's thoughts under the wedding canopy, never wondering how Leah felt about betraying Rachel. With the progress of the story, the envy between the sisters deepens. Rachel hangs about Leah's son's cradle, and her helping with the baby is not what it seems. Leah's consoling words on Rachel's barrenness are double-edged as she observes that their master goes to Rachel four to six times as often as to herself. Finally, the narrator explains the degeneration of Rachel's character and her once loving relationship with Leah by appeal to "woman's nature":

> She was friendliness itself, but it was more than a woman's nature could bear and not feel jealous of her sister; and envy is a solvent to the emotions in which much else besides admiration unfortunately comes to the surface, and the reaction simply cannot be the best in the world. It could not but undermine the sisterly feeling between the two—in fact it already did so. Leah's maternal status outweighed the advantage of her infertile co-wife, whose appearance was so much that of a virgin that the other must have been a hypocrite to be able to betray in her manner no trace of consciousness of her superior worth.[14]

At last, Mann concludes: "thus, sisterly tenderness was at an end, and Jacob stood embarrassed between the two."[15] If classical Midrash struggles to create a bond of love between the sisters, Mann systematically erodes their love. His representation of these founding mothers leads to a larger conclusion about women, namely, that it is in "women's nature" to envy one another. This belief was a particularly congenial one in societies that were worried about sisterhood.

DICKENS AND HIS WIFE'S SISTERS

The suffragist movement in nineteenth-century England was a time of growing political sisterhood, and Victorian novels represent many and various relationships among sisters. Important fictions also explored the extent to which a wife should be a kind of sister to her husband. Charles Dickens's autobiographical fiction, *David Copperfield*, represents the ideal wife, Agnes, as sisterly; the development of romantic love between a man and his surrogate sister is already common in Romantic fictions (such as *Ivanhoe* and *Wuthering Heights*). Yet, to the extent that *Copperfield* is autobiographical, the sisters whom Dickens loved in the place of his wife were not his own but rather his wife's sisters.

What is interesting in this context is not so much Dickens's relationship with his sisters-in-law, nor how his relationships were rearranged and fictionalized, but the biographer's art, specifically as he or she approaches the question of a real life hero's possible affair with his wife's sister. Dickens's wife, Catherine Hogarth, eldest sister to Mary, Georgina, and Helen, was no sooner married to Charles than fifteen-year-old Mary came to live with them in their three rooms. Such arrangements were not unusual in Victorian homes. Mary and Dickens idealized each other, and when she died suddenly in his arms, she became monumental and inspirational to the artist (depicted in, among other characters, Little Nell); he reverenced mementoes, and he wished to be buried in her grave. Georgina later replaced Mary in the Dickens's home, helping her sister with the house and the children. As all of the biographers report, Dickens felt that Mary's spirit "shines out in *this* sister," and Georgina, displaced her sister Catherine as mistress of the house and as the wife of Dickens's affections.[16] Finally, when Catherine and Dickens separated after twenty-three years together, the youngest sister Helen, together with the women's mother, is said to have spread the deceit that Georgina and Dickens were, as they would have seen it, "incestuously involved."

In their biography of Dickens, the MacKenzies assert that though Georgina was pretty and admired, she preferred her brother-in-law to her suitors. They write: "Such a part in life was common for a maiden aunt in Victorian families. . . . What was uncommon in this case was the manner in which Georgina gradually assumed all of the functions of a wife, except those of sexual partner. . . . The Victorian conventions made many men ambivalent about their sexuality."[17] They interpret Dickens's treatment of his wife and her sisters as a psychological strategy for overcoming the Victorian classification of women as virgins or whores, a split that interfered with a man's sexual happiness with his wife. By this logic, Catherine's motherhood is what triggers Charles's disaffection, identifying her with his own mother, about whom he had bitter feelings. Fred Kaplan explains: "Unlike his mother, Georgina would never undervalue or reject him. Unlike Mary, she would never desert him. . . . Unlike Catherine, she was feminine without being sexual or maternal."[18] Here, the Leah-Rachel story takes a peculiarly Victorian turn, conforming to our era's interpretations of Victorian sexuality: the sister is the virgin wife; the man still possesses both women, however now one is loved virgin (a Christian variation on the barren matriarch Rachel), and the other is fertile whore (the unloved but productive Leah).

The MacKenzie biography was written in 1972. It is astounding that the authors characterize Catherine as a "weak and self-pitying woman who found it difficult to make the best of life . . . unsuited to the strains of the part in which marriage cast her." Then immediately: "It is true that she had suffered five miscarriages and the birth of ten children over the twenty years."[19] To conclude that this mother of ten lacked the vitality to keep up with her writer husband seems, on the face of it, a dubious judgment.

When it appeared in 1988, Kaplan's biography was previewed in an essay in the *New York Times Book Review*. In the synthesis that he created for the *Times*, Kaplan promises to go beyond the existing biographies in desentimentalizing the great writer, and his corrective in the *Times*'s essay focuses in particular on Dickens's relation with women. He writes: "Most biographers have not been aware that Dickens was widely rumored to have had a longstanding affair and numbers of children with his sister-in-law Georgina Hogarth. . . . It was claimed that they had had as many as three children together. The rumors depicted a ménage à trois in which he went from one bedroom to the next as it pleased him. Almost certainly the rumors were false."[20] In vilifying the great man, the Victorians put him in bed with his wife's sister. Did these imaginings also magnify the greatness of his larger-than-life persona, making him patriarchal on the model of Jacob?

Kaplan suggests that the rumors are false because the sister-in-law as virgin-wife better answered Dickens's Victorian psycho-sexual problem. He goes on:

The sister-wife fantasy was encouraged by the prevalence in Victorian society of husbands considerably older than their wives. Dickens had a special attraction to that confusion of images and roles. Sexual relations with mature women of his own age had too much of the maternal element. As she grew older, Catherine became increasingly matronly. . . . His ideal woman was always young, slim and sisterly. And when he made his break with the marriage, the woman he fell in love with [Ellen Ternan] had some features shared by his real and fictional sisters and daughters. In the combination of Georgina and Ellen he was able to fulfill his ideal. Georgina served his domestic needs; Ellen served his romantic needs. Together, they made the perfect wife. Catherine had not been the perfect wife, among other reasons because she had been the prolific mother.

In her fecundity, Catherine is cast by Kaplan in the role of Leah, while Georgina, the younger, more beloved sister without children becomes Rachel, who for many years was childless.

There is an untold story in the biographies of Dickens, a story that no one is imagining. Even though all agree that rumors of a sexual liaison with Georgina are unfounded, the biographers do not for a moment hint that the affair is unlikely because neither Mary nor Georgina, who were Catherine's companions, would have betrayed their elder sister by sleeping with her husband. Agency and moral responsibility rest with Dickens alone. None of these life stories deplore the appearance of sisterly betrayal because the biographical emphases deprive the sisters of the intimacy that is requisite for there to be a betrayal, in spite of the physical (and possible emotional) closeness among the sisters.

If the neglect of attention to the nature of Leah and Rachel's attachment may be attributed to the text's single-minded focus on building up Jacob for his heroic role, so too Dickens's position at the center of a family of women may function to reassure us that Dickens retains control of the system. The relationships among the five Hogarth women may, however, have posed a threat to Dickens that generated stories about Dickens's sleeping with sisters to empower him as family patriarch. As the story is usually told, Dickens betrays his wife by loving first Mary then Georgina, and then the youngest sister Helen and the mother betray Dickens in revenge by lying about his relation to Georgina. The real scandal here is the deeper plot that divides these women. Perhaps Dickens's psychological anxiety was not about the matronly wife at all but about female intimacies. The compensatory story has two sisters, separately, discount their sister in favor of the man she loved, and a mother and a third sister who are prepared to ruin the reputation of their own sister and daughter with the ugly report that she was having an incestuous affair. I venture to counter the biographers' amateur diagnoses of Dickens as substituting a virgin wife (his sister-in-law) for his fertile (sexual) wife with an alternative psychological speculation.

Dickens's biographers make clear his anger against his own mother for having tolerated his degrading labor in a factory while his own sister attended school. He blamed this female connection in his childhood for an emasculating humiliation. This defining fact of Dickens's childhood and the lifetime resentment it engendered, a resentment against what he perceived to be a threatening conspiratorial bond between mother and sister, echoes in the sexually scandalous reports about his adulthood. The fantasy about Dickens and his sisters-in-law functions to divide the matriarchy—mother and three daughters—that he feared would control the adult home that he was desperate to control. The rumor that his sister-in-law had some of his many children added to the myth of this hyperprolific, hyperenergetic (but traumatized and insecure) writer.

A FREUDIAN SLIP AND UNSPOKEN TABOO: HIS WIFE'S SISTER

Sigmund Freud, son of Jakob Freud, is heir to this biblical-Victorian tradition, and he recapitulates it in his life and work. A tyrannical element in Sigmund's love for his fiancée, Martha, was his excluding envy of her relationship with her mother and brother Eli (whom Freud's own sister Anna later married). Peter Gay writes that "Martha Bernays refused to countenance his jealous demands that she break with them. This generated strains that took years to dissipate."[21] When Martha had borne six children to Freud, her younger sister Minna joined the household to help out. Ernest Jones's early biography of Freud, famous for its reverential qualities, reports of Minna that:

> [I]ntellectual, and particularly literary, interests absorbed her life. Tante Minna was witty, interesting, and amusing, but she had a pungent tongue that contributed to a store of family epigrams. She and Freud got on excellently together. There was no sexual attraction on either side, but he found her a stimulating and amusing companion and would occasionally make short holiday excursions with her when his wife was not free to travel. All this has given rise to the malicious and entirely untrue legend that she displaced his wife in his affections. Freud always enjoyed the society of intellectual and rather masculine women.[22]

Peter Gay's biography of Freud also doubts this legend (he will later have reason to change his mind), and his reasoning, while not relying on the connection of intellectuality and masculinity, is equally Freud centered. Without considering any evidence from the relationship between Martha and Minna or the likelihood that the women would be restrained by their Victorian values, Gay thought it unlikely that Freud and Minna had a sexual relationship because Minna was not pretty enough.

Gay characterizes Martha as disinterested in psychology but attentive to all household matters and "one childhood ailment after another."[23] Of Minna, Gay writes that after her fiancé's premature death she "grew heavier, more jowly, becoming exceedingly plain; she looked older than her sister Martha, though she was in fact four years younger. . . . She was the intellectual sister. . . . In the pioneering years, Freud thought her his 'closest' confidante, along with Fliess."[24] With the abiding biblical prejudice that favors the younger matriarch, Gay argues for Freud's preference for the elder sister by explaining that she seemed to be younger.

In a bibliographical essay, Gay directly addresses the question: "Did Freud have an affair with his sister-in-law Minna Bernays?" Gay explains that Carl Jung, the first to make this accusation, claimed to have met Freud's wife's younger sister and found her "very good looking." Minna, deeply guilty, confided the affair to Jung, and later Freud reported disturbing dreams about himself, his wife, and her sister. Gay finds substantive reasons for doubting Jung, and he doubts that Minna would have confided in a stranger. But most of all he doubts Minna's attractiveness: "I submit that the photographs we have do not show Minna Bernays to have been 'very good looking.' She may indeed have been to Freud's taste, but it seems highly implausible that Jung, who had an eye for feminine beauty and was himself highly sexually active during those years, beyond the bounds of marriage, would really have found her so." Peter Swales, using the dubious evidence of Freud's dreams, corroborates the legend and goes further than Jung in supposing that Minna became pregnant by Freud. The end of Gay's account of the matter is: "If dependable independent evidence . . . should emerge that Freud did indeed have an affair with his sister-in-law and actually (as Swales argued in some detail) took her to get an abortion, I shall revise my text accordingly."[25]

Dependable evidence in the form of a hotel log surfaced and was reported on the front page of Sunday's *New York Times*, on Christmas Eve, 2006. The registry from a hotel in the Swiss Alps dated August 13, 1898, shows that Sigmund Freud signed in with Minna as husband and wife.[26] The *Times*'s article revisits the speculation that not only was there a liaison between Freud and his sister-in-law, but Minna shortly thereafter got an abortion. As in Dickens's case, Freud is also rumored to have impregnated his wife's sister.

In an earlier essay that appeared as the feature on the front page of the *New York Times Book Review* (January 29, 1989) titled, "Sigmund and Minna? The Biographer as Voyeur," Gay promotes his biography of Freud by reporting on his "pleasure" at having been "the first to go through the precious bundle" of correspondence between Freud and Minna Bernays.

Gay's portrait here is of himself as an intimate participant in the lives of which he writes, and Gay describes himself at his "familiar table" in the Library of Congress going through the letters: "Freud's German script, after years of study an old companion, offered no resistance. Minna Bernays's was more problematical. . . . Soon her handwriting too, yielded to me." "Resistance" and "yielding" suggest the biographer's erotic involvement, and Gay confesses that he does not expect but almost hopes to find something erotic in the letters. As in the biography itself, Gay's essay for the *Times* speculates about but fails to discover a love affair between Freud and his sister-in-law. Here, the evidence is the letters of these two alone; of Martha, the woman who would have been betrayed by such an affair, we learn only that she remains a "shadowy figure."

What is most interesting for this discussion, however, is the intensity not only of Gay's interest in the question of Sigmund and Minna in the 1980s but our collective interest, as was evidenced by the fact of this series of essays, with provocative headlines, claiming their place on the front page of the paper of record (at a time when this plot's detail also appeared in a cluster of popular movies). Moreover, as in the cases of the Dickens's biographies, during the years of speculation, the conjectures about Sigmund and Minna are never based on the evidence of the sisters' relationship, and there is a strange mixture of judgment and detachment in the reports of the hero's sexual relations with his wife's sister. In both cases, the most recent biographers raised the possibility, in order to discount it as unlikely, that the great man actually impregnated his sister-in-law.

In the Levitical incest laws, sex with one's wife's sister is expressly prohibited, and in the traditional Jewish wedding ceremony the groom veils the bride, a ceremony that at once effaces the woman and assures the man that he has Rachel and not Leah. Although a man may marry his deceased brother's childless wife, Jewish law forbids marriage to one's wife's sister. Freudian theory teaches us that the taboo is greatest where the desire is strongest.

Writing about incest taboos, Freud himself puts the sister-in-law under erasure. *Totem and Taboo* addresses in close detail the temptation to the young boy of his mother and sisters. Freud then goes on, omitting any mention of sisters-in-law—often fixtures in Victorian homes, including his own—to talk about how the early incest temptation shows up in the relation of sons-in-law to mothers-in-law. Following an impressive list of evidence from "primitives" that literally keep this pair apart, Freud jokes: "Although laws of avoidance no longer exist in the society of the white races of Europe and America, much quarrelling and displeasure would often be avoided if they did exist and did not have to be reestablished by individuals."[27] Freud points out dismissively that one reason for this antagonism is the possibility of an excluding closeness between the mother and daughter. (Here one recalls Freud's own jealousy of Martha's relationship to her mother.) Freud's surer explanations displace the envy: mothers, because they live through their daughters, can fall enviously in love with their sons-in-law. For the man's part, his mother-in-law "actually represents an incest temptation" because she reminds him of his own mother. The ambivalence comes of a likeness to his wife but as the older, less lovely woman he fears she could become. Since Freud's discussion of the incest taboo includes sisters as equal to mothers, it is surprising that he has nothing to say about sisters-in-law, who also may remind a man of his wife without the "matronly" qualities that the biographers of our eminent Victorians find so unattractive.

Freud's emphases and omissions in *Totem and Taboo* scream a powerful but overlooked temptation, one codified in texts as venerable as the Bible and as recent as Woody Allen's *Hannah and Her Sisters*. Freud omits this taboo, though rumors about Freud and his sister-in-law circulated in his lifetime. The temptation of the sister-in-law exists less because she may remind a man of his wife and his own sister than because the wife and sister together threaten a man's patriarchal power; having both women undermines their intimacy as it reassures the man of his exclusive and excluding desirability. It is a way to make Sigmund into Jakob, a familiar Freudian story, the son into the father.

HANNAH AND HER SISTERS: THE VIRILE *NEBISH*

Allen's film alludes to the Hebrew Bible in the heroine's name. Hannah names the barren mother of Samuel (this Hannah has a fertile co-wife, Penina) and the prolific mother in Maccabees who martyrs herself and her sons. The film's title suggests that this is a movie about women, but it opens with a chapter title, "God she's beautiful," articulated in a voice over by Elliot (Michael Caine), Hannah's husband, going on about her (no antecedent for the pronoun) pretty eyes and sexy sweater, wishing he could get her alone, wishing he could tell her he loves her, and most emphatically wishing he could take care of her. Then: "Stop it you idiot, she's your wife's sister," he tells himself. We learn that he has been consumed with Lee (Barbara Hershey) for months and that he thinks it is "disgusting." We soon hear Elliot compliment his wife's sister's catering, and we come to realize that he means Holly (Dianne Wiest), Hannah's other sister. Only then do we see the three sisters together in the kitchen, chatting about Thanksgiving and their parents; Lee, we learn, would like to work with children; Hannah's first husband, Mickey (Woody Allen), is mentioned ("crazy as ever"). The viewer cannot see this scene and accept comfortably the sisters' evident intimacy. Hannah's husband, in his absence, governs our reading of the sisters together. We already know about Elliot's obsession, and we wonder how the man's lust for his wife's sister will affect the relationships within this family enjoying Thanksgiving. A man is the absent center that controls the viewer's reading of the sisters' relationships.

When Hannah (Mia Farrow) is complimented for her successful performance as Nora in *A Doll's House*, the allusion suggests that the film functions within a tradition of narratives about women who assert themselves. Hannah then gives the now familiar speech about how the role tempted her return to the stage, but she is glad to be back doing what she loves, caring for her husband and children. The film both celebrates these nostalgic values, even as we appreciate the ironies; after all, this husband to whom Hannah is so devoted lusts after her sister.

Meanwhile Hannah's first husband, Mickey, becomes a character in his own right, a typical Woody Allen "nerd" in contrast to his handsome and successful former partner. Mickey visits Hannah and their twin sons, and he observes that he likes and identifies with Hannah's new husband: "he is awkward and clumsy and under-confident—a loser like me." Both of these men, both Hannah's husbands, are characterized as losers, yet these losers will win not only the very attractive Hannah, but Elliot will seduce Lee, and Mickey will end up married to the talented Holly, whom we learn he always had a crush on, the clear implication being that he lusted after Holly even while he was married to Hannah. Because of the doublings in this plot, Hannah has two sisters, one for each husband. Moreover, Mickey's sons are not his. His dubious virility is epitomized by his infertility and small sperm count. The twins (a product of the patriarchal virility that generated Jacob and Esau) were conceived by artificial insemination; the donor was Mickey's manly former partner.

Hannah's new husband Elliot intends to seduce Lee, and a parallel plot develops in which Holly and her best friend April (Carrie Fisher) begin dating the same man. David takes them out together on the famed architectural tour of New York, and when we are in Holly's consciousness for the first time, she is conflating her sister and her friend, comparing herself first to Hannah and then to April. As she listens to April joke with David, Holly regrets that she cannot tell jokes as Hannah can. She thinks, "I hate April. She's pushy. I really like him a lot." April replaces Holly's older sister as an object of envy, and we hear the ease with which envy becomes hate when a man enters the arena. April and Holly are best friends and business partners; they have known David for less than an evening.

Elliot begins his seduction. He directs Lee to a sexy e. e. cummings poem, and he offers to accompany her to an AA meeting. It is a cheap and silly seduction, but it works. Referring to Elliot's lies about his marriage, Lee muses, "Hannah never said anything. We are very close. Poor Hannah." She repeats that she and Hannah are close. In the next scene we see Hannah caring for their mother, who is drunk, and the mother tells Hannah that Lee worships Hannah. Immediately, we see Elliot and Lee in bed; the sex was "perfect." In Allen's film, this betrayal is the price of the sisterly worship so often emphasized by the characters.

Competition and rivalry—sexual and professional—underlie the sororal intimacies that are betrayed by Hannah's sisters in conversations with her husband and ex-husband. Lee says to Elliot, "I was so worried that I wouldn't compare to Hannah," and Lee confesses to having such thoughts all the time. She imagines that her sister is passionate. Elliot admits that Hannah is warm but not needy enough. Lee reassures him, saying, "I want you to take care of me." Soon Elliot is in bed with Hannah, thinking how cozy it is with her and how passionate it is with her sister.

Mickey's memory of his love for Hannah triggers a memory of his first date with Holly after his divorce. On that occasion Mickey compared Holly's taste in music unfavorably to that of both of her sisters. Holly shouts like a child in the throes of sibling rivalry: "I am my own person." Hannah, like Leah, the eldest and the fertile sister, wants more children. She already has four. She tells Elliot that she would be destroyed if he were in love with someone else, echoing Elliot's earlier thought that he would prefer to hurt Lee a little rather than destroy Hannah. The nebishy Elliot's ego expands as he feels his destructive power.

The three sisters go out to lunch. Holly asks Hannah for money to pursue her writing. When Hannah agrees, Holly accuses Hannah of condescension. More competitiveness. Lee rushes to Hannah's defense. For the viewer, Elliot is the absent presence at the table. We are encouraged to see Lee's former alcohol dependence and Holly's former cocaine dependence as symptoms of sisterly rivalry.

The movie is punctuated with Mickey's cancer terrors and quest for a god in whom he can believe. In one particularly Allenesque moment, Freud is invoked as a great pessimist. Indeed, in Allen's version of the family romance, sexual taboos are twice violated, as three men prove that they know what women want, managing to win sisters and best friends with no consequence to themselves. Freud's version is significantly more pessimistic.

One Thanksgiving later, Holly has written a play in which Hannah sees her marriage represented, and she says to Holly, "You make it sound like I have no needs." Confronting Elliot, Hannah says, "I have enormous needs." Elliot yells back, "I can't see them and neither can Lee or Holly." In the married couple's next lovemaking scene, Hannah begins weakly, "I feel lost." Elliot becomes reassuring, and the viewer knows that because Hannah showed vulnerability (reversing Nora's progress in

A Doll's House), the sex will be as satisfying as that which Elliot enjoyed with Lee.

Hannah's flaw is that she appears too self-possessed and confident. Her sisters (for whom she provides) resent her competence as does her husband. The message is that to be loved, a woman should be weak. A husband needs to be generous, and female jealousy may lead to malice. Hannah, like the fertile Leah of scriptures and the fertile Catherine Dickens, feels unloved because, for all of her children and successes, both men, husband and ex-husband, turn to her (ambiguously) "weaker" childless sisters for satisfaction. The sisters, to calm their envy, accept the offers.

As the plot signals closure, Lee has a new boyfriend, and we are led to believe that this relationship will succeed because with him she can become a mother. Mickey and Holly date, and Holly produces some wonderful scripts. Coda: one Thanksgiving later, the fairytale is complete. Hannah, perfectly happy with Elliot, has a new role as Desdemona. Lee is married to Doug. A sign of the conservatism of the script, in the background the black maid dims the lights in the dining room. Holly, who has arrived late, is looking at her beautiful face in the mirror as Mickey, whom we now discover has become her husband, kisses her neck and thinks that it would make a great story, a man married to one sister, it doesn't work out, and years later, he marries the other. Holly speaks: "Mickey, I'm pregnant." They kiss. Like Sarah and Rachel, late to conceive compared with their fertile co-wives, both "barren" sisters will now have the satisfaction of children, as the film ends with this biblical miracle that impregnates the more beloved barren wife.

Hannah and Her Sisters repeats the same story three times, and yet reviewers barely notice this scheme. Three neurotic and essentially unworthy men succeed in bedding down with two women each, two women who, in each case, we have reason to believe, should be more loyal to each other than to the men who succeed, with precious little effort, in seducing them. Thus, the "schlep" is made patriarchal. How to make the "Jewish" boy virile is the subject of many Woody Allen films. It is also the story of Isaac and Ishmael and of Jacob and Esau. At what cost?

The film is touted as a great comedy, and it is a comedy in the classic sense. Ending with the sisters' father playing "Isn't It Romantic" on the piano, all four women (the three sisters and April, whose friendship is sacrificed out of the picture because of her disloyalty to Holly) have found their appropriate mates, and all will live happily ever after. No guilt, recriminations, or retributions. The reconciliation among the sisters seems genuinely grounded in their intimacy. Thanksgiving, the dust settled, everyone has what to be thankful for. A funny allegory complete with miracles.

The principle gain is virility. Once more Allen succeeds in making a man of the inadequate self beneath the male persona. Even the infertile Mickey—the Allen alter ego—can impregnate a woman if she is the right woman. No loss? Only if we accept the movie's assumptions, part of the subconscious of the culture, about women, their relationships, their loyalties, their needs, and their priorities. These assumptions are rearticulated in this popular form in the 1980s because they provided the soothing voice of tradition (feminist backlash) to those worried about the sisterhood that feminism promised.

The message hides behind the plot's familiarity so that viewers ironically regard this as Allen's feminist film. In the *New York Times* review of *Hannah and Her Sisters*, Vincent Canby cannot contain his praise. He concludes from this movie that Allen "is our only authentic auteur," and introduces the film as a "beneficent, funny, psychologically complex family chronicle."[28] Although he will later point out that Mickey, the character played by Allen, is the movie's "lodestar," Canby's paraphrase of the plot implies that the movie is essentially about the sisters of the title; it is, Canby writes, "about three Central Park West-bred sisters and their emotional entanglements with their husbands, their lovers and their mother and father." In this review, Canby promotes the film by implying that its values are feminist: "It is as if Mr. Allen had liberated . . . the three sisters of 'Interiors,' to allow them to become their own women in this new work."

Steven Soderberg's 1989 film *sex, lies and videotape* challenges precisely these gender stereotypes by playing with the roles in the sleeping-with-sisters plot. In this story the sisters are classic doubles, complementary and antithetical: the one fully restrained, the other uninhibited. The younger sister, Cindy ("Sin" played by Laura San Giacomo) is sexual, desired by and in bed with her elder sister's husband, John (Peter Gallagher). Enter the feminine "brother" Graham (James Spader), John's aimless, sweet, impotent frat brother who videotapes women talking about sex and who has grown distant from his mightily successful friend John. The sisters compete for Graham. Dramatically reversing the gender positions in the mythic plot, here John, the man who betrayed his wife by having relations with her kid sister, loses everything: his fancy job, both women. The elder inhibited sister Ann (Andie McDowell) triumphs, apparently cures Graham of his inability to have unmediated intimacy with women, and the sisters move toward one another, each more like the other. The viewer hopes for a developing connection between them. Here, uniquely, the betrayal *is* between sisters, is discovered, and is consequential. *sex, lies and videotape* thereby challenges a "truth" rooted in scriptures and biography.

The story of the weak hero, his wife, and her sister is a special variation of the ubiquitous erotic triangle, and its modern American manifestations demand ideological analysis. Sedgwick concludes her introduction to *Between Men* with this observation:

> Thus, Lacan, Chodorow and Dinnerstein, Rubin, Irigaray, and others, making critiques from within their multiple traditions, offer analytical tools for treating the erotic triangle not as an ahistorical, platonic form, a deadly symmetry from which the historical accidents of gender, language, class and power detract, but as a sensitive register precisely for delineating relationships of power and meaning, and for making graphically intelligible the play of desire and identification by which individuals negotiate with their societies for empowerment.[29]

In *Nostalgia and Sexual Difference*, Janice Doane and Devon Hodges demonstrate how many superficially feminist plots (they are discussing John Irving's *The World According to Garp* and I am thinking of *Hannah and Her Sisters*) are actually nostalgic for an illusory past when women were domestic and quiet. Doane and Hodges conclude that in fiction "truth is structured in such a way as to guarantee paternal authority and to silence women, no matter how much they may seem to speak."[30]

Allen's film sustains this conclusion. Its heroines seem to be considerably more outspoken than Leah was when she took her sister's place as Jacob's bride. But Hannah, Lee, and Holly wear veils insofar as the triumph of the men in their lives depends on their silences as partners in a misogynistic deception. The real deception is the one that the narrative works on the viewers. From Genesis through *Hannah and Her Sisters*, women are inexplicably, but necessarily, silenced in their relationships to one another. Allen's seemingly weak and dominated men, like the victimized and relatively effeminate biblical Jacob, become patriarchal through a plot that divides the matriarchy.

The story of the hero who sleeps with his wife's sister, like the Cinderella story, is often told: sister rivals, sister meanness. The other story is more rarely developed, but it is the story beneath this story: Jacob is off center, not so important; Leah and Rachel love each other and each other's children. Their feelings are complex and strong and various, and they do not worry about Jacob nearly as much as he worries about them.

5

Coats and Tales: Joseph and Myths of Jewish Masculinity

The ambivalent and self-contradictory masculinity of Isaac and Jacob culminates in the history of representations of Jacob's favorite son, Joseph. Joseph, as he is represented in Genesis 37–50, is a relatively complex figure whose heroism finds expression not only in the grand acts of vision and planning that save his family and, indeed, all Egypt from famine, but also in the seemingly more incidental details of his beauty and chastity. Although the Joseph of Hebrew scripture is not without his character faults, his beauty and chastity have unambiguously positive connotations. In rabbinic and medieval midrashic literature, in the Koran, and in subsequent art and fiction, however, re-creators of Joseph find it increasingly difficult to reconcile Joseph's heroism with his chastity. The beauty that is sexually unproblematic in the biblical story becomes effeminate in later renderings of Joseph, and what has come to be remembered as the "coat of many colors" is reshaped accordingly. In this sketch of several transfigurations of Joseph, I will suggest that one effect of the exaggerations of succeeding literary reinterpretations of this hero is to make him flamboyant.[1] Joseph's gender alterity maps onto his outsider national identity as a successful Hebrew in Egypt, creating an implicit association between Joseph's appearance and behavior and his rise to power as an assimilated foreigner. This exceptionality—along both sexual and political axes—later extends to the ambivalent image and self-understanding of Jews.

At once an object of exaggerated desire and unnaturally chaste, a figure who experiences extreme highs and lows, Joseph becomes increasingly parodic—a drama queen—over the history of representation. Joseph, a former slave who makes himself so useful and attractive to the Egyptians that he rises to high political position, reads increasingly over time as a prototype for the Jew as improvisation artist, immigrant mimic, and a stand-out (queer?) fellow who is too good to be true.[2] In Joseph we have an origin story for the changing image and self-image of the Jew as an outsider within, an identity approximation like that of conscientiously assimilating immigrants. Joseph contains the seeds of both the Jew as an idealized good citizen and an ominous resident alien. Joseph and Moses, who bracket the Israelite sojourn in Egypt, are both welcomed into the intimate space of foreign power even as the reader retains a consciousness of their national difference as a potentially disruptive threat.

The sibling rivalries of early Genesis extend to Joseph, who is Jacob's preferred son born of Jacob's barren and beloved wife Rachel, and Joseph's story conforms to the pattern that we have seen of the barren mother longing for and losing (in some form) her late-conceived child. The textual pattern that reverses the rule of primogeniture may also have a political rationale. Perhaps the early Israelites favored these myths because they were a relatively small, militarily weak, and young people. Thus, in the cases of Isaac and Ishmael, and Jacob and Esau, Joseph and his brothers, and later, King David and his brothers, and Solomon and his brothers, it is the younger son, the child of the more beloved but less fertile wife, the physically smaller, less hirsute, more delicate, more domestic son, the son closer to the mother, a hero of intellect rather than of brawn, who is selected by God over his brothers to dominate the story and direct its future. As we have seen, however, because the victorious son's advantage over his stronger brothers owes much to his mother's position or support, he comes to be read as a "mama's boy."

This hero-type may be further aligned with women in that these family constellations typically identify no daughters, and so the young son who is the mother's favorite may occupy the daughter position in the reader's unconscious. An actual daughter materializes in the last of this Genesis chain: in the family full of boys, Dinah is sister to Joseph and his eleven brothers. Dinah's role in the story is limited to being raped by a neighboring prince, and while Dinah's narrative seems to interrupt the Joseph story, it serves to highlight Joseph's similarity to her. Joseph and Dinah both attract the lust and harassment of a foreigner with power. These details also contribute to other later stereotypes of Jews, such as that of a harmless, if distastefully feminized, people controlled by their women. Finally, this negative image of relatively weak Jewish masculinity develops in correspondence with a developing image of the Jewess or Hebrew beauty, built from biblical seduction stories, as sexually overpowering and insatiable.

INCIDENTALLY BEAUTIFUL IN THE BIBLE

The biblical Joseph, characterized as an instrument of divine will, is a typical hero. Singled out equally as an object of love and an object of envy, Joseph's status as hero is plainly a function of his having been pre-selected for a special role in the Genesis narrative history. Everything in his personal story conforms to the type of the biblical hero: not only is he a beloved son born of a "barren" favored wife, but there is also an early attempt on his life, and he eventually achieves a position of political influence, making him like Moses, Oedipus, Jesus, and other classic heroes.[3] In spite of his being identifiably a hero, Joseph's acts of pride compromise him in the eyes of the reader. Joseph is a complex hero in part because his human ambitions and faults are necessary to actualize God's plan.

Jacob gives Joseph a striped coat. This detail in the story would seem superfluous, but added to Joseph's dreams of power and mention that Joseph tattles on his brothers, the reader sympathizes with the brothers' jealousy. Even Jacob evidences slight annoyance with his favorite son's pretentiousness. When Joseph tells his prideful dreams, Jacob rebukes him, asking if Joseph really expects that his parents and brothers will someday bow down before him (Genesis 37:10). The biblical Jacob, by contrast with the Koranic Jacob, is unsuspicious of his older sons and encourages Joseph to join his brothers on the day that the brothers will abandon Joseph in a pit and return to their father with a concocted story of Joseph's death, furnishing Jacob with the coat that had been his gift as "proof" that his beloved son has been slaughtered by wild beasts. Whatever may have been Jacob's parenting mistakes and Joseph's flaws, this fate seems excessive and undeserved, and Joseph is more sinned against than sinner. The rest of the narrative is generated by the injustice of the brothers having sold Joseph into slavery.

The fact of Joseph's beauty occurs as a single line in the text that serves only to explain why the wife of Potiphar, his Egyptian master, lusts after him. Once more Joseph's garment, this time left behind in his flight from the seductions of Potiphar's wife, is the material sign of a lie: it "proves" that Joseph came "to insult" his lord's wife. Again Joseph is unjustly punished—this time by imprisonment—but once in jail, he has the opportunity to prove himself a reader of dreams. In the context of the false readings of Joseph's clothes, Joseph distinguishes himself as a true interpreter and eventually earns release from prison because of his interpretive powers. His administrative and interpretive skills make him indispensible, until he is appointed Pharaoh's vizier, and of course, the day does come when his brothers do bow down before him. The fact that Joseph knows his brothers while they do not recognize him is unremarkable in the story but does suggest that Joseph has effected a radical transformation over these years and that Joseph's beauty is neither exotic nor distinctively Hebrew; his appearance is not so singular as to betray his identity to his unsuspecting brothers. Joseph's withheld identity creates suspense and the narrative possibility for the brothers to prove the fullness of their repentance. Jacob descends to Egypt, and these episodes end happily, God's promises and Joseph's prophecies alike fulfilled.

Although Joseph is God's pawn, his personal heroic qualities are evident: he is wise, chaste, loyal to God, to his own people, to his master Potiphar, and to Pharaoh; he is a skillful politician (he manipulates both Pharaoh and his brothers to get what he wants) and a skillful administrator (he manages Egypt so well that he acquires people and property for his lord, transforming a system of private land ownership into a feudal economy). What is it about the Joseph story that so troubled later readers as to necessitate that Joseph's beauty—incidental in the Bible—would become his most remarkable and memorable trait?

PRETTY BOY IN THE JEWISH COMMENTARIES

In the Bible, Joseph's beauty is a vehicle only to present the lusts of one woman and the chaste virtue of the hero. The commenting tradition projects Joseph's beauty back to his youth. Jacob's particular love for Joseph is explained not only by Joseph's being "the child of his old age" but also by their sharing beautiful features, an interpretation developed from a pun latent in the Hebrew.[4] The first-century historian Josephus, writing in *Jewish Antiquities*, and comments in the Midrash Rabbah, explains that Joseph's beauty is inherited from his beautiful and favored mother, Rachel.[5]

The attitudes toward this exaggerated beauty range widely. Writing in first-century Alexandria, the Jewish philosopher Philo betrays unease in his treatment of Joseph's character. In spite of the Bible's nuanced characterization of Joseph, to Philo, Joseph is principally a man of carnal lusts. In Philo's *Allegorical Commentary*, an exposition of the Bible possibly aimed at assimilating Jews in his own community, Philo places Joseph in an allegorical scheme that presents Egypt (a stand-in for contemporary Rome) as the type of the body and its passions.[6] To paint Joseph as wicked, all body and pleasure, Philo omits those biblical episodes and comments uncongenial to his thesis. Philo's purpose appears to be to warn his Jewish readers against the sins of materialism. In *De Josepho*, a work directed to a more general readership, Philo apparently recognizes that Joseph's character is not monolithic. In this work, Philo promotes Joseph's leadership. In the former account, Philo depicts Joseph as vain and spurious; in the latter, Joseph is lordly. Philo's English language editors collect the descriptive language in which Philo depicts Joseph: "prepared to subordinate truth to the expediency of falsehood; . . . eager for vain glory, self-opinionated, presumptuous, swollen-headed with vanity. . . . Joseph is the lover of the body and its passions, the champion of the body and externals, fond of luxury. From his mother he inherited the irrational strain of sense-perception."[7] A unique passage praises Joseph for controlling himself with Potiphar's wife,[8] but generally, Philo's distaste for Joseph seems related to Joseph's easy assimilation into the role of a well-stationed Egyptian.

If Joseph's association with Egyptian carnality and decadence troubles Philo, Joseph's sexuality, a midrashic preoccupation, confuses and irks the rabbis. The Midrash Rabbah glosses Genesis 37:2 ("Joseph, being seventeen years old . . . being still a lad"): "It means, however, that he behaved like a boy, penciling his eyes, curling his hair and lifting his heels." The biblical indication of Joseph's youth is thus translated into meaning that he was immature, an immaturity that is characterized by beauty, effeminacy, and vanity. The Midrash, while not justifying the brothers' behavior, makes Joseph more deserving of their contempt. Abel, the first biblical victim of fratricide, is analogously not an entirely blameless victim in Midrash, and Abel is identically described as "penciling his eyes, curling his hair, and lifting his heels."[9] In the rabbinic imagination, murderous rage in these brothers is made partially explicable by the rabbis' imposition of a fantasy of particular behaviors of primping on the victim brother, behaviors that, in rabbinic times, may have been associated with women.

The Midrash invents another misdeed that more closely fits the biblical Joseph's punishment: Joseph, guilty of slandering his brothers to their father, more specifically claims that they are lustful. God exacts vengeance by inciting "a bear," that is, Potiphar's wife, against Joseph himself. The harassment of Potiphar's wife is rendered retributive by this midrashic addition. In this way too the Midrash taints the brothers with an accusation of lustfulness, which, however false, is likely to have been generated to implicitly contrast with Joseph's famed chastity. One might interrogate the rabbis' unconscious motives in inventing the content of this slander. Like Isaac relative to Ishmael, and Jacob relative to Esau, over time, Joseph became encoded as less masculine than his brothers. Because Joseph's brothers, uniquely, are also tribal patriarchs in Israel, for the rabbis, these misbehaving ancestors, maligned with an accusation of lust, may function as a corrective to the hero who pencils his brow and lifts his heels.

The Midrash magnifies and spreads the lust around: Joseph's exaggerated beauty provokes all of Egypt's noblewomen to lust, and Joseph's chastity motivates rabbinic expansions in two directions, each based on the premise that Joseph's self-control requires explanation beyond ordinary piety and duty. The first explanation makes Potiphar's wife repulsive; the second calls Joseph's manhood into question. We are told in the Midrash Rabbah to Genesis 39:16 that she "speaks like an animal," that she let Joseph's garments "grow old in her keeping, embracing, kissing, and fondling them," and that she went to great lengths in her seductions: "she went as far as to place an iron fork under his neck so that he would have to lift up his eyes and look at her."[10]

As much as these midrashic stories betray the rabbis' uneasiness over Joseph's chastity, others go to great lengths to assure the reader that chastity is a great virtue; in so doing they protest too much. Joseph's self-control is made to go beyond the lusts of one noblewoman: "The Egyptian women, daughters of kings, desired to gaze upon Joseph's face, yet he would not look upon any of them. He therefore merited both worlds, because he entertained no impure thoughts about them." An alternative tradition elaborates: "You find that when Joseph went forth to rule over Egypt, daughters of kings used to look at him through the lattices and throw bracelets, necklets and ear-rings, and finger-rings to him, so that he might lift up his eyes and look at them; yet he did not look at them." Again, just as the rabbis marvel at the self-discipline of their hero, they feel obliged to account for it: "Rabbi Huna said in Rabbi Mattenah's name: He saw his father's face which cooled his blood. Rabbi Menahema said in Rabbi Ammi's name: He saw his mother's face, which cooled his blood."[11] The commenting tradition exaggerates the fact of Joseph's chaste beauty and creates a parody of female desire and male restraint, with hot-blooded women desperate for even the chance to gaze upon Joseph's face, and Joseph in possession of a degree of control that, under the pressure of these elaborations, distinguishes him from the average man.[12]

In the biblical story, Joseph's innocence of the charges by Potiphar's wife is known only to the reader; Joseph leaves prison because Pharaoh requires his assistance in dream interpretation. There are midrashim that are less able to tolerate this unjust accusation against Joseph remaining undiscovered, and these suggest that if Potiphar had believed his wife, then Joseph would have been killed rather than imprisoned. The rabbis supply Potiphar with an additional line of dialogue: "'I know that you are innocent,' he assured him, 'but (I must do this) lest a stigma fall upon my children.'"[13] Joseph is rewarded with Potiphar's vestures of fine linen, not because of his administrative talents, as the Bible implies, but because "his body had not cleaved to sin." For these rabbis the politics of the body had become more important than the politics of the state.

Midrash constructs two she-bear fables. The first excuses Joseph's reticence: the she-bear (that is, Potiphar's wife) is arrayed in expensive jewels; the crowd declares that whoever is brave enough to attack her may keep the jewels. The wise man looks at her fangs, not at her attire. In the other, a man who is "penciling his eyes and curling his hair" declares, to the amusement of the crowd, that he is a man. "'If you are a man,' the bystanders retort, 'here is a she-bear, up and attack it.'" The implication of the latter story is that if Joseph were a man, he would not apply makeup to his face; if Joseph were a man, he would attack the woman. Apparently Joseph is not much of a man.

The rabbis' mixed messages betray discomfort with the sacred hero's chastity and beauty. Declining to articulate their doubts too directly, the blunt question is put in the mouth of a woman who doubts that a hot-blooded youth would have resisted the advances of his boss's wife: "A matron asked Rabbi Jose: 'Is it possible that Joseph, at seventeen years of age, with all the hot blood of youth could act thus?'" Although Rabbi Jose confidently replies that the Bible is clear on the matter, another rabbi finds reason to argue that Joseph's intentions, at least, testify to "hot blood": "On examination he did not find himself a man,", and in a footnote, a modern editor explains: "He actually went to sin, but found himself impotent."[14] The biblical Joseph is an ambivalent figure because the combination of paternal favoritism and his own arrogance is understandably irritating to his older brothers. Midrash deepens the ambivalence; in their historical context, more particularly, it is Joseph's beauty and innocence that strike the rabbis as unnatural and effeminate.

Joseph's brothers, like Ishmael and Esau, might be justified in their distress over Joseph's usurpation of their father's affection and leapfrogging their position as elders. But the Bible seems to require the characters' acquiescence to any textual favoritism that is God's will. (Jonathan's love for David may be an idealized representation of graceful acceptance of the deserving, chosen usurper.) The Midrash rebels against the Bible's untroubled accounts of possible mistreatment of Ishmael and Esau and goes out of its way to vilify the first-born sons in gestures that vindicate the Bible's self-serving patriarchs and their biased mothers. In the case of Joseph's brothers, however, their behavior is made more excusable. Of course Ishmael and Esau are not patriarchs but instead become the founding figures of rival nations. Joseph's brothers, progenitors of the tribes of Israel, would have been the rabbis' own mythic forefathers, and as such, Joseph does not have their unqualified approval. What is relevant here is that the rabbis express their resistance in part by withholding complete endorsement of Joseph's pious sexuality, perhaps disassociating themselves from Joseph's sexual disinterest.

Cignani, Carlo (1628–1719), Joseph and Potiphar's Wife. Ca. 1670/1680. The interpretations of Joseph's piety, chastity, and beauty increasingly translated into weak masculinity. Bildarchiv Preussischer Kulturbesitz / Art Resource, New York.

UNCONTAINED DESIRE IN THE HOLY KORAN

The Holy Koran, which generally avoids narrative as a vehicle for religious teaching, chooses to develop but one sustained narrative, Sura Yusuf, "the fairest of stories," the story of Joseph.[15] Intolerant of divine injustice or deception, the Koranic version departs from the biblical account in order to clarify the story's morality. With an emphasis on religious values, Allah frequently interrupts his narrative to make meaning and moral explicit. The Koran's didacticism and clarity eschew narrative suspense and ambiguity. The Hebrew Bible, more compatible with a modernist literary sensibility, places limited value on the story's role in improving the reader. Although the Koran's departures from the Hebrew Bible basically serve to underscore cosmic justice, they also suggest that Mohammed was no less troubled than the rabbis by Joseph's chaste beauty.

More prophetic than the biblical Jacob, the Koranic Jacob discourages Joseph from telling his dreams lest his brothers "plot against him" (12:5). Neither does the patriarch in the Koran harbor illusions about his sons' characters, jealousy, and murderous propensities. While the biblical Jacob urges Joseph to follow after his brothers, the Koranic father is more anxious and reluctant: "a wolf may devour him" (12:13). The coat, designed to justify this fear, is returned to Jacob "with false blood." In the Koran, unlike in the Hebrew Bible, no mention is made of its being torn. Seeing that the coat is whole, Jacob is not deceived by his sons. Later, at the home of Joseph's Egyptian lord, the coat, which is dropped in one piece in the Bible, is ripped off his back by his master's wife. The tear, displaced from the first coat, is replaced here. Just as the whole coat bore witness to the brother's lie, the torn one testifies to Joseph's honesty. Joseph could not have been the aggressor as the position of the tear indicates that he was running away from the woman. In the Koran, a witness of the fold explains that because the coat is torn from behind, Joseph speaks the truth (12:26–28).

The Koranic story, otherwise more concise than the biblical version, adds several details about Potiphar's wife: "She verily desired him, and he would have desired her if it had not been that he saw the argument of his lord" (12:24). Thus, Joseph is transformed into a man with natural sexual desires. The Koran sees a double problem: if Joseph's innocence is proved by the torn coat, why is Joseph imprisoned? And if Potiphar's wife is proved guilty, how does she survive the women's gossip in court? The Koran explains that Potiphar's wife invites the women to dine and equips each with a sharp knife and blood oranges:

> [12:]31. And when she heard of their sly talk, she sent to them and prepared for them a cushioned couch (to lie on at the feast) and gave to every one of them a knife and said (to Joseph): Come unto them! And when they saw him they exalted him and cut their hands, exclaiming: Allah Blameless! This is not a human being. This is no other than some gracious angel.
>
> 32. She said: This is he on whose account ye blamed me. I asked of him an evil act, but he proved continent, but if he do not my behest he verily shall be imprisoned.

The women see Joseph and bleed. Although Potiphar's wife is not vindicated in the eyes of posterity, a silent consensus is reached among the court women as Joseph's heavenly beauty justifies her lust. Clearly the women would have done the same. Joseph prefers imprisonment to submission and warns Allah: "if Thou send not off their wiles from me, I shall incline unto them and become of the foolish" (12:33). Thus, once more, Joseph's beauty is exaggerated and his natural urges are clarified. "And it seemed good to them (the men-folk) after they had seen the signs (of his innocence) to imprison him for a time" (12:35). If Joseph had remained free, his sexual urges would have proved too strong. He asks to be incarcerated to protect himself from the women's lust and his own ignited passion.

Finally, the Koran adds a third coat to Joseph's wardrobe. The ordinarily prescient Jacob (the Koran's patriarchs are all prophets) does not know what has become of Joseph, though he knows enough to disbelieve his sons' explanation. The prophet's metaphorical blindness is relieved when Joseph sends his coat home with his brothers. Jacob wipes his eyes with it, and his prophetic vision is miraculously restored. The third coat comes to reveal that which the first tried—but failed—to conceal. Thus, the deceptions that motivate the biblical story are not tolerated in the Koran, which makes every sign a readable expression of divine justice.

In spite of his simplifying effort to elucidate meaning, Mohammed, like the Jewish exegetes, betrays an anxiety over Joseph's masculinity and accordingly elaborates upon both Joseph's beauty and the extent to which he must have been tempted. Although the Bible shows no concern over either male beauty or what in the intervening years came to be called "healthy" male sexuality, over time male beauty became suspect if it were not used to seduce women. As the association of masculinity with predatory sexuality comes to be normalized, vigorous sexuality became a more important heroic trait than spirituality. The biblical Joseph's chastity therefore leads later interpreters to doubt his masculinity; by exaggerating Joseph's beauty, these writers virtually deprive him of beauty, imagining an effeminate man who, ironically, is a less than attractive role model.

THE DECLINE OF THE SPIRITUAL MAN IN THE MODERN ERA

With the advent of early modernism, there are signs that the dominant conceptualization of male sexuality was being refigured in opposition to his spirituality. Although angelic beauty was increasingly reserved for heroines, more heroes could boast a beastly appeal. In Henry Fielding's *Joseph Andrews* (1742), the deliberately and aptly named title character embodies this transition. He begins exemplary for his chastity, but he learns to be a "real man." Explicitly like the biblical Joseph, Joseph Andrews refuses the seductions of a noblewoman, but as it turns out, he is saving himself for a more deserving heroine. Fielding's fiction works to solve the problem of Joseph's beauty by balancing Joseph's spiritual nature with an equally strong animal nature.

As masculinity was ever more often identified with animal drives and femininity with angelic spirituality, male chastity—Joseph's trademark virtue—lost its appeal, and female chastity became the heroine's most obligatory virtue. Samuel Richardson's tragic early novel *Clarissa* captures the tension of this system in the contest between the attractive villain, Lovelace, and the chaste heroine, Clarissa, whom Lovelace is ambitious to seduce. When Lovelace succeeds in overcoming Clarissa, narrative logic requires that she die. These ideals are mutually destructive. By the time of the Byronic hero of romanticism, the suggestion of sexual wildness had been culturally revalued into a symptom of virility. The man represented as a beast (Byron, Heathcliff, Rochester) became more appealing than the once-revered fine gentleman. The Joseph figure, vain of his talents and elegant in his fancy coats, had increasingly less to recommend him in the eyes of readers who preferred physical strength and bare-chested sexual power.

SEXUAL VICTIMS AND POWER POLITICS: JOSEPH AND DINAH

The relationship between sexual and political power evolves along gender and ethnic axes in complicated ways. The rape victim, when represented as a troublemaker, exemplifies one of many paradoxes in this evolving system. Similarly, the younger son for whom the rule of primogeniture is reversed is both victimizer (of the older, entitled brother) and victim of his brothers' revenge. He is a feminizing agent, aligned with his mother in ways that compromise his father's authority; he is also a high achiever but has a tenuous hold on power.

With only one exception the Bible makes no mention of daughters in the first families, though Midrash occasionally supplies them. One effect of the rivalry between brothers along a gender divide is to position the less masculine brother as daughter in the nuclear family, with the daughter in the position of sexual powerlessness. Joseph's sister, Dinah, the only daughter mentioned as having been born to the matriarchs and patriarchs, epitomizes sexual powerlessness because she is a rape victim. Outside of the community of men represented by his brothers, Joseph aligns with the daughter. Like Dinah, Joseph is also a sexual victim who fraternizes with outsiders, and both behave in ways that inspire their brothers to violent reactions. Excluded from the homosocial bonding among real men, hardworking and pious, Joseph is the most successful man, the businessman before whom his brothers will have to fall prostrate, dependent on his good offices. Here too is the foundation of another Jewish stereotype, that of the man who is not a typical guy's guy, but rather someone who stands apart, someone with financial and political clout, someone whose vanity must be indulged for favors.

Although the Bible's narrator objects that Shechem, Dinah's rapist, "ought not to have done such a thing," the story's larger point is that Dinah's full brothers, Leah's sons Simeon and Levi, overreact in their acts of vengeance. At Jacob's request, they agree to Dinah's marriage to her rapist on condition that the tribe into which she marries circumcises all of their men. Again, these brothers are represented as devious and as liars, and on the third day, when the men would have been most sore, they slaughter them all, with the excuse that their sister has been treated like a whore. What is relevant here is that the Bible takes no interest in Dinah as a character. Although the Bible does not question her innocence, her victimization is presented without demonstrable sympathy for her. The focus remains on Jacob, his sons, and their relationship with the Hivites, the neighboring tribe. The excessive vengeance of Dinah's full brothers, Simeon and Levi, accounts for the relatively small portion of their tribal inheritance.

In Midrash, however, Dinah presents as wicked, a victim who invites the crime. The Bible's statement that she "went out" to visit with the women of the land is interpreted to mean that she went out to seduce. According to the Midrash, what we learn from her story is "why man must master his wife, that she go not into the marketplace, for every woman who (like Dinah) goes into the marketplace, will eventually come to grief." Every woman who is said to "go out"—and the list includes Leah, Jael, and Dinah—is immoral, a designing prostitute.[16] In the Bible, Dinah's brothers are said to remove her from Shechem's house, but according to one rabbinic reinterpretation, the men must drag her by force because "when a woman is intimate with an uncircumcised person, she finds it hard to tear herself away."[17] This principle that a woman must find an uncircumcised man irresistible painfully summarizes the Jewish male anxiety about control in the larger world, a fear expressed in terms of relative sexual allure.

The impotence ascribed to Joseph in Midrash at once makes him the antithesis of the uncircumcised and aligns him with Dinah in their shared position as bait for unwelcome gentile sexual attention. The midrashic revision of the rape victim into a woman eager for adventure with foreign women and someone who develops a preference for uncircumcised men is consistent with the lack of rabbinic enthusiasm for Joseph's chastity. Both Joseph and Dinah explore foreign parts and stir up political trouble by being sexually attractive. The elaborations on the Bible's stories betray the rabbis' sexual insecurity about being Jewish men, expressed in part as a need to control their women. Indeed, the daughter's vulnerability (that of Dinah) and the seductress's sexual power (that of Potiphar's wife) expose the Jewish man's sexual, social, and political insecurity. This constellation of texts together reveals that the biblical definition of heroism comfortably embodied by Joseph could not be sustained by the commenting tradition, which expresses its own anxiety about virility in increased ambivalence toward Joseph.

In biblical narratives, just as the mother acquires political advantage through her son, so too another type of biblical woman, the seducing heroine, differently acquires political power through her sexuality. Joseph's beauty and his self-restraint, sources of both power and vulnerability, come to signify weak virility relative to representations of women and as sexually overpowering and insatiable. In the biblical context, sexual self-control indicates male power. On the model of Samson, succumbing to the femme fatale devastates the heroic man, in Samson's case, resulting in symbolic unmanning, a haircut (because of which he loses his strength) and blinding. The struggle between Potiphar's wife and Joseph is about sex, power, and explicitly about loyalty to authorities higher than either of these actors, namely, "the lord" in the story, a designation that refers to both Potiphar and God, both of whom would be cheated by this threatened infidelity. In her power grab, Potiphar's wife might have compromised her husband's mastery and asserted her commanding power over Joseph as well. Cheating on his God, Joseph would have stood to lose his good standing with both of his masters, while surrendering to a woman. In the biblical context, the servant Joseph's power is bound up with his resistance, and his loyalty manifests independence. In the evolving gender dichotomy loosely charted here, however, masculinity becomes increasingly beastly and instinctual, proudly uncontrolled. The sinful rebelliousness of that seductive, single-minded disembodied snake in the Garden of Eden—a representation of primary, libidinal, animal drives activated by women—becomes paradoxically admirable.[18] Joseph's resistance to the noblewoman begins to read, over time, as unnatural self-righteousness and participates in positioning the Jewish man as the cautious, good boy student, the teacher's pet, the man whose success is born of obsequiousness and comes at the cost of male privilege and pleasure.

Daniel Boyarin and others have argued for a Jewish masculine difference that is approved by the tradition.[19] This sensitive Jewish man—Alan Alda in the Yeshiva—represents a happy, feminist alternative to secular, aggressive ideals of masculinity. I am suggesting instead that a variety of Jewish masculine differences may indeed have empowered and distinguished the Jewish man, but ambivalently, and at a cost to his sexual (self) image. If Jacob's marriage to sisters works to recuperate his masculinity, Joseph's well-controlled sex drive and beauty remain both valorized and suspect. Joseph's success as a Hebrew in a foreign environment is connected to his dutiful behavior, intelligence, and effectiveness. At the same time, his wilder, more aggressive, rebellious, and sinful brothers have a less-than-secret appeal.

We have seen that the narratives in Genesis are driven by sibling rivalries as the sons of the patriarchs vie for their place in the all-important biblical genealogies. Jacob, I have argued, comes to be seen as "passing as a man" by pretending to be Esau in order to inherit the patriarchy: that is, he enacts his brother's masculinity. He then actualizes himself as a man, like the original man, Adam, by leaving home (going far for many years), working (hard and very successfully), marrying (twice: to sisters), and fathering sons (twelve, for the tribes). These details are developed with energy. Joseph, too, leaves home, goes far for long years, and works very hard and with exaggerated success. It is achievement and material success that establishes the tribal fathers of Genesis. Being the son of the beloved wife at once guarantees the success of these heroes and stains him with her femininity. The version of the smooth, high-achieving Jewish man who is more brain than brawn, who is a power behind the throne, finds his closest antecedent in the biblical Joseph. His history is one of mixed appeal, of ambivalent beauty (at once irresistible and flamboyant), and of ambivalent sexual appetite. The Jewish man predicted by Joseph contains our culture's mixed message about male sexual aggression, a persistent confusion about how controlled male sexual passion should ideally be.

6

Miriam's Fluid Identity

SOLID SURFACES

The fullness of Miriam has been created and elaborated over the generations into something solid from a handful of short brushstrokes of biblical text: a character, a woman, a leader, one in the sibling triumvirate who
guides the people through the wilderness that is a biblical metaphor for life.
Admitting textual ambiguities, readers have nevertheless assembled narrative details into a biography of the ancient Miriam, a model of a woman
leader who is explicitly neither a wife nor a mother, but rather, and even
uniquely, foremost a sister and daughter. She is a character and a set of
roles that apparently expands the biblical range of female possibility.

I will suggest that this elaboration of Miriam from limited text into a
full characterization is at the same time a restriction of her character, not
only into recognizable paradigms of women's leadership as they have
been made familiar by Western culture, but also, a restriction into the narrative parameters of the story into which she has been made (somewhat
awkwardly) to fit. I invite us to consider Miriam as a name that functions
as a container for her watery self: a proper noun, "Miriam" is a vessel that
shapes contents that might have been differently held. Miriam's story and
its history clue us into yet another strategy by which our culture has used
the Bible to install the categories of our gendered world.

Parts of this chapter are excerpted from *The Women's Passover Companion: Reflections on
the Festival of Freedom* © 2003 Edited by Sharon Cohen Anisfeld, Tara Mohr, and Catherine
Spector (Woodstock VT: Jewish Lights Publishing). Permission granted by Jewish Lights
Publishing, P.O. Box 237, Woodstock, VT 05091 www.jewishlights.com

I am making a double argument. First, the textual details, when reassembled outside of the story into which the biblical editors have placed them, allow us to imagine an alternative Miriam, an even more ancient heroine who had been refashioned to be assimilated into the biblical Exodus story, the most enduring myth of Jewish peoplehood. This refashioning accommodates the Bible's theology and truths about gender and power. Second, I want to generalize from the case of Miriam to deepen, in another way, the claim that I hope to have been justifying throughout the analyses in this book, that is to say, that biblical characters always evidence an alternative self, a self that undermines its own superficial coherence. Just as Eve and Adam are each both fundamentally seducer and seduced, and the "barren mother" self-contradicts in principle, and Isaac and Jacob are patriarchal by virtue of an enacted and false masculinity most fully realized in its contradictions in Joseph, so Miriam is literally a fluid self. And just as the meanings of Sarah's laughter refuse to be tamed, so Miriam's associations with water metaphorically express the doomed effort to fix the boundaries of her identity.

Miriam's readability is like the readability of a caricature, which derives its power as likeness as much from the viewer's imagination as from the skill of the artist. Indeed, when the details are sufficiently evocative, their very sparseness guarantees successful similitude because the persona develops fully formed (and thus perfectly approved) in the mind of the viewer and transfers effortlessly to the page.[1] Textual fragments tempt us to fill in, according to our own prejudices, what we perceive to be missing. As Page duBois has demonstrated with respect to Sappho's poetry, and by analogy to the surviving fragmented sculptures left from the ancient world, our modernist Western aesthetic and psychological needs drive us to complete what we experience as lacunae rather than simply tolerate the ambiguity of mystery, appreciating the art of the fragmentary artifact in its incompletion.[2] The fullness of Miriam's story—inasmuch as it derives from so little evidence—reminds us that character, identity, self and ego, and related concepts such as woman and man, mother, father, son, lover, daughter, sister, or brother are constellations and consolidations, conceptualizations that solidify under the pressure of repetitions, patterns, and increasingly confident assumptions about their meanings over time.

Miriam's scattered presences in the books of Exodus and Numbers evidence an under-the-text stream of water of the sort that Ilana Pardes encourages us to discern in her groundbreaking book *Countertraditions in the Bible*. Contrasting the Bible with a work of modern fiction, for example, Pardes explains that "a confounding mixture of dispersed language . . . best represents the art of Biblical narrative," and therefore, "dealing with a text that is not divided into chapters and parts composed by sundry authors during approximately a dozen centuries requires a different hermeneutic suspicion."[3] Exposing heteroglossia is Pardes's strategy for discovering feminist counter-traditions within the Bible. Although I am not certain that the "counter voices" are necessarily female per se, my reading shares Pardes's impulse to "explore the tense dialogue between the dominant patriarchal discourses of the Bible and the counter female voices which attempt to put forth other truths."[4]

MIRIAM'S WATERSHED LEADERSHIP

The Red Sea divides. This miracle is the stuff of legends, paintings, and dramatic movie scenes. Moses leads the people through the parted waters and then sings a beautiful song of victory and gratitude. Only after this dramatic scene, with its bold poetry, do we come to the more understated sentences that describe the women following Miriam in instrumental dance. She leads them in a chant that scholars observe is a one-sentence summary of Moses' *Shirat Hayam*, "The Song of the Sea" (Exodus 15:21). Those Bible scholars who date the constituent parts of biblical text speculate that the song of Miriam is among the oldest passages of the Hebrew Bible. Source critics of the Bible therefore suggest that *Shirat Hayam*, Moses' long poem, may actually be a later elaboration of what had begun as Miriam's song, or a response to her call.[5]

Although the reader of the Bible is familiar with Miriam from before this moment—we meet her at the Nile when she sets her baby brother Moses in a basket—she is named for the first time at the sea, identified as "Miriam the prophet, sister of Aaron." Why, the Midrash asks, is she named as the sister of Aaron? Acknowledging his sense from the text that Miriam is somehow primal, with an authority that predates Moses, the rabbi in the Midrash responds that it is to indicate that she was a prophet even before the birth of Moses.[6]

Aside from an incidental mention of her name in Micah 6:4 that reinforces her co-equal leadership with Moses and Aaron, Miriam appears four times in the Bible. When the Pharaoh decrees that all of the baby boys born to Hebrew slaves must be killed, the midwives, Shifrah and Puah, disobey the death decree. What follows is the story of Moses' mother Yocheved, who creates a water-proof basket and sends her young (as yet unnamed) daughter to place the baby Moses in the Nile. Yocheved tells her child to hide in the bulrushes and discover the fate of the baby who will grow up to be the reluctant hero of the Hebrew people.[7] While Miriam stands watch, Pharaoh's daughter, the princess herself, comes to bathe and takes pity on this baby in the basket. She declares her intention to adopt him, and Miriam steps forward, offering Yocheved as the wet nurse for her own child.

The reader senses a remarkable, utopian conspiracy among women. The midwives, a slave mother, her daughter, and a princess cross boundaries of age, race, and class to save the life of a baby. The male realms of politics and economy loom large in the Bible—with decrees against whole populations—while in a smaller female domestic space, a single baby is saved. And in this act begins an epic redemption.

The large number of female characters in the episodes surrounding Moses' birth contributes to building his boundary-crossing heroic identity. At the same time, this plenitude is rare and therefore disconcerting. Midrash Rabbah accordingly suggests that Shifrah and Puah are other names for Yocheved and Miriam.[8] In the world of the Bible, we see very little suggestion of women in community. Instead, we typically meet women alone or in pairs. Although readers must have been aware of women's community in their own experience, the presence of five distinct women finding their way into sacred story in so short a space seems unrealistic or unwelcome to the commentator, who reduces the remarkable group into a single pair. In a characteristic rabbinic move, this consolidation increases the heroism of Moses' relatives—and thus of Moses—by collapsing the identity of the midwives into that of the leader's mother and sister. In the biblical story, however, women proliferate: mother, sister, midwives, and princess all work together. As with barren mothers, the text asserts women's heroic capacity to generate history—as individual women and in community—but a subsequent counter-impulse (like restraining women's public presence) works to contain them, in this case, by limiting the women's numbers.

More remarkable than Miriam's functioning in the company of other women (both as a child and then as the leader of the dance at the Red Sea) is that the Bible reports a story about her as a child. Because heroines are generally defined by their roles as mothers, wives, or seducers, they typically enter into the story on the threshold of sexuality. Accordingly, no other woman in the Bible has a recorded childhood. Miriam's childhood story is a miracle story set at the shores of the Nile River. Even the etymology of Miriam's name brings us to the sea. As Ellen Frankel suggests in *The Five Books of Miriam*, Mir-Yam derives from the Hebrew words *Mar* and *Yam*, bitter Sea. Alternatively, "Mir" comes from the Egyptian word *Mer*, Beloved, making her name "Beloved Sea."[9] Women's proliferation swells at the Red Sea, where Miriam will lead all of the women in dance. Rashi's interpretation that Moses led the men in song while Miriam simultaneously led the women conjures up an image of the Israelite party departing Egypt and marching along a gender divide (mirroring the partition of the medieval synagogue?), with Miriam leading the full complement of women in separate community.

A woman leading the women may be less surprising than the image of all of these women brandishing musical instruments. Although this text presumes that the women would each have been carrying a drum, the larger context emphasizes the extreme haste with which the people left Egypt. Indeed, the haste of their departure accounts for the main religious obligation derived from this central foundation myth: because there was not have enough time for the dough to rise, eating *matzoh*—unleavened bread—is basic to the observance of Passover, the holiday that commemorates the Exodus. How is it that these women who were so busy rushing that they could not pack adequate food all packed their *toopim*, their timbrels? Because women are depicted elsewhere in the Bible celebrating victories with dance and with timbrels (the judge/general Jephtha's daughter, who greets her victorious father playing the timbrel, is another tragic example [Judges 11:34]), we might imagine that these timbrels had the status of religious ceremonial objects. Were pious Jewish women to leave home in haste today, they might remember to take the family candlesticks. In the world conjured by biblical stories, an Israelite girl made sure she had her tambourine.[10]

After overcoming the formidable obstacle of the sea, and almost immediately following Miriam's verses, the problem of water in the desert asserts itself. Arriving in *Marah* ("bitter," a word that may be related to Miriam's name) after a three-day journey, the water proves too bitter to drink, until Moses is given directions for sweetening it. The people, newly out of Egypt, complain, as they will continue to do tirelessly in the desert. Still later, there is no water, and God will tell Moses to hit a rock with his rod to get water. Midrash devises its own miracle to solve the problem of limited water in the desert based on the biblical description of a pillar of smoke that leads and protects the people by day and a cloud of fire that accompanies them at night. A Talmudic commentary to the text adds that smoke and fire accompany the people because of the merit of Moses and Aaron. The commentary goes on to say that the people were also accompanied through the desert by a well. The presence of this well of water, essential to their survival in the desert, is attributed to the merit of Miriam.[11]

The third time that we meet Miriam is when she and Aaron have a complaint to lodge against their brother Moses, possibly against his wife or, on the contrary, on behalf of his wife. The content of the complaint and the motivations in this story are ambiguous, but the text suggests at least that the elder siblings think that their younger brother is arrogant. They ask: "Aren't we prophets too?" (Numbers 12:2). God responds angrily. He calls the team of Aaron and Miriam outside, and God appears as a cloud upon them. When the cloud lifts, it is Miriam who is leprous, covered in white from her intimate, physical contact with God's presence. Here, as elsewhere in the Bible, the female body is a kind of drawing board upon which God's messages are written. Just as Lot's wife turns to salt (Genesis 19:26) and the body of the anonymous wife/concubine in Judges 19 is cut into twelve pieces, an apparent symbol of the fragmented body politic, Miriam's leprosy is a sign, and her body is the site of mystifying representation.

More interesting than the fact of Miriam's leprosy, however, is the way Miriam's brothers, and indeed all of the people, respond. Aaron and Moses see Miriam, and they react instantly on her behalf. Moses utters the shortest and the most urgent prayer in the Bible. He calls out to God: "*El nah, refah nah lah.*" In staccato rhyming Hebrew, he calls, "Please God, heal her." God replies: "If her father had spat in her face, would she not bear her shame for seven days?" (Numbers 12:13–14) (JPS translation). Miriam's leprosy turns out to be a consequence and effect of contact with divine metaphoric spit. The people will not go farther without Miriam. She is quarantined, and only when she recovers and rejoins the leaders are the people willing to continue their journey.

Miriam is mentioned only once more. In the passages leading up to the Israelites' entry into the Promised Land, God declares that Aaron will not enter Israel. Aaron's death is couched in a detailed description of the removal of his vestments and the investiture of his son Eleazar, followed by a report of the people's thirty days of mourning (Numbers 20:22–29). By contrast, Miriam's death is reported with little comment. From the proliferation of women beginning with the conspiracy to save the baby to the swell of women at the Red Sea, Miriam's death, especially by contrast with the pomp that surrounds Aaron's death, is apparently lonely and spare. The text says simply, "Miriam died there and was buried there." The next verse, in an apparent non sequitur, reads, "and the land was without water" (Numbers 20:1–2). Perhaps the earth itself is mourning: Miriam's death brings drought. The Talmud takes this hint, explaining that Miriam's well disappeared upon her death but returned because of the merit of Moses.[12] The ongoing legend of Miriam's well emphasizes its timelessness. Having been filled with the waters of the firmament at creation, Miriam's well still exists in the world as a resource for healing.

After Miriam dies (but without reference to her death), the people yet again decry their fate and rail against Moses for taking them out of Egypt to die of thirst in the desert. Again Moses prays, and again God tells him to go to the rock. This time God says, "Lift your rod and tell the rock to give you water" (Numbers 20:8). Moses strikes the rock (as he had been instructed to do in the past), and although the people do get their water—in abundance—Moses is punished for his disobedience. Because he strikes the rock instead of talking to it, God declares that he will not be allowed into the Promised Land. If ever a punishment were disproportionate to the crime, it is here. Moses, who put up with so much, who twice climbed a mountain to get the law, who led this endlessly cranky people through wars and wanderings, who was ever humble and ever great, is to be denied entry into the Promised Land because he hits a rock. Not a person, but a rock. Moses is the hero who risks his life and his position because he could not bear to see a slave beaten. On the one hand, even heroes die, and always it is untimely and always, unfair. On the other hand, the association of Moses' death with his having hit the rock after Miriam's death suggests censored details in this story.

MIRIAM IMPORTED AND ADAPTED: WATER GODDESS OR PRIESTESS

Beyond the sad truth that death asserts itself unfairly, perhaps something else is going on here. Miriam, whose name means either Bitter or Beloved Sea, is always associated with water miracles. In mythology and legend, gods and goddesses, heroes and heroines often have a characteristic miracle story associated with their childhood, a proto-feat that predicts the nature of their distinctive heroic capacities. Miriam protects her baby brother by watching over him at the Nile. Later, she leads the women in triumphant celebration after the parting of the Red Sea. When she and God get into an intimate power contest, God makes her leprous, but neither her brothers nor anyone else will proceed without her. One begins to sense some fear among the people that without Miriam there will be no water.

When she dies, this fear is confirmed. God reassures Moses, but Moses nevertheless overreacts, for the first time. He does not talk; he strikes. Perhaps he panics; perhaps he too thinks that without Miriam, there cannot be water, and perhaps this is the serious crime, the reason that Moses' faith is questioned. Alternatively, Rivkah Walton observes that the text indicates that God tells Moses to talk to *the* rock.[13] Which rock is *the* rock? Walton remembers that in the ancient world, as we know from the Christian scriptures, great people were buried in caves, and a boulder was set to cover the mouth of the cave. God says "talk to the rock," and Walton interprets this to mean, "Go to the rock that blocks Miriam's grave, and ask for water." According to this reading, Moses' crime is against the memory of Miriam, and God is defender of her honor. Angry that even after her death they must depend upon Miriam for water, Moses impatiently strikes the stone that blocks her grave. God punishes the little brother's impertinence. Because the narrative here is sparse, as it is in much of the Bible, the explanation for Moses' crime and God's response is, of course, indeterminate.

The Hebrew Bible is a layered document, and we can find hints of constituent older stories hidden at the lowest levels of the text. In its overarching structure, the Bible's One God is the hero, and God acts through a long series of brave men who lead God's people. But here we have Miriam whose name means Beloved Sea, whose song is likely to be among the oldest pieces of the text, who performs a sea miracle as a child, who claims leadership after the parting of the Red Sea, who confronts God and retains that people's loyalty, and whose death apparently causes the earth to go dry. If Moses' brother Aaron, the prophet, is high priest, then Moses' sister

Miriam, the prophet, had perhaps been Water Priestess, or the revision of a more ancient heroine with access to the divine water pipe, a water goddess. Miriam's exceptionality has been appreciated as part of the movement from the biography of the first Hebrew families in Genesis to the biography of the people Israel in Exodus.[14] The book of Exodus accordingly departs from the family patterns of Genesis, with its repeated representation of rival brothers competing to inherit the narrative line, parental favoritism, and dramatic negotiations within small family units that presume particular roles for mothers, fathers, and sons. Exodus, by contrast, represents a model of sibling cooperation that effaces hierarchy and gender differentiation. In their roles, however, the brothers and sister effectively function as parents to the newly born people. Alternatively, but equally fancifully, this egalitarianism may reflect the text's domestication of a pantheon that included a water goddess who is assimilated into the story as the hero's saving sister.

Miriam, uniquely, is characterized without explicit reference to her sexuality, in striking contrast to the full complement of biblical women who are mothers, wives, or seductresses (the matriarchs—Sarah, Rebecca, Rachel, and Leah—Samuel's mother and Samson's mother, Tamar, Yael, Esther, Judith, Ruth). So, too, in subsequent literature women have been represented in domestic roles more often than as leaders in the public sphere. If the preponderance of stories confines women to roles as mothers and seductresses, we also have hints of female leadership as priestesses, celebrants, judges, and prophetesses. The songs of Miriam, Deborah, and Hannah, from early layers of the Bible's composition, invite us to imagine the possibility that biblical heroines in particular are redrawn from earlier characters with stronger social power. Savina Teubal similarly speculates that Sarah and other barren mothers are revisions of pagan priestesses.[15] How the Bible appropriates and reshapes gender roles for heroes and heroines is less important, however, than an awareness of a process by which readers reconstruct a (pre)history of characters in ways that mirror our own fantasies about gender and power.

Miriam has also been read as a variant of Isis. Pardes' analysis of the famously enigmatic "bridegroom of blood" episode that features Moses' wife Zipporah (Exodus 4:24–26) imports Isis, another saving sister/wife, into her interpretation. She makes a connection between the Moses' narratives and Egyptian mythology, finding in Zipporah ("Zipporah" in Hebrew means "bird") an echo of the winged bird-goddess, Isis.[16] Zipporah effects some kind of rescue through the act of circumcision, and Pardes reminds us that Isis saved her brother/husband Osiris by reconstituting his dismembered body, in some versions, by rebuilding his missing phallus (the sign of fecundity in this fertility myth). Echoes of Isis—the saving sister/wife—may be found in both Miriam and Zipporah (and Pardes observes also in Shifra, Puah, and Yocheved), all of whom are associated with healing.[17] Miriam saves her brother in a basket in the Nile, just as Isis rescues Osiris from a coffin in the Nile, and Midrash credits Miriam with promoting generativity differently by bringing her father and mother together to be willing to have another baby when her reluctant father would have preferred to divorce her mother sooner than have a son who would be born under Pharaoh's threat of death.[18] Thus, although Miriam seems not to be defined by her own sexuality, she is elevated by these readings into an agent of national fertility.

In *The Particulars of Rapture*, Avivah Gottlieb Zornberg also explicitly associates Miriam's leadership and women's heroism with seduction and fertility, first in their legendary seduction of reluctant slave husbands and second in their singing at the sea, which Zornberg suggests comes from the womb (borrowing from Stanley Cavell and Catherine Clément's discussions of women's operatic voices) at an "intersection of pain and pleasure." The singing women may appreciate God's role as midwife at the Red Sea, aware of the danger and miracle of coming through parted waters.[19] "*Mitzraim*," the Hebrew for Egypt, read as a pun ("*mi-tzraim*" means "from narrowed straits") evokes the birth canal. The Exodus story, a birth story of the people of Israel, renders first the Nile and then the Red (or Reed) Sea ambivalently, with the potential to sustain life, source of both flooding or drowning and life-saving miracles. Like childbirth, as it would have been apprehended in the ancient world, the Nile represents the extremes that evoke ultimate ambivalence, the awesome potentiality for regeneration and life and a high risk for death.

This fractured collection of texts is an assemblage of fertility legends of the Nile, including such details as bird-women, sister/wife heroines whose rescuing powers concern a threatened phallus (that of Osiris and Moses), an ambivalent Nile River and Red Sea (which can save or drown Moses and the people of Israel, respectively), and multiple water miracles. In the biblical national birth story, as in each birth story, a woman is situated on the razor's edge, between life and death. Mir-yam, Bitter or Beloved Sea, contains this ambivalence; neither mother nor lover herself, her fluid identity includes traces of fertility myths and water's power to both support life and create tsunamis. As Miriam's story was elaborated by the tradition, Miriam is recognized more simply as a leader of women, celebrated for what came to be appreciated as distinctively "female" qualities. This domestication of Miriam is like the Nile at its best: a fertile source when contained within its banks.

JEWISH TIME

This reading of Miriam has limited respect for historical time. Discerning subtexts opens an imaginative mythic space, outside of historical time, and I submit that this challenge to history is congenial to Judaism and Jewish theology. In their transformations from biblical narrative into the Jewish religious imagination, the liberation from Egypt, the crossing of the Red Sea, and the Sinai experience in particular transcend linear, historical time. Like the fantasy of Miriam's eternal well—filled at creation, activated for the forty years of desert wandering, and still present in the world—another identity-defining legend explains that all Jewish souls (past and future, Jews by birth and Jews by choice) were present at the Red Sea to witness the miracle and at Sinai to receive Torah. This timeless assemblage is ceremonially acknowledged in synagogues when these portions of the story are recited from Torah and the congregation suddenly rises, transforming themselves from passive listeners into participants in the event. Similarly, the Passover Seder, which includes the telling of the Exodus myth (the work of the "Hagaddah"), is supposed to be not so much a re-creating or narration, nor even a reliving of departing Egypt, as an experience of liberation (every year), like a skip in an old-fashioned record. These principles and practices insist on a Jewish conception of sacred time as nonlinear, locating God in a place of infinite simultaneity, where, from a cosmic perspective, everything is already known and redeemed. A God's-eye view is outside of time; as per the Talmudic principle that: "there is no 'late' or 'early' in the Torah."[20]

The story that we tell about the deep, dark past depends on who is holding the candle and what she is looking for. Because foundation myths, like history, account for the present, the future changes our apprehension of the past. Discerning a subtext of Miriam's power over water, or a pretext of a social world in which women and men had more varied roles, challenges the Bible's gender boundaries. Miriam, like Sarah and Hannah, at once resists the presumption of patriarchal authority at the same time that liquidity of expression—as signified by laughter, prayer, songs, and sea—encourages an unconscious perception of humanity that transcends the formulas for male and female family roles.

Classical Midrash and contemporary midrashic poetry share a confidence in the people's right—indeed obligation—to return to Sinai to clarify foundation stories and their meanings. As we have seen in women's poetry in Lilith's voice, a substantial body of feminist poetry about the Bible adopts the midrashic strategy of reimagining biblical heroines, filling out their stories, for a purpose similar to the goal that Milton specifies in *Paradise Lost* to "justify the ways of God to man." Justifying God's ways to women through reclamation of the inner lives of female characters and women's relationships makes sacred stories compatible with the values of the poet in the same way that Midrash accommodates scripture to changing ethics.

I have suggested that biblical heroines' association with fluidity of expression—Sarah's laughter, Miriam's identification with water, and

Hannah's grievous noise—are textually rebellious. This rebelliousness finds its way into contemporary poetry that embellishes the stories of these characters. Eleanor Wilner, for example, creates an imagined "Sarah's Choice" and revises "Miriam's Song."[21] In the former, when Sarah is imagined to have been ordered by God to sacrifice Isaac (presumably before God resorted to making this demand of Abraham), she refuses ("for such is the presumption of mothers") and she then approaches her son, asleep in his "too short bed," to encourage him to join her in making peace with Hagar and Ishmael. Isaac, "afraid of being nothing," asks his mother what will happen if he goes, and Sarah replies that she does not know but that history records what will happen if he stays. The poem invites the reader to imagine that through the mother's agency, history might have been (or might yet be?) otherwise.

In "Miriam's Song" Wilner conjures Miriam on the banks of the Nile, her ears full with the "wail of Egypt's women" grieving the deaths of their first-born sons. This Miriam pulls her blue and white shawl (adapting the *tallit*, classically male Jewish garb, for the ancient heroine) tightly around her and enacts what may be a ritual of regret. Like a distracted child, Miriam tosses rocks into an empty basket until it sinks, thinking that she had meant only to save the life of a baby. In the background the march of armies becomes timeless, the march of men in armies in all places and all times, warriors, who had once been the babies of protective mothers. The poet's Miriam reflects that we "exchange one Egypt for the next."

These anti-war poems, like other women's literary and critical responses to Bible, imagine an alternative foundation story, playing with reversals and gender, creating fantasies of a redemptive time-out-of-time where women make alternative choices for life. Judaism's traditional approach to Bible encourages readers occasionally to position themselves above the text from where it is possible to assume a cosmic perspective, where the future can alter our perception of what has been. What I hope to have suggested here is that like Sarah's laughter and Hannah's grieving articulations, Miriam's watery self—her generativity outside of sex roles—exposes textual fissures through which can flow fantasies of alternative realities, including alternative constructions of gender in the social world. Efforts to contain Miriam within the strictures of roles that are familiar from later formations of the nuclear family, when up against efforts to reconstitute her as a goddess fragment, highlight the reader's role in making Bible characters legible to us by familiarizing them. An awareness of the role of the reader in making the biblical family like our own can open up other and more possibilities for identity enactments.

7

Bedrooms and Battlefields: Command Performances of Femininity

THE SECRET OF THE BEDROOM

In the Hebrew Bible, the bedroom is the battlefield where men always lose. There is no shortage of examples. Tamar, widowed and entitled to seed from her father-in-law Judah's line, addresses Judah's reluctance to comply in the guise of a cult prostitute (*kedeisha*); she escapes the death penalty by proving Judah's paternity and bears twins, one of whom is the ancestor of King David, and, by extension, the Messiah (Genesis 38; cf. Ruth 4). Jael lures the enemy General Sisera into her tent, lulls him into defenselessness, and kills him with a tent pin through his temple (Judges 4–5). Samson, a strongman superhero, succumbs to Delilah's pestering, losing his strength with his hair, then his eyes and his life, apparently because he ultimately found his lover irresistible (Judges 13–16). Esther, the closeted Jewish beauty queen, marries the king, positioned to save her people. To do so, she dresses elaborately in hopes that her powerful husband will choose to allow her presence by touching his royal scepter (rather than kill her for impertinence); she hosts parties and undoes the villain Haman when he is caught prostrate before her, and the king misinterprets his intentions. Like Esther, Judith (a Hebrew beauty who names a book in the Apocrypha), exchanges mourning clothes for brocade and jewels to seduce the enemy general Holofernes. Under Judith's spell, Holofernes literally loses his head. And the Jewish American princess (JAP), at her most successful, is a material girl who wins over men, controlling first her indulgent father and, later, her helpless lover(s). She descends

111

from these biblical ancestors, who are immensely popular in the history of art: sensual subjects, poised between sex and death.

In these stories, the women exploit their sexuality for political ends, in imbalanced contests between a man made to want a woman and a woman who pretends to want a man but actually wants access to his power. In the surprise substitution of violence for sex—the woman often seems to promise sex and delivers violence—woman's punishment in the Garden of Eden is exposed as a wish: "you will yearn for your husband, and he will lord over you." In these seduction stories, the repetition of Adam's vulnerability—man at the mercy of a snake-charming woman—challenges the essence of the sexes and of sexuality as well as the basis for desire.

First, the women in these stories are all pretending. The dangerously elaborate masquerade of femininity dramatizes Joan Riviere's early psychoanalytic definition of "womanliness as masquerade," suggesting that women's coquettishness is an enactment of their very womanhood.[1] "Woman," being all pretend, has no actual, discernible content. Second, the women play games of sex-role reversals, alternately pleadingly submissive and dominant, a dangerous game, with a woman placing herself at mortal risk but penetrating when there is an expectation that (almost by definition) she will be penetrated. Playing at femininity, her truer self plots and slaughters like a man. Third, the woman acts less on her own behalf than on behalf of her community, her body a stand-in for the body politic and her agency an extension of both corporate and divine will. As such, God and Israel act through and are represented by a woman alternately enacting femininity and masculinity. Finally, the seductress and seduced are not the only actors in these dramas, and the other characters interfere with the appearance of a straightforward boy-girl competition. For example, Yael doubles for Deborah, and Esther doubles for Vashti, each heroine accomplishing a victory that the text first constrains her double from managing. Judith is a widow apparently in primary relationship with her maid, who partners with her by managing her estate and by abetting in the murder.[2] Esther is married to King Ahasuerus but maintains a primary relationship with her uncle Mordechai. And God, too, is a third-term actor, asserting his control over political outcomes by channeling his power through a woman, effectively extending himself through her, a variation on Elaine Scarry's demonstrations in *The Body in Pain* that God wields authority vertically, in his capacity to wound.[3] As Lori Rowlett suggests in her analysis of the Samson story as a sadomasochistic game, Samson and Delilah are "role players without fixed identities or essences," playing with control in reversals of top and bottom that includes Yahweh's self-assertion as the ultimate "top." Because "[t]he titillating play of Samson and Delilah mirrors the cat-and-mouse game

Yahweh plays with the Israelites," Rowlett shows how queering Samson and Delilah "calls into question by analogy the divine/human dichotomy as well."[4]

A long, strong pattern of seduction stories suggests a strict economy of male and female desire, one that promotes the myth of the femme fatale over the opposite social conviction that it is women who are sexually vulnerable. These opposing constructions nonetheless lead to the identical conclusion that women must not be allowed to leave home. The rape victim, susceptible to blame for inviting lust, embodies the contradiction of women's simultaneous power and powerlessness, attested in the rabbinic commentary on the rape of Dinah that a woman who goes out, goes out to seduce.[5] Enacting femininity and exploiting men's sexual vulnerability, the biblical femme fatale and her descendants in popular culture, notably the JAP, testify to and promote a terror of female sexuality even as they reveal the extent to which gender and sexual identity are elaborate performances and even as their story structure (one of reversal) depends on the premise that it is women who are ordinarily at risk of sexual violence. These stories, like the other dynamics we have seen in biblical narrative, assert two sexes and their meanings with energy even as they leave in doubt both the fact of two sexes and what characterizes each.

Another peculiarity of this collection of stories that explore the edge between male and female power is that they are situated along the other significant boundary of the biblical world, that which divides the Hebrews from others. These power-play stories double as Hebrew and gentile: Yael the Kenite stands in for Deborah, the Israelite judge; Esther, the Jewish queen, takes Vashti's place in Ahasuerus's bed; Samson's lovers are Philistine women; and as we will see more fully in chapter 9, Tamar doubles for—or predicts—the Moabite Ruth, the woman who seduces Boaz and becomes great grandmother of King David, extended from the line begun by Tamar and Judah. Perhaps it is this very sensibility—one that assimilates the foreign threat into the body of Israel—that unconsciously informs a Talmudic commentary that Rabbi Akiva descends from Sisera, presumably from his imagined union with Jael.[6]

WOMAN IN THE MIRROR: JUDGE-WARRIOR

Chapters 4 and 5 of the book of Judges tell the story of Deborah and Barak, Jael and Sisera in a classic table of battles and beds. With designations rare for women in the Bible, Deborah is identified as a judge and a prophetess. As the story begins, Deborah, sitting under the tree where she does her judging, summons the Israelite General Barak to tell him that it is time to go to battle against the enemy General Sisera because God has given her assurances of Israelite victory. Barak agrees, conditionally, to go to battle, asking Deborah to accompany him into the battlefield. He apparently needs his prophetess at his side. Deborah goes, having first cautioned him that if she does accompany General Barak, then Sisera, the enemy general, "will be delivered into the hands of a woman." Under the circumstances of this story and since there are few active women in the Hebrew Bible, it seems clear to the reader (as it must be clear to Barak) that the woman into whose hands Sisera will be delivered will of course be the prophetess-judge in the battlefield, Deborah herself. But that is not what happens.

The Israelites do win the battle, as Deborah had predicted, but Sisera manages to escape and run away. It is at this point that Jael materializes, a literary double, a stand-in for Deborah, and it is Jael who becomes the heroine who will be victorious over the enemy general. Breathless, Sisera reaches the tent of Jael, who invites him inside. He asks for water, and she gives him a skin of milk. One Midrash embellishes the text, imagining that Jael went to meet Sisera "arrayed in rich garments and jewels. She was unusually beautiful and her voice was the most seductive ever a woman possessed."[7] The Midrash reads "the skin of milk" that Jael substituted for the requested water as a euphemism, setting us up for a graphic sexual seduction that is not explicit in the biblical narrative itself. In the Bible, Jael gives Sisera this milk and covers him with a blanket. And then—in a move that surprises the reader as much as it surprises Sisera—instead of being penetrated by him, she penetrates him, driving a tent peg through his temple. The text, ordinarily relatively spare in details, is painfully explicit: Jael drives the tent pin through his temple, "until it reaches the ground." The ordinary penetration of seduction narratives is painfully reversed along the axis of gender.

Deborah's professional identity as judge and prophet, stated as if unremarkable, does challenge sex norms, a challenge evidently exacerbated by the male general's requirement that she attend him in battle. The textual substitution of Jael for Deborah only seems to function as a corrective by restoring female activity to the tent, because in the surprise ending, Jael's violent penetration of the general again destabilizes the apparent restoration of gender norms. At the same time, bedroom violence against men is a biblical convention, a clichéd power reversal in domestic space so familiar as to seem natural. Indeed, it is this convention that makes the rabbinic interpretation of the murder of Sisera as a sexual seduction effortless. The Talmud supplies the more precise detail that Jael had intercourse with Sisera seven times, an interpretation derived from the seven verbs in a rhythmic, repetitive verse in Judges: "Between her feet, he sank, he fell, he lay; at her feet he sunk; he fell; where he sunk, there he fell down dead" (Judges 5:27).[8]

After a battle and a flight from the field, the rabbis also required Sisera to have superhuman sex to adequately sap him of enough strength such that he could be physically defeated by a woman. That Jael herself would have been too tired to lift the hammer does not seem to trouble the rabbis and may be explained by ancient science that located virility—masculine energy—in semen. In draining Sisera, as it were, Jael was, effectively, bulking up, and even if this model no longer has biological explanatory power, it retains a hold on our unconscious convictions.

This biological belief smuggled into the rabbinic interpretation reinforces the myth of fatal female sexuality but is only incidental to the rabbis' articulated ethical concerns. The Midrash's investment in asserting that this biblical story of violence is also a story of sexual seduction is to establish a biblical case to pose a religious question more central to the rabbis' own legal and ethical agenda. Using the example of Jael, the rabbinic interpreters ask when, if ever, it is acceptable to sin in order to achieve a more important goal. May we tell an innocent lie to protect someone's feelings? ("Yes," they conclude elsewhere because even God lied to Abraham when explaining why Sarah doubted that she would have a child in old age, eliding that what she really said was that her husband was too old.[9]) Imagining Jael's military strategy, the rabbis up the ante: Is a fornicating woman a sinner if her purpose is to defeat an enemy general? In rabbinic fashion, they persist: Does it matter if she derived pleasure from the sex?

Man's fantasies, and anxieties, about the extent of women's pleasure and insatiability are accidentally revealed in the rabbinic elaboration of the scene of Jael and Sisera in the tent and their curiosity about the possibility of Jael's taking pleasure. It is reminiscent of the question that Juno and Jove posed of Tiresias, who having lived as both a man and a woman was able to settle an Olympian dispute with the information that a woman's pleasure in sex is much greater than that of a man (for which judgment Juno blinded him and Jove gave him prophetic powers). That Tiresias chose to return to his masculine form in spite of this knowledge confirms that, in Robert Scholes's words, "Tiresias knew what the phallus was all about—not pleasure but power." Women "may have more pleasure but men have more power."[10] This Midrash and the tale of Tiresias both imply male feelings of intimidation in the presence of female sexuality, but not convincingly enough that we suspect that the men would choose to trade places.

Whether or not this rabbinic dilemma about the boundaries of sin still engages us, we retain the exegetical assumption in the cultural unconscious that the bedroom is the battlefield where men always lose. Because Deborah went into the battlefield with Barak, the story needs to fulfill the promise that the enemy will be delivered into the hands of a woman, and the Bible knows only one way to make that happen. Although the narrative sets up the possibility, the text is actually unable to imagine Deborah defeating Sisera in the field of war. Instead, the text manufactures Jael to accomplish inside the tent that which a woman could not accomplish on the battlefield. In so doing, this story is made to conform to the pattern of women's victories over strong military heroes in the bedroom.

SAMSON AND DELILAH

Samson and Delilah, a story of abiding popularity, represents a hero of exaggerated strength and accordingly exaggerates the power of the seductress' threat. Also in the book of Judges (13–16), Samson is famously represented as the strongest man on Earth. No army of men could defeat him. He breaks people like straws and tears a lion with his bare hands. He falls, however, to his third and most persistent Philistine lover, Delilah, who manages, with a combination of sweet talk and whining, to succeed where legions of men had failed. Using a peculiarly potent weapon, she nags him until he reveals that the secret of his strength is in his hair, even though he had every imaginable warning that Delilah could not be trusted. Three times Samson attempts to mislead Delilah about the source of his extraordinary strength, offering the misdirection that he would lose his strength if he were bound by various styles of ropes or if his hair were braided, and each time Delilah acts on the information. Nevertheless, unable to tolerate her accusations that he does not love or trust her, Samson ultimately confesses the real secret that leads to his destruction.

When Milton re-creates this story in the dramatic poem "Samson Agonistes" (1671), Dalila (Milton's spelling) is embellished with perfume, ornaments, and powers of seduction so formidable that the reader is inclined to excuse Samson's bad judgment. Samson is made to lament that he has fallen into the snare "Of fair fallacious looks, venereal trains / Soft'n'd with pleasure and voluptuous life" (ll. 533–534); these "venereal trains"—or the traps of the goddess Venus—are tricks of seduction, and Dalila is characterized by "fair, fallacious looks," falseness and beauty mutually implicated, with some ambiguity as to whether it is her appearance (her looks) or her way of looking that is at once attractive and false. When Dalila appears, contrite, at the poem's end, she is described as a ship of state, "bedeckt, ornate, and gay," preceded by "an Amber scent of odorous perfume" (ll. 712, 720). In the Bible, Samson is represented unselfconsciously as a fool who is given every reason to know that Delilah is not to be trusted. Elaborations on the text vindicate Samson by exaggerating the woman's power—aided by charms and scents—to compromise his judgment. The man is split in the conflict between his libido and reason.

The secret of Samson's strength is in his luxuriant hair, a sign of sexuality and a lifelong reminder of his mother and the pact she made with God on his behalf. The angel who came to Manoah's barren wife to predict Samson's birth secures a promise from Samson's soon-to-be mother that while she is pregnant, she will live by the vows of the Nazirite by refraining from wine and not cutting her hair. Moreover, she promises that her son will live by the same rules. Samson's hair functions then as a sign of his mother's role in his heroic identity—the special status of the sons of barren mothers—and his subservience to both his mother and God, who together conspire to direct his life choices. Strong as he is, Samson—like Isaac and Jacob before him—is subject to the fate of the sons of biblical barren women, favored and controlled, antecedents of the successful Jewish man who lives under the obligation to please his mother. As Rowlett points out, Samson—characterized by his enormity and his strength—is actually infantilized by the text's women, first by his mother and then by the wife in whose lap he is pictured. Samson's mother and Delilah are doubles, just as the Jewish mother, controlling and ambitious for her son, and the JAP, controlling and self-interested, bookend the life of the Jewish boy and trap him between them.

Once in possession of his secret, the Philistines cut Samson's hair and pluck out his eyes. This violence is expressed as cutting (like circumcision), for Freud, gestures specifically of castration: Oedipus blinds himself for seeing his mother's nakedness. In the oedipal drama, the mother and wife are literally one and the same, and the son/husband's punishment is symbolic emasculation. A precursor to Rowlett's appreciation of the possibility of reading Samson and Delilah as playing a consensual adult game in which Samson pushes ever closer to the point of mortal danger, Mieke Bal's analysis of this story detects narrative sympathy for Delilah, who effectively gives birth to the adult Samson, making Delilah a kind of mother to the man. Bal persuasively finds this interpretative possibility implicit in both Rembrandt's and Rubens's paintings of Samson and Delilah. Moreover, for Bal, Delilah competes less with Samson's actual mother than with God, with whom Samson is bound up. Delilah represents a projection of Samson's sexual insecurity.[11]

The psychoanalytic and psychosexual tendencies of these analyses increasingly elide the meanings of the terms man and woman, which are superficially critical to the story and its later history. Here, God and mother duplicate each other; Samson and Delilah mirror each other; God and Samson mutually resolve into each other. This story at once reinforces the images of the controlling mother and deadly lover that become the Jewish

Rubens, Peter Paul (1577–1640), Samson and Delilah, about 1609–1610. Delilah "births the man" and by taming Samson, the politically motivated woman deprives a sexually exhausted Samson of the power contained in his hair. © National Gallery, London / Art Resource, New York.

mother and Jewish princess even as Delilah's feminine masquerade (she sells her husband's secret for money) reveals her sexuality to be a cover for political, military, and business motives.

THE QUEEN IN THE CLOSET

The Scroll of Esther, the Diaspora romance communally read on the Jewish carnival celebration, the upside-down holiday of Purim, features a heroine savior, and her uncle, the hero behind the heroine. This biblical book is named for the Jewish winner of a beauty contest, Queen Esther, while God's name is omitted as the saving agent of the people. As such, this story balances the God-centered story of the Exodus read liturgically at the Passover Seder during the holiday that most immediately follows

Purim. In this way, Esther and God mirror each other in these minor and major tales of redemption. Each of the seduction narratives can be read as mini-dramas that lead to redemption: Tamar seduces Judah to begin the Messianic line; Deborah, through Jael, fulfills God's promise of victory; Delilah is God's agent of vengeance, punishing Samson for disobedience even as Samson recovers enough strength by story's end that he is able to bring the Philistines down with him.

The book of Esther may be part Persian folktale, and the hero and heroine's names, Mordechai and Esther, are possibly Hebraicized versions of the Babylonian Marduk and Ishtar or Astarte. In spite of these markers of the exotic, generally this tale of seduction conforms closely enough to biblical models to have been canonized. The story begins and ends with drunken revelry, the deliberate human effort to corrupt judgment, and a fitting frame for a tale of reversals. In the opening scene, the drunken King Ahasuerus invites his wife, Queen Vashti, to leave her party of women and dance before him and his men. When she refuses—the reader might speculate that she is unwilling to suffer the humiliation—the king's advisors persuade him that Vashti has set an example of disobedience to all women and she must be banished. A new queen should be found to replace her. As with Deborah and Jael, the text doubles women characters. Vashti functions to set an example both for the reader and for the new queen by illustrating the consequences of refusing to obey the king's command to appear or, equally forbidden, to appear when a command to do so has not been issued. If the king and his advisors are at pains to maintain gender roles and the power dynamic that guarantees male control over boundary crossing into the other's sociosexual domain, the rest of the story undermines these efforts. Esther will succeed in wresting control where Vashti failed.

Vashti and Esther appear to be opposites, and indeed, the rabbis vilify Vashti and valorize Esther. Vashti and Esther, however, actually duplicate each other in that both refuse to comply with the same rule: appear when you are summoned and only when you are summoned. Vashti declines to show off her beauty when she is called; and Esther shows herself off with a vengeance when she is not called. The threat posed by Vashti's refusal is greater than her defiance of the king. Instead, she threatens the definition of woman's place: because the queen sets the example for all the women of the realm, her brazen disregard of her husband's drunken command could lead to women generally declining to be subservient to their husbands. In this way, the text both acknowledges the conventionality of women's subordination and insists on maintaining it, demanding that the boundaries of the sex roles be well policed.

Esther, whose Jewish identity is deliberately kept secret, wins the beauty contest to become queen after Vashti's banishment. (The implication of

Esther's hidden identity and how it does and does not work as a parable for sexuality in the closet is discussed by Eve Kosofsky Sedgwick in *Epistemology of the Closet*.) This closeted queen finds precedent in both Joseph and Moses, as well as court Jews close to power whose identities were sufficiently hidden that we might presume they had forsaken any tell-tale Jewish practices. When Esther learns from her uncle Mordechai that her people are under a death sentence, she removes her finery and dresses in sackcloth and ashes. And then, as part of her strategic plan, she changes her dress to masquerade as a seductress for a higher political military purpose. Though presumably terrified and sad on the inside, she makes herself especially glamorous and goes to the king, aware that he may kill her for the impertinence of her uninvited visit. But she touches his royal scepter—a gesture that begs for a Freudian reading—and in this way, on three separate occasions, she gets Ahasuerus and his murderously anti-Semitic advisor Haman to attend her parties. At last, she reveals her purpose, outing herself as a Jew and begging for mercy for her people. It is not, at this moment, however, that she wins her husband's favor. Instead, the story makes clear, the royal husband leaves the room, and Haman, afraid, falls prostrate before Esther. When the king returns, he misinterprets the meaning of Haman's posture, and, convinced that Haman is making advances on his beautiful wife, the king devises the punishment that gives Jews the happy ending of the Purim story. Like Jael and Delilah, Esther creates a feminine text of her body and invites a misreading of her sexual intentions to achieve a military victory in the bedroom.

In even the most religious Jewish communities, where gender roles are strictly defined, it is permissible for men to dress as women and women to dress as men on Purim, the holiday that is the Jewish day of carnival and masquerade, Mardi Gras, upside-down day. The folktale upon which the holiday is based opens the way for these enactments of sexual role reversal, which, like other carnival practices, at once reifies and undermines the boundaries that define identity categories. Carnival and masquerade do their work within categories of class and gender: peasants dress up as nobility and women as men.[12] Reversing the axes of power only to right them again when "normalcy" is restored has the effect of reifying oppositions more completely, stabilizing the poles that delimit our identity categories. At the same time, the subversion of roles during carnival leaves a trace effect: the peasant may recall with some pleasure seeing one of their own as king, and a woman may smile at the memory of wearing pants. These traces permanently challenge the inevitability of things-as-they-are, the inherency of identity, and the naturalness of our assumptions about who we have to be.

JUDITH AND HER MAID

Stories of biblical femmes fatales are preserved in the tradition of high art in many graphically realistic paintings that work to capture the contradiction of deadly femininity. And as Germaine Greer has argued, these Bible stories provided excuses for the depiction of lusty women in compromised dress.[13] One favorite in the tradition of art is Judith, the heroine of the apocryphal book that bears her name. Legend associates Judith with the Hasmonean rebellion commemorated on Hanukah on the basis of a sentence in the Talmud that women are required to participate in lighting Hanukah candles because "women participated in the miracle."[14] Because the nature of this participation is unexplained, the rabbis developed a range of possible accounts.

Some rabbinic interpreters understand this participation to mean simply that women, like men, benefited from the Hanukah miracles, usually identified as either a military miracle or a miracle of magically long-sustaining oil to light the eternal flame. The sites of these miracles—the battlefield and the temple precincts—are exclusively males domains, and so it is that various traditions attempt to identify heroines whose participation in the miracle was more explicit. Competing explanations include the conjuring up of Hannah, a daughter of the Matathias, the priest, who rebels against the edict of *jus primae noctis*, which permitted each virgin to the governor on her wedding night. This Israelite daughter tears her clothes under the wedding canopy, shaming her father and brothers with her self-exposure, until she incites the rebellion by asking how they could be more shamed by her nakedness than by allowing her to be raped by an uncircumcised man.[15] Invoking the brothers of Dinah, who avenged their sister's rape (Genesis 34), Hannah uses guerrilla theater and sexual display to begin the guerrilla war. Thus, a woman is credited with the Hanukah miracle by exposing a paradox around sex and shame. Refusing the role of modest, passive bride, she takes action and substitutes the idea that the woman's nakedness shames the men with the revelation that the men are shamed by their own disempowerment, by those edicts that make Jewish men as passive as women.

By analogy with the Purim story of Esther, Judith became the favored explanation for women's participation in the Hanukah miracle as another female savior who achieved a military victory in the bedroom. The apocryphal story of Judith tells how a beautiful widow saved her people. Enemies surround the Israelites on all sides. The situation is represented as hopeless. Inside the camp is the beautiful and expressly modest widow Judith, who is known for piety and intelligence. Again, in a text otherwise spare in descriptive details, the reader is treated to an elaborate description of her dressing up, her masquerade. We are told that she has worn nothing but widow's weeds in all of the years since her husband Manessah's death. Now, in detail reminiscent of Esther's story, when circumstances are most dire, Judith puts on her finest dress from the days when her husband was alive, and she adds perfume and jewels:

> she removed the sackcloth which she had been wearing, and took off her widow's garments, and bathed her body with water, and anointed herself with precious ointment, and combed her hair and put on a tiara, and arrayed herself in the gayest apparel, which she used to wear while her husband Manasseh was living. She put sandals on her feet, and put on her ankelets and bracelets and rings, and her earrings and all her ornaments, and made herself very beautiful, to entice the eyes of all men who might see her. (Judith 10:3–4)[16]

Thus armed for battle, she leaves the camp with her maidservant. When this incomparably beautiful woman is met by an enemy guard, she explains her intention to defect and supply the invaders with secret information in exchange for safety for herself and her family. Her help is eagerly welcomed, although seeing Judith's transcendent beauty, the guard thinks that her people must be destroyed down to the last person because if Judith is any kind of indication, the power of this people must be irresistible. Again, the masquerading woman is identified with the people Israel. Judith is escorted to Holofernes, the enemy leader, and coyly admits that she believes he is destined to destroy the Hebrews. She lets him know that she is prepared to do a great deal to save herself and her family. After establishing a pattern that allows her and her maid some freedom of movement, Judith accepts Holofernes' invitation to the party after which he intends to seduce her.

Holoferenes drinks copious amounts of wine in anticipation of his night with the rare beauty Judith, in some versions, his thirst aggravated by the salty cheese that Judith supplies as a gift. And then Holofernes loses his head. No sooner does Holofernes succumb to the soporific effects of the wine than the modest widow prays to God for superhuman strength. This prayer, which brings God into the bedroom, is like Samson's prayer to God for restored strength before bringing the house down on himself and the Philistines. In the Midrash, Jael also precedes her murder of Sisera with a similar prayer. God's presence is part of what switches the register from sex to politics, as God enters the stories—and possibly the bodies—of biblical mothers and seductresses to affect the course of history. After her prayer, Judith, together with her maidservant, cuts off and bags Holofernes' head. In some medieval and Renaissance representations, Judith is pictured naked (interpreting that the seduction had gone at least this far) with a head held by the hair in one hand and a sack in the

Gentileschi, Artemisia (1597–ca. 1651), Judith and Holofernes. Ca. 1620. In this triangle, the two sexually powerful women literalize the General's losing his head. Alinari / Art Resource, New York.

other. The women now slip back to their own camp, erecting his head on a stick at the top of the hill. In the morning, the terrified enemy sees their general's head magically aloft and they are convinced of the superiority of the Hebrews' God. The enemy flees, and the people are saved.

These biblical stories bring the reader to the threshold of sex. Although the rabbis invent the details of Jael's sexual seduction of Sisera in order to inquire into the possibility of her having taken pleasure in this illicit sex, in their biblical contexts, when these heroines doll themselves up for battle, none of them actually experiences the sexual desire to which she pretends. Each heroine masquerades. Each has an ulterior motive. Each pretends to want a man, when what she requires is not the man himself but access to his power.

DESIRE AND ITS LACK: THE JEWISH AMERICAN PRINCESS

The beautiful woman's murderous sexuality and the masquerade of desire persist well beyond these biblical representations. The symbolism of lost vision as punishment for sexual crimes persists in fiction, as, for example, Charlotte Brontë's Rochester in *Jane Eyre* is diminished for his unlawful sexual appetites in a fire that compromises his vision and use of a limb. His unbridled virility thus reduced, he is made fit for the heroine. By the end of the nineteenth century, Samson's fate, like that of Holofernes, was an oft-reproduced image of masochism. Bram Dijkstra writes: "The masochism, then, of the late nineteenth-century male, and his manipulation of the image of woman as an all-destroying, rampaging animal was an expression of his attempt to come to terms with the implications of his own marginalization." Dijkstra cautions us against reading this preference as any kind of "back-handed compliment to woman's power over him" but "it was rather the creation of a surrogate master who could be sacrificed—indeed, destroyed if necessary—once the true masculine, the true 'Aryan' master-slave bond . . . had established itself." Dijkstra cites Sacher-Masoch's hero Severin's pleasure in reading the book of Judith, Ezra Pound's obsession with woman's lust for the man's severed head, and the persistent replication of images of Judith and Samson and Delilah.[17] Most interesting for this history, however, is Dijkstra's observation that women's classic lust for power over man translated by the fin de siècle into a lust for his money: "Even a daughter could participate in the unmanning of her own father."[18] On the eve of the twentieth century, when the JAP would enjoy center stage as a stereotype of consuming Jewish femininity, the images of castrating, head-severing biblical women, on the model of Delilah and Judith, was refigured as a monster of materialism. In a post-Holocaust suburban culture, the JAP was the latest "surrogate master," who could be sacrificed by men who feared their own marginalization.

The JAP persona was the victim of much derision on college campuses, the subject of graffiti and riddles. What does she make for dinner? Reservations. What does she say after sex? "Darling, the ceiling needs painting." The message of this stereotype was consistent with her biblical forebears:

her passion is pretended. She is also distracted, selfish, and inattentive. Mostly, she is spoiled and materialistic, and she uses her feminine wiles, her vain and purchased beauty, to lure people or inveigle them in her games. She is represented as pampered by her parents. Young men were advised to steer clear of her and were taught to worry that if they get too close, they would be helpless. Riv-Ellen Prell has analyzed the mixed messages of JAP humor and concluded that the Jewish woman's body is a sustained symbol of production and reproduction that reveals a great deal about American Jewish culture.[19] JAP humor evidences the persistence of "gender systems" in American Jewish culture.

The Jewish woman as a lusty, politically motivated seductress asserted itself energetically again at the most recent turn of the century. In 1998, as Israel was expecting renewed pressure from the Clinton administration to withdraw from the settlements, the public was distracted by headlines that broke the Monica Lewinsky scandal. More than one relieved Israeli journalist dubbed "Monica" the modern "Queen Esther" whose access to the royal scepter saved the Jews, even as radical Arab media represented her as a plant by the Jewish community in the royal palace, not unlike Mordechai's strategic positioning of Esther in the Purim story. The Israeli newspaper *Haaretz* reported that "Monica will go down in history as the woman who had sex with an American president and saved an Israeli prime minister."[20] A parody of the book of Esther circulated on the Internet that featured Lewinsky as Esther and Clinton as the king.

STEREOTYPES AND PERFORMING GENDER

On the level of the stereotype, just as the biblical seductress is the corollary of the biblical barren mother (discussed in Chapter 3) and as the madonna correlates with the whore, so too the JAP in American popular modernism is the corollary of the other overwhelming stereotype of the Jewish woman, the Jewish mother. If it takes three JAPs to screw in a light bulb (one to get the diet sodas, one to get the ladder, and one to call Daddy), it takes no one to screw in the bulb for the martyred, self-sacrificing Jewish mother ("It's okay, I'll sit in the dark."). The Jewish mother made famous by American Jewish writers of the 1950s and 1960s, most famously in Philip Roth's early fiction, seems to have little in common with the JAP. The Jewish mother is all self-denial, and the JAP is all self-interest. But in fact, they share a great deal.

These mothers bear their beloved sons out of desperate longing for them, and they are ambitious on their favorite son's behalf. But the stories all entail loss in this longing: Isaac is brought to the altar in a mock sacrifice, and in the next chapter, Sarah dies. Jacob must flee his mother's home for fear of Esau's revenge; Joseph, also hated by his manly brothers, is sold into slavery; Samuel is weaned and given over to temple service in recompense for his birth; and we have seen Samson's terrible fate: his haircut, loss of eyes, and eventual martyrdom. The mother's losses are almost as immense as her longings for a baby. She'll sit in the dark.

Recent stereotypes of the Jewish mother, JAP, and mamma's boy have roots in the earliest layers of the textual tradition, and while we may have long since publicly dismissed these stereotypes, biblical origin narratives fix categories of Jewish personae in the collective unconscious. Categories of men and women develop from performances of sexual and gender identity, approximations into which real people are made to imaginatively—and inadequately—fit. Different as they are, both the Jewish mother and the JAP disempower men. The Jewish mother, like the matriarch, does not cut off her son's head, but she is overcontrolling and ambitious, self-sacrificing, and manipulative. Her situations are extreme: longing and loss. The message of the stories of heroine-seducers is that women have inordinate power inside the tent. Partly on this basis, women in biblical legislation are not allowed into the market place or the board room. If she is so controlling and powerful at home, these stories imply, what would happen if she were unleashed?

Jewish masculinity is imagined to be physically weak by comparison with the stronger men—the Ishmaels and Esaus—whom he sees around him. The most celebrated version of this stereotype of a frail, neurotic Jewish boy with a controlling Jewish mother and dreaded dates with girls who graduated from Brandeis is of course Woody Allen. In his movies, as in his life, Woody Allen becomes powerful, even virile, by dividing women from one another (discussed in Chapter 4).

The stereotypes that emerge from these stories are not inevitable. They did however prejudice a generation so that Jewish women enjoyed an unfortunate reputation in popular culture and often—whether JAP or Jewish mother—a Jewish woman feels like the loudest person in the room, even if she has not said a word. These images reflect anxieties about Jewish masculinity that blame an invented Jewish femininity for its own low self-esteem. The stories that give women too much sexual power and men too little domestic power have had consequences in the real world: Jewish men became wary of Jewish women, even as they applied a false and heterosexist standard of hardened masculinity to themselves. The trajectory of these narrative traditions led to mixed feelings about the presumed value of Jewish domesticity and inspired negative reactions to women's intimacy with one another. Recognizing the source of stereotypes in habits of reading the family dramas in scriptures loosens their hold on us.

Mythology and history imagine false power to justify oppression. The black slave was imagined to be a man of brutal sexual impulse, so he had to be shackled lest white women be harmed. Jews have been imagined to control banks and governments to justify their destruction. Woman too needs to be enchained if a little perfume is all it takes for a man to lose his head. The powerful Rebecca of *Ivanhoe* stands trial for witchcraft because, as Sir Walter Scott demonstrates in his Romantic novel, medieval Europe imagined the Hebrew beauty as a creature of dangerous sexual allure. These motifs echo still in popular culture. Jewish women are represented as overpowering and not easily satisfied. The Jewish man is said to make a good husband: he does not drink, does not tend to domestic violence, is submissive, domestically responsible, is perhaps too loyal to his mother, but is also faithful to his wife. This mythology urges the Jewish man to assert himself, to free himself of the Jewish woman.

Often when we think about the representation of women in Hebrew scriptures, we presume that they are relatively powerless, that their roles are circumscribed, that they do not do much of importance. On the contrary, women in the Hebrew Bible are overinvested with power, but their power is always sexual and when it is used, it is devastating to men. The JAP descends from Jael, Delilah, Esther, and Judith insofar as she inspires fear, though for all of her allure, the cultural stereotype succeeds in making her far from irresistible. Although this body of stories proffers reasons to fear female sexuality, they function as inoculations against desire.

Understood differently, the stories of Tamar (in Genesis), Jael, Delilah, Judith, Susannah, Esther, and even Ruth provided the excuse for centuries of graphic depictions of lush and murderous female sexuality. All acquire political potency—in some cases deadly power—by enacting a heightened and deceiving femininity that conforms to the psychologist Riviere's characterization: "women who wish for masculinity may put on a mask of womanliness to avert anxiety and the retribution feared from men."[21] In this articulation, rather than raising male anxiety, the woman's display of sexual interest works, on the contrary, to disarm men who might otherwise resent her competition in the workplace (much as Deborah's threat is transferred from the battlefield to the bedroom).

Stephen Heath, situating historically Riviere's influential essay, refers us to Nietzche's characterization of woman in *The Gay Science* as fundamentally unknowable, "women produced as 'the woman,' *das ewige Weibliche* the function of this discourse of mask and behind, that mask behind which man suspects some hidden danger."[22] (The "eternal woman," like *das ewige Jüde*, the "eternal Jew" is a sign of emptiness.) Heath observes that for Freud, both sexes repudiate femininity, because femininity is masquerade and evil; and for Lacan "adornment" *is* the woman. Juliet Mitchell accordingly identifies woman as phallus insofar as woman and the phallus share a status of being "potentially absent," the "signifier of a lack."[23] Heath writes that "alienation is the structural condition of being a woman," and finally that "[t]he masquerade says that woman exists at the same time that, as masquerade, it says that she does not." He refers to "this tourniquet of disturbance and reassurance."[24] In "Imitation and Gender Insubordination," Judith Butler, describing not the condition of being a woman but the game of gender appropriation indicated by drag, suggests that both sexes enact gender: "[d]rag constitutes the mundane way in which genders are appropriated, theatricalized, worn, and done; it implies that all gendering is a kind of impersonation or approximation."[25] These Hebrew heroines who pass as harlots and the consequences of their heightened femininity dramatize, in particular, the appropriation of masculine authority in the form of military, political, or social victories in an infinite regress of gender appropriations.

Gender identity and ethnic identity are always performative, represented in these stories as role play and as forms of passing. Tamar, Yael, Delilah, Esther, and Ruth enact femininity to achieve military, political, or other narrative ends. Jacob pretends to be Esau, to be man enough to be a patriarch. Joseph, as secretary of state to Pharaoh, has become unrecognizable to his brothers and only outs himself as their brother under the pressures of the story to self-reveal. Like Esther and Joseph, Moses too is a court Jew with a hidden identity until the narrative requires him to reclaim his birth identity. Both gender identity and Hebrew or Jewish identities are susceptible to being alternately removed and put on. These women sometimes act as men, Hebrews double for non-Jews and vice versa; God enters them and they enter into God, and in these maneuvers, these narratives highlight the dangerously unstable borders between very old countries: man/woman; Jew/gentile; God/human.

8

Other Boundary Crossings: Of Talking Beasts and Bodies Fragmented

BODY SYMBOLS AND EXCHANGEABLE BODIES

In the Bible, bodies are sometimes objects of exchange and sometimes interchangeable. At such moments, the characters who are actors in the stories are also symbols in foundation texts, individual bodies that represent bodies politic.[1] Even a partial list of literary doubling and body bartering in stories discussed thus far suggests the body's narrative utility in the Bible. As we have seen, Jacob pretends to be Esau (and thereby gets the blessing intended for the first born). Leah pretends to be Rachel (acquiring the husband to whom her sister was betrothed). Rachel purchases Leah's mandrakes with Jacob's favors, effectively commodifying the husband they share. (Each sister conceives.) Deborah predicts that the enemy will fall to "a woman" (presumably herself), and Jael materializes in her stead to accomplish in bed what could not be accomplished on the field. Esther replaces Vashti; Mordechai rides the prize horse that Haman intended for himself, and Haman, in turn, replaces Mordechai on the gallows. Lot's wife, the biblical Orpheus who disobeys God by looking back, is transformed into a pillar of salt, and Miriam, when she disobeys God, is enveloped in a cloud from which she emerges covered in leprosy, these sulfuric women's bodies drawing boards on which God composes judgment. Sarah gives her slave Hagar to Abraham to conceive in her stead, as Rachel will give Bilhah to Jacob, and Leah will proffer Zilpah, doubling the wombs that produce the tribes of Israel without adding to the number of matriarchs. In another kind of surrogacy, Ruth and Naomi, two bodies in one, also symbolize the barrenness and fertility of the land.

A character's symbolization is often most apparent when most acutely defined by his or her carnality: at the thresholds of birth and death, during sex, and when subject to violence and violation. If repeated patterns of representation reveal sexual identity and life roles to be performances (for example, of masculinity or femininity, motherhood, patriarchy, or fraternity), these moments of bodily barter or boundary crossing undermine the "effect of the real" produced by self-styling characters and locate the reader in the alternative reality of allegory, myth, and fantasy. From the wife-sister exchanges of the patriarchs to the incest of Lot's daughters, to the threats of homosexual gang rape in both Genesis 19 and Judges 19, the bodies of women are especially susceptible to incarnating the body politic. The parallel plots of Genesis 19 and Judges 19 represent the threats of violent sodomy and rape not so much as crimes against persons but as violations of the rules of hospitality. As Sheila Delany's analysis of Judges 19 demonstrates, the biblical body is often best understood as the polity, and doing so counteracts the "horror" that might be inspired by a literal reading of textual violence and violation.[2] Bodies—human and polis—are mutually informing inventions.

This chapter discusses how the Bible's routine violation of identity and body boundaries necessarily fails to restore a stable system of sexual identity and mores. I begin by suggesting that the identity categories neatly established at creation and reestablished on Noah's ark are repeatedly violated in reprise after reprise of the first disobedience, which associates forbidden fruit with sexual transgression, exile, and consequences for subsequent generations, hopelessly upsetting the norms of Eden's classification systems. Future generations—including the reader—are implicated in the cycle of sexual, social, political, and religious infringements on regulated boundaries that (fail to) define the (utopian) land of the normal. If Adam and Eve's disobedience leads to the fate of mortality, suffering, and loss for all humanity, subsequent protagonists in biblical foundation texts violate sexual rules to explain the fates and circumstances of the particular nations or tribes that they conceive. I then focus on the uses and meanings of the body in two strangely difficult stories: that of Balaam and his talking donkey (Numbers 22–24) and that of the *pilegesh* (concubine), who is multiply raped and whose body is cut in twelve pieces to send a message to the tribes of Israel (Judges 19). These stories exemplify a range of narratives in which the body represents the polity and carnal violations and transgressions allegorize geopolitically. Moreover, these are "queer" stories to the extent that their transgressions of normative social, sexual, and political boundaries expose the self and the land as textual configurations unreliably maintained by border police.

Eating forbidden fruit and discovering shame in the naked body at once disrupt the perfected order of Eden and lead to long-term consequences. As the history of God's creation proceeds, there are radical ruptures, as if the text, unable to control human productivity and reproduction, and God, unable to control humanity, attempt to go back on its own beginning. The first such rupture comes as early as the story of Noah. With humanity multiplying exponentially, the narrative can no longer contain all the stories, and overwhelmed by both overpopulation and humanity's insistent violation of God's regulations, human sin drives the Creator to cleanse the world and begin a reordering process. Noah's ark, that ideal, floating, controlled microcosm, reiterates with clarity a human/animal universe of life, each species in perfect pairs, male and female, with people further organized into families. No sooner has this cleansing been effected, however, than Noah plants the first vineyard, drinks too much wine, "uncovers himself," and invites renewed disorder. Reversing Adam and Eve's self-covering, Noah immediately reintroduces nakedness as shame into the world, defeating God's intention to restore the ordered boundaries of creation and initiating a long series of stories that reiterate the Edenic association of fruit, transgression, and the naked body as origin myths of enemy nations.

"Noah, the tiller," plants the first vineyard, gets drunk and naked, and inspires his son Ham to sin by witnessing his father's nakedness, bringing curses upon Canaan, the nation Ham fathers. Conversely, Shem and Japheth, the brothers to whom Ham will be enslaved, are blessed with increase because they cover their father without looking at him. After the next totalizing destruction of Sodom and Gomorrah, Lot's daughters, wrongly imagining that they are the only survivors in the world, ply their father with wine in order to have sex with him, and through this incest, birth the fathers of the Moabites and Ammonites. Thus, biblical narrative extends the connections between the double shames of Eden—transgressing God's command and human sexuality—in stories that substitute eating forbidden fruit with drinking wine. Wine leads to the relaxed defenses, which permits extended sexual boundary crossing. As in the instances of Ham's flagrant disrespect of his father's privacy to the incest of Lot and his daughters, the effects are manifest in the fate of the tribes and nations that descend from the transgressing founding figures.

Within Israel too, the political fates of the tribes are ascribed to the sexual boundary crossing of their founders: Rueben loses the leadership priority of the first born (Genesis 49:3–4) for lying with his father's concubine (another metaphoric instance, in biblical parlance, of "uncovering his father's nakedness") (Genesis 35:22). Dinah's full brothers, Simeon and Levi, are similarly punished for excessively avenging their sister's rape by murdering the rapist Shechem and his newly circumcised tribe (Genesis 34). The rape of Dinah, which is narrated powerfully but with little attention to the victim's feelings, is best understood as one in a long series of political origin stories cast as sociosexual family allegory that explains the later fate of tribal Israel's nation-states. Dinah's rape, which accounts for her brothers' rage, bad behavior, and relatively small land portions, does not otherwise insist on a sympathetic response from the reader because Dinah is experienced as instrumental.

Indeed, the textual function of daughters, relatively rare in these early patriarchal narratives, seems largely to provide sites for transgression in origin accounts of the descendants of the men to whom they belong. In the midst of stories of fathers and sons and patriarchal inheritances, Lot's four referenced daughters are at once precious possessions for barter, objects of loss, and producers of competing tribal leaders. The first daughter mentioned is the virgin daughter that Lot offers to the crowd of townsmen who come to sodomize the angels, another exchangeable body, the purpose of which is to potentially stand in for the angels and so prove Lot's exemplary hospitality. Lot's two married daughters do not leave Sodom because their local husbands disbelieve Lot, and their presence as precious transferred property left behind in the burning city may explain Lot's wife's inability to obey God's command not to "look back." Finally, Lot's misguided surviving daughters seduce their father to found enemy nations. The daughters' lack of meaningful personal identity is signaled by their anonymity.[3] And like Dinah's rape, the potential horror of all of these stories is mitigated by the extent to which the reader experiences the women's bodies as metaphors in political allegories.[4]

The created world's order is disrupted by wine and illicit sex, both of which prove irresistible from Eden forward. Stories that combine wine and sex perpetuate the association initiated in Eden of compromising behaviors with compromised national futures. Drunk, Ahasuerus launches the book of Esther by inviting Vashti to display herself (the rabbis read: naked, except for her crown); Esther uses wine to interfere with the threatened genocide and evade Vashti's fate; Judith uses wine to compromise Holofernes before murdering him, and Samson's power and undoing are associated with his hair and with refraining from wine. The dynamic of history reduces to key players' failure of "self"-containment.

BETWEEN ASS AND ANGEL:
THE HUMAN SITUATION IN NUMBERS 22–24

Biblical narrative presumes a heterosexual norm, well-regulated family and communal life, and populations living within their borders. Beyond Eden and Noah's ark, however, story after story represents and manages the inevitable border crossings and category violations of which mythic history is comprised. These border violations of both person and territory expose the artificiality of all identity boundaries, and biblical norms prove themselves more exception than rule.

The story of Balak (Numbers 22:2–24:25) is replete with boundary crossing and ambiguous identity categories: a beast talks; angels walk among us; and the protagonist-prophet Balaam, who ultimately blesses the people Israel, is a gentile sorcerer and, in the Bible and later commenting tradition, is characterized as both friend and foe, an ambiguous hero. Interrupting the well-ordered regulations of temple worship and stories of Moses, Aaron, and the priesthood, which are more typical of the book of Numbers, this narrative intrudes and is distinctive in its failure to observe the conventions of biblical realism. Instead, we are treated to a fabulous story—indeed, a fable—with some of the upside-down, and therefore subversive, features of carnival. This counter-text may be intentionally comic, a corrective and expansive vision of reality. Like the dream work, this text, which is populated by anomalous beings, reminds the reader that the identity categories to which people are assigned—especially categories of gender and sexuality—are optional to the extent that their borders are arbitrarily drawn and must be rigorously policed.

The episode about Balak presents as a fable. An ill-intentioned, powerful, and wealthy king Balak twice offers riches to the skilled diviner Balaam to curse the Israelites in hope of ridding them from the land; a protagonist prophet, in possible need of moral strengthening, reluctantly agrees (fable-style, on second request) to travel to see these Israelites but insists that he can only say the words that God puts into his mouth; a journey (the road of life, where knowledge is acquired) is interrupted by a sharp-talking, sword-brandishing, angelic presence en route who can choose to whom he manifests; a loyal donkey protectively avoids the angel, who is invisible to Balaam, and so provokes her master's violent reaction (he beats her three times), and when the talking donkey objects to this mistreatment, she finds support in the formidable, threatening angel, suddenly and terrifyingly visible to Balaam. The angel secures Balaam's promise of obedience. Still, in an effort to influence fate, Balaam has Balak offer three hilltop sacrifices, each with seven altars, seven bulls, and seven rams (magic numbers), but the will of heaven will not be thwarted. Including the famous lines preserved in Jewish liturgy, "How goodly are your tents, O Jacob, your dwellings, O Israel!," the people are blessed in a clear, poetic conclusion that affirms the unyielding power of fate and definitively supplants the evil king's intended curses with abiding blessings from heaven.

A second, darker ending (Numbers 25) in which the fickle, idolatrous people cease to deserve these blessings, a functional postscript rife with illicit sex and murder, breaks from the genre of the fable and restores the more usual conventions of biblical narrative realism.

The story leapfrogs identity boundaries by situating humanity between talking beasts and interfering angels. Insofar as angels are asexual (non-carnal) men or ambiguously sexed fantasies, the angel's presence reinforces the reader's sense of a world in which identity is not what it seems. The angel's careful decision about when to out himself, as it were, further enforces the message of a ubiquitous unknowable population that walks unseen among people. Even a great seer cannot tell where an angel may be. This story is about power and perception, and ultimately, about the power of perception. What the seer sees governs the fate of a nation. The reader, through identification with Balaam, receives a small education in human limitation and the life and death consequences of interpretation.

The angel's surprise manifestation is like the several significant instances of identity revelation in the Bible, each of which demonstrates the power and danger of the closet. Joseph, Moses, and Esther, as court Jews whose Jewishness is a potentially threatening secret, are variations within a biblical pattern of concealment and revelation of identity that includes angelic presences, such as those who manifest to Abraham, Lot, Jacob, Samson's mother, and Balaam. Not knowing who may be an angel—not knowing who may be a Jew—is analogously dangerous, such that over the course of history, the ambiguity of Jewish racial identity, especially for Ashkenazi Jews, has repeatedly proved to be dangerous.

If the Great Chain of Being goes from the lowliest of creatures to the loftiest, from bugs and fish up through four-legged beasts to humanity, angels, and God, then the donkey and the angel are situated outside the extremes of humanity, which is, at its best, angelic, and, at worst, beastly. In this story, there is a brief alliance formed between beast and angel against the main human character, Balaam, who would more conventionally be in relationship with either of them than they with one another.

First the angel stands in the way of the donkey, who is beaten; then the angel backs the donkey into a wall, squishing Balaam's foot and earning the donkey another beating, and finally, the angel forces the beast to lie down altogether, earning the donkey not just a beating but the murderous threat that if Balaam had had a sword, he would have done away with his incorrigible ride. When the poor donkey protests and asks her master if she has not been loyal all her life, the angel manifests in the donkey's defense. Wielding a sword of his own, the angel exchanges Balaam for the donkey as the object of threatened violence. Indeed, Balaam might imagine here that his having conjured a sword to be used against the donkey produced the vision of a sword that could be used against Balaam himself. The power relationship between master and beast is reversed by an unseen force that stands, as a corrective, on the donkey's side of the scale of justice. And to the extent that the sword represents a hypermasculinity that Balaam wishes for but does not have, the angel—who has no carnal or material needs or appetites—uses his sword to keep Balaam from misusing such power as he has. Even though Balaam has already made this commitment, the angel forces Balaam to promise yet again that he will only say what he is told to say, will function, essentially, as dummy to the divine ventriloquist.

If Balaam has limited autonomous power, the human king evidently has even less. The king, Balak, and the prophet, Balaam, represent classes of people who possess different kinds of power, material and spiritual, respectively. The king, despite his wealth and authority, requires the skills of the diviner if he is to effectively curse the Israelites and end their obnoxious reproduction on the land. Balaam is in turn dependent on God to earn the riches promised by the king, and so Balaam sets about instructing Balak on the sacrificial offerings that might turn things his way: three times with seven altars, prophet and king work together to influence God, and three times, Balaam delivers blessings, though Balak had ordered curses, for which he was prepared to pay handsomely. The king is irate.

Anger, like laughter, is a disruptive force: an expression of lost control, unpredictable in its ability to be checked. Sarah's ambiguous laughter, unreadable even to God, reminds us that laughter has a gendered history and that the laughter of women has been encoded as monstrous, associated with witches and hysterics. Like female laughter, male anger threatens to exceed its bounds. Anger is important in this story. The king is an angry man: first at the Israelites and ultimately at Balaam, and the combination of anger and power threatens the safety of stasis. Balaam is afraid to provoke God's anger, another terrifying prospect, but Balaam himself is capable of anger against his loyal ass.

The wonder of this fable is that powerful, angry men prove impotent, their threats idle, and their anger at thwarted desire proves futile and fizzles. After his lesson from the angel, Balaam says nothing further to the ass. Balak rails weakly and impotently against Balaam, and Balaam ventures not a syllable against God. King and diviner have no choice but resignation. Although neither resigns his lofty post, both must be resigned to self-limitations. In this story, the strict boundaries of biblical order are violated; the rules of the world are upturned; power is reversed and restored; wishes thwarted, anger diffused, and bullies are put in check.

Reminding us of life's mystery and unpredictability, this story represents all identity as carnivalesque: the ill-intentioned king is a paper tiger. This fictional world locates real power with God, who animates angels and animals, controls his sorcerer prophets, and wins contests with kings. Because God's agent in the story, the angel, is not susceptible to greed or misdirection, he, like the simple donkey, acts with pure intention. Although biblical angels manifest as men, they are not debilitated by male desire or sexuality and as such they are personally free and agents of liberation. This aspect of the biblical angel is echoed in two of the late twentieth century's most powerful American dramas that attend to the triumphs and tragedies of queer America. Jonathan Larson's award-winning musical *Rent* and Tony Kushner's *Angels in America* feature sexually transgressive, boundary-crossing "Angels" who function to tame rage and exemplify the joy of loving self-expression. Kushner's Angel is a comic and powerful revision of the biblical prototype. She warns: "You can't outrun your occupation, Jonah. / Hiding from me in one place you will find me in another. / I I I I stop down the road, waiting for you." And in her triumphant conclusion, the angelic voice yells: "FOR THIS AGE OF ANOMIE: A NEW LAW! / Delivered this silent night, this silent night, from Heaven, / Oh Prophet, to You."[5] Angels remind prophets—Balaam, Jonah—that they neither can "outrun their occupations" nor define their missions.

But angels are there for wrestling and invite showdowns of conscience, most memorably in the case of the patriarch Jacob. Balaam's story evokes Jacob. When Balaam blesses Israel, he blesses the "good tents of Jacob," and Israel is identified in this episode repeatedly as "Jacob," named for the patriarch who saw angels ascending and descending a ladder, and who famously wrestled an angel, from whom he wrested a blessing, and who left him marked on the thigh. These encounters with fighting personal angels in ambiguously homoerotic engagements (Balaam's angel wields a sword; Jacob wrestles his angel in the night, and Jacob will not release him) also expose the psychic dream work beneath biblical narrative.

With Balak effectively disarmed, the text abruptly departs from the other world outside of Israel, with its envious kings, gentile prophets, talking donkeys, and sword-brandishing angels. Back in those goodly tents, the story becomes grimly realistic. The people sin and worship Baal-peor. The men whore with Moabite and Midianite women. God's anger becomes serious, and the punishing plague visited on the Israelites is only checked by the public murder of two flagrant sinners. It is as if the story's postscript aims to reverse its earlier effects: it ends by putting an end to the comedy, refusing permission to cross ethnic or sexual boundaries, and planting the reader firmly in a world with God and sinners, one without angels and talking donkeys.

But it is too late. This counter-text has worked its magic, surprised our expectations, and subverted the categories that the Torah often insists upon with too much protest. It is good to recall here Moe Meyer's discussion of queerness as a challenge to the concept of "self." He writes in *The Politics and Poetics of Camp* that "What 'queer' signals is an ontological challenge that displaces bourgeois notions of the Self as unique, abiding, and continuous while substituting instead a concept of the Self as performative, improvisational, discontinuous, and processually constituted by repetitive and stylized acts."[6] In this sense, the fable with a talking donkey is a "queer story," with king and prophet desperately and rather futilely enacting their life roles, and angel and beast disrupting their self-assessments. In the fashion of all carnival texts, this brief biblical story reminds the reader that because everyone improvises a self, the self is queer, by definition.

THE FRAGMENTED BODY POLITIC IN JUDGES 19

Judges 19 is apparently as gruesome a text as is imaginable, including gang rape, murder, and mutilation. The narrative affect is, however, relatively flat, and the claim that I will make here is that for the reader, the story is less disconcerting for its violation of the rules of morality and humanity than for its deliberate, ingenious violation of the rules of narrativity and textuality. The story constitutes an interchapter between Judges and the books of Samuel and is designed explicitly to exemplify "those days when there was no king in Israel," "a time when everyone did as he pleased," signaling the need for the rule of judges to yield to the presumed tighter rule of kings. This hero is nameless, an anonymous Levite, an Everyman whose travel maps a political and geographic landscape; from Ephraim to Bethlehem in Judah through Jerusalem and Gibeah of the Benjamites, his journey twice traverses tribal Israel. By story's end, the cultural and social classification system that had been carefully developed since the opening chapters of Genesis will have been thoroughly undermined.

In these penultimate chapters of Judges, the last judge figure travels through the whole of Israel to recover his *"pilegesh,"* a woman who has, for reasons not told to us in the story, gone back to her father. The man lingers there day after day, and the reader becomes anxious, suspicious of the apparently excessive hospitality that detains him—and us. Finally he starts home late in the day with his belongings and his woman. In spite of approaching night, the man and his entourage choose not to stay among strangers, and they travel on to an Israelite tribe, the Benjamites, where they are taken in by the only good man in the town. The townspeople, in a story that resonates with the crimes of Sodom and Gomorrah, wish to rape the guest, and they bang on the door so that he might be sodomized. The host is appropriately outraged and offers to send out his virgin daughter instead. But it is the Levite's woman, the one whom he had traveled so far to retrieve, who is thrown out to the men; she is multiply raped, and in the morning, the Levite, the man, finds her lying across the threshold. The Levite says, "Get up; let us go," but she cannot; perhaps she is already dead. The Levite travels home to Ephraim, having now traversed all Israel, all twelve tribes twice—this last part of the journey with the woman's body. No longer personally useful, the woman's body is politically useful. Once home, he cuts her body into twelve pieces, and as if in a parody of his own journey, repeats the original journey in fragmented form, mailing a piece of the corpse to each tribe in Israel. Each part thereby becomes a mobile and multiple signifier: it signifies brutality (but the text is ambiguous about the agent of the brutality: the Levite? the Benjamites? all Israel?); it is a call for vengeance against the Benjamites, and (for the reader) the parts are metaphors for the fragmented body politic, the land itself. This fragmented people require a king to unify them.

The narrative strategy works with psychological effects. The hero is nameless; he goes to recover an equally nameless woman from the home of her nameless father, to which she had returned (having played the harlot?), for no specified reason, four months earlier. The days of the Levites' visit are marked by the anticipation of his ready departure, which is twice deferred when the "father-in-law" presses his visitor to tarry. This time, during which the man, his concubine, and his attendant might have been en route home, is spent instead over male feasting followed by nighttime pleasure: the girl's father and "master" dawdle over food and retire. The hospitality is explicitly "warm," but the excess seems unmotivated, and after three days, a summary statement leads the reader to expect that the departure will come on the fourth day. But the fifth verse actually slows the pace even further, beginning with the man's intention to leave and the father-in-law, urging, in direct speech, more food. Again, he stays and is invited to stay the night—with night now established as a time of pleasure rather than danger—and again the guest begins to leave but the host prevails. When the pattern repeats in verse eight and they dawdle until past noon, the reader becomes tense. When once again they begin to leave and are urged to stay at least until morning, the reader becomes off-balance: Will the man move on so that there can be a story? Is the hospitality true? Should he wait until morning?

These few verses have raised many subtle questions: What is a *pilegesh*, a wife or a harlot, or some intermediary sexual partner, like a concubine? Why did she leave? And once she left, why did the Levite make such an effort to retrieve her? Should we trust the warmth of her father's reception of the Levite? Is this father-in-law's home a place of gluttony and dangerous detention or a site of generous hospitality? In a violation of classic narrative realism, these motivating enigmas all remain intact.

At first, this final story in Judges seems to fit the overall pattern of Judges classically described by Kenneth Gros Louis: "Israel does evil, God is angry, he raises enemies to punish the Israelites, they repent, a judge is chosen to save them, there is a brief period of peace and the cycle begins again as Israel does evil."[7] But in this story, the pattern is truncated: there is only the evil and the vengeance. The narrative syntax is left incomplete, and the story is left relatively unresolved, without the restoration of order. Ambiguity persists, and the story refuses the reader's attempts to pass judgments on the judge: Is this Levite, this ultimate judge, a cold, cruel victimizer who determinedly traveled to retrieve an unwilling woman from her home only to throw her to rape and death? Or is he the ultimate victim, a man who so loved a woman as to have traveled far to reclaim her affection only to lose her to the vicious Benjamites? And how are we to judge her: is she a whore who left her husband and brought all the trouble of the story upon Israel and by poetic logic deserves a nasty fate, or is she the silent picture of innocence violated?

Judges 19 rests on a social order defined by a set of cultural and social oppositions more sophisticated than those of Genesis, which divided the created world into land and sea, sun and moon, light and dark. The divisions on which this story depends are variations on home/away; safety/danger; day/night; inside/outside; stranger/compatriot; licit relations/illicit sex; hospitality/inhospitality; wife/harlot; masculine/feminine; fair trade/theft; lawful punishment/excessive brutality; and life/death. Although ordinarily the left side of the pair would have been positive, here those values are also unstable. At the story's climactic moment, the woman is lying, in a poignant image, at the door, her fingers on the threshold, unable to get up. This image is a metaphor for the story's situation of the reader. The story sits on the threshold, on the line between the oppositions that will not stabilize. Just as we cannot be sure if the woman is alive or dead, neither inside nor outside, neither wife nor whore—just as fellow Israelites are less trustworthy than strangers—and we cannot know who is family and who is foe, where safety and danger lie, so too we experience the absence of order in a social world in which the dependable classification system of social order no longer applies.

As a mediating figure, the girl threatens the story's polarities of difference and opens the space for sustained ambiguity. A *"pilegesh,"* she is linguistically and (because she left her husband) both a wife and a harlot. As such, she is both deserving and undeserving of narrative punishment, and because the circumstances of her departure are unclear, the man acts both wisely and unwisely in his attempt to woo her back. Her father is equally ambiguous as he is both a close relative and a stranger, and his home is potentially a safe haven and dangerous. His tent is marked as a place of gluttony and detention, where night offers enjoyment. The depraved men are fellow Israelites as opposed to the members of the stranger community among whom the Levite chose not to stay and who might have proven more hospitable than the Benjamites. The Benjamites are "strange relations." The old man who offers sanctuary in his home is identified as a resident alien (is he more resident or more alien?), and though he keeps the Levite from the open market, the refuge he provides proves unsafe. He too makes a morally ambiguous offer when he offers to throw his own virgin daughter to the crowd. Finally, "the hero"—if he is that—mediates each of the narrative oppositions because it is continually questionable whether he should have undertaken this journey and crossed the literal and figural borders of the text. Although he is ultimately the wronged victim, his suffering is a displacement, and he may be responsible and, as the judge, accountable for both the most brutal acts of violence in the text and the lawlessness that made them possible.

To read this story allegorically requires one transformation: the individual, carnal, sexual body stands for the body politic. The characters are unnamed because each represents and is represented by tribal affiliations and geographic locations, places of origin and residence. The man's mission is personal and sexual, and the story's first questions concern the nature of fair exchange and hospitality, first in the father-in-law's home and then in Gibeah, where the man's body is first indulged and then threatened with exploitation ("the depraved lot" who wish to be intimate with him). The text reiterates that the man has adequate means and goods with which to pay for proper hospitality, but since the mission is sexually coded, regular trade resolves itself into sexual exchange and exchange of the sexes. The text forces a substitution, again, a gender substitution, as the woman's body replaces the man's body; her body is thrown out to the rapists instead of that of the Levite or the host himself or even the host's virgin daughter (who is offered), and the woman's corpse is fragmented to symbolize the fragmented polity.

There is a chain of substitutions. Instead of the man's goods, the lawless townsmen want the man himself; instead of the man, they are given the commodity for whose sake the journey was undertaken, the woman. In twelve parts, the broken body is precisely the political landscape that needs to be rendered whole again through a military act of revenge and restoration. And true to the biblical translation of the political into the sexual, the Benjamites will first be punished with the loss of women, and their restoration takes the form of replacement of women. These bartered women are again symbolic; they are commodities, possessions that resist being experienced in the fullness of even narrative humanity.

The oppositions usually stabilized at the end of the stories in Judges remain unbalanced in this final version. The man, as ultimate judge, is really no judge at all, and he has been drained of value and power. Samuel must come to anoint Saul because the story ends with a lawlessness that is structurally paralleled by the story's refusal to stabilize the oppositions that it establishes. The story's conclusion does not restore the order upset by the threats of sodomy and the woman's murder. The scandal here is less the threats and transgressions on the surface of the plot—disruption of the family order, violation of hospitality, threatened sodomy, rape, and murder—than the quiet transformation through which the woman's body replaces the man's body as the site of violent representation. The land is intact, but not so the social order; and although the judge represents the social order and the sexual woman represents the land, in a classic reversal, the man's body (though threatened) remains whole, while the woman's body (which replaces him) is mutilated.

Like Helen of Troy, whose beauty is made responsible for the Trojan War, the anonymous *pilegesh* ends the rule of the judges. Like Dinah and other biblical women, she was sexually threatening and sexually vulnerable, ultimately powerful and powerless, requiring protection and possessing that from which men must protect themselves. In multiple ways, the characters in these stories disrupt bourgeois notions of a stable self. Because the judge cuts the woman's body into twelve fragments that become telegrams to the tribes signifying the fragmentation of the people Israel, this story reconfigures national identity, anticipating the unifying vision of the books of Samuel and Kings.

A more culturally sophisticated classification system than that of the first chapters of Genesis, Judges 19 undermines its own social oppositions and reversals: night and day; wife and harlot; safety and danger; excess and restraint; licit and illicit relations; family and strangers; hospitality and violation; and finally, masculinity and femininity are among the oppositions that are rendered unstable in these unstable times. It is a story about thresholds and transgressions, and they are geographic and political. This judge has no name because he is an everyman identified by place, and the unruly body wishes to violate him because it is lawless; the system has failed, making way for the books of Samuel and the rule of kings.

Judges is characterized by sexual reversals: Deborah is a woman on the battlefield; Sisera is penetrated instead of penetrating. Samson, the strong man, is shorn and has his eyes removed by a whining woman. The townsmen desire to rape a man as if he were a woman.[8] In the time of judges, men were not men; the land and the people are a metaphoric, fragmented, feminized corpse. The book of Ruth, an antidote text, revisits the landscape and dichotomies of Judges, resolving the most intractable of biblical dichotomies with a shift in attitude toward biblical boundaries. In Ruth, again, the female body will stand for the body politic, but the boundaries defining national boundaries and sexual roles are relaxed. In Ruth, women journey safely and the stranger is safely integrated. In a small taste of the messianic future, predicted by the birth of a Davidic ancestor, the story imagines domestic and national peace and order, where people find consolation for the hardships and losses that define the human condition after Eden.

9

Oy! Was That a Close Call: Ruth and the Fundamental Jewish Story

The book of Ruth resonates with life hungers. The urgent flight from famine with which the story begins is balanced by abundant gleaning in fields of grain toward the story's end. The untimely, unexplained deaths of sons that mark the story's start are answered by a birth and genealogy at the story's conclusion. Departure and return, barrenness and fertility, desperation and redemption, depletion and replenishment are the extremes between which the narrative occurs. Among the themes and meanings in this pastoral romance, most compelling is the story's implied message that although meaning is elusive, life fragile, and our fates unpredictable, the small individual persevering in the impulse to satisfy life hungers can play the most crucial role—unknowable even to the self—in the vast plan of history. Here, a biblical lesson culminates: the source of Jewish vitality is procreation and persistence against all odds. The book of Ruth suggests itself as the ultimate text about the triumph of faith over fear, a romance that resonates with life hunger and resolve.

The main metaphors in the book of Ruth are food and sex. The book of Ruth begins with famine in the land and barren women, and it ends with plenitude, a successful seduction in fields of waving barley, and an unusually promising baby on Naomi's, his grandmother's, lap. As in many stories in the Hebrew Bible, the individual female body, the land of Israel, and the body politic symbolically stand in for one another—alternately barren and fertile, depleted and blessed—and it is the individual who perseveres to satisfy life's hungers who moves humanity forward on the road to ultimate redemption.

Also resonant in Ruth are other biblical narratives, and this small story's plush texture comes from its allusions to other places in the larger text, its multiple threads, and its subtle but powerful reenforcement of both a biblical sensibility and the biblical patterns of representation that have been the subject of this book. Although God and the Law play only supporting roles in the drama, God and Law are its invisible center. Strands from Adam and Eve, Rachel and Leah, Judah and Tamar, and the book of Job, against a background of variations on the Deuteronomic and Levitical laws of gleanings and Levirate marriage, broaden and deepen the story. Variations on the patterns that I have described in scripture are reiterated in the book of Ruth almost systematically, as if to summarize and seal their inevitability. Yet the wide perspective offered in the book of Ruth gives us enough distance on the constructs of sex, gender, and family roles as to effectively challenge their certainty.

Although the book of Ruth reinforces biblical patterns and ends with a birth that hints at a messianic future, the particular variation on biblical themes and meanings in Ruth transcends the boundaries typically proscribed by biblical narrative. For example, Ruth is both a seductress and a mother, putting her in the uniquely distinguished company of Eve and Tamar, as the primary progenitors of humanity and Judaism, respectively, with Ruth advancing that lineage toward David and the Messiah. At the same time, Ruth and Naomi resemble the Bible's journeying heroes, although they are two women. Working cooperatively across a generation, as one body, they succeed in fulfilling the commandment to Adam to multiply, and the result is an unconventional family that includes a prominent mother-in-law, a daughter-in-law who functions as a surrogate, a man and a baby: no envious co-wives or competing sons. Most notably, Ruth—the figure from whom redemption will come— begins as a Moabite, a daughter of the place most accursed in the Bible, and she ends incorporated into the Jewish future. The gender, sexual, and national identities that the text had worked so hard to fix in earlier moments are here revealed to be relatively incidental. The story ends with a Job-style restoration because, in another variation on biblical patterns, Boaz abides by biblical laws that require making selfless choices. In this story, the boundaries between man and woman, Jew and gentile, rich and poor, like gender roles, sexual identities, and roles within the family, seem arbitrary and relatively unimportant.

Boaz, Ruth, and Naomi are infinitely important in the great scheme of things and yet, as individuals, their identities are irrelevant: The baby who is born at the story's end has no story himself and technically belongs to the men whose names are briefly mentioned and with whose deaths the story begins. This is the story of how Elimelech ("My God Is King,") Machlon ("Disease"), and Chilion ("Destruction")—men with allegorical names and about whom we know little—come to be contained in the body of the Messiah through someone else's son. Although the Genesis narratives seem to promise that the Bible will be a history of the world (and then a history of the Hebrews) with characters who are the founding heroes of the epic history of God's creation, the book of Ruth suggests a different generic possibility for the biblical corpus and a more democratic view of character. This pastoral romance within the epic abandons the hero model and tells the story of lives that might have otherwise gone unrecorded, illustrating the unpredictable promise of each life and every relationship in any combination. It is the story of Everyman as Everywoman, a pilgrim's progress about how the corporate body of Israel beats the odds, whatever the vicissitudes of individual lives and history.

COMEDY AND TIMING

Almost not making it is a fundamental biblical plot, a storyline that Jews in recent generations popularly embrace as one version of the Jewish historical experience. Abraham, credited with being the first monotheist and by extension the first Jew, is promised descendants as numerous as the stars in the sky and the grains of sand on the beach. Time passes, and the text is not shy to tell us that his old wife Sarah has reached menopause. At last Isaac is miraculously born to these aged parents, but no sooner is his older brother Ishmael banished and declared the father of a different people than Abraham is commanded to sacrifice Isaac on the altar. Famously, Abraham agrees, Isaac is bound, the knife is poised at his neck, and in the nick of time, comes the angel, frantic, "Abraham! Abraham!" Oy! Was that a close call!

Abraham is promised that he will father myriads, and then almost loses his "only" son. Were it not for that sudden, last minute intervention, the promise would have ended there. Among the many patterns that the book of Ruth reiterates is the pattern of rescue in the nick of time. Tragedy, by time-honored definition, ends in death, a cutting off of the future, and comedy ends in marriage, an opening up of the future. Ruth is a classic comedy because it ends in marriage. A more nuanced difference between comedy and tragedy is whether the hero, while on life's journey, knows what he needs to know in time. Like Odysseus, Dorothy, Jacob, Joseph, Moses, and the people of Israel, Ruth and Naomi take a journey. In literature, the journey is a metaphor for life. The road is knowledge and the destination is always the same: home. The trick to a comic outcome is to discover what you need before it is too late. Success—staying alive—is all about timing.

One aspect of the Jewish self-image includes neurotic survival anxiety, epitomized in Woody Allen's hypochondria. A story from the canon of popular culture expresses this Jewish ethnic distinction: A Frenchman, a German, and a Jew are wandering in the desert. The Frenchman says, "I'm tired; I'm thirsty; I must have wine." The German says, "I'm tired; I'm thirsty; I must have beer." And the Jew says, "I'm tired; I'm thirsty. I must have diabetes." In another story, the Jew is wandering in the desert alone, and with each step he groans, "Oy, am I thirsty. Oy, am I thirsty!" Suddenly, he finds himself at an oasis, complete with a soft drink machine, where he drinks to his full satisfaction. As he resumes his walking, he groans, "Oy! Vas I thirsty." These familiar characterizations portray stock types with the recognizable Jewish qualities of kvetching and anxiety; worrying about what may be and worrying about what has been, and a comparative disinterest in life's pleasures (the Frenchman and the German want wine and beer) because of a distracting preoccupation with what may go wrong.

The introductory hallway to the Diaspora Museum in Tel Aviv, Beit Hatefutsoth, in its first permanent exhibit in the 1980s gave witness to one close call after another: a catalog of powerful enemies, Babylonians, Assyrians, Romans, Crusaders, Cossacks, Nazis—most of whom no longer exist on the planet—who tried and failed to annihilate the Jews. In the twentieth century, there was some marvel that the European Holocaust did not succeed in erasing the Jewish people, followed by hand wringing that prosperity and assimilation would succeed where murderers failed. Historian Simon Rawidowicz famously coined the paradoxical term "the ever-dying people" to refer ironically to the people of Israel.[1] The comic plot of eleventh-hour survival is at once an inoculation against doom and a source of consolation and hope.

PILGRIMS' PROGRESS

The book of Ruth is a story of survival against the odds, a fairytale that accepts disease and death without intimidation. Presenting the extremes of desperation and recovery, the story quickens the dead through the birth of a namesake. Ruth begins: "In the days when the Judges judged," there was a famine in "Bet-Lechem" (which literally means "House of Bread"). Alternatively: "Once upon a time, there was no bread in the House of Bread." This is a formula for an origin myth. In this case, it is an origin story for the Davidic line, from which will descend the kingdom and, eventually, the Messiah. As the story begins, however, there is a famine at home, and Elimelech (an Everyman, "My God Is King,") his wife, Naomi ("Pleasantness"), and their sons Machlon and Chilion—Disease and

Destruction—move to Moab, a place that is encoded in the Bible as especially "Enemy Territory, the Accursed Place," so much so that Jews are
not permitted to marry Moabites. Within only a few verses, ten years have
passed, Elimelech is dead, his sons have married Moabites, Orpah and
Ruth, and both young men are also dead. There are no children. (Once
upon a time, there was no bread in the House of Bread, and God-is-my-
King, his wife Pleasant, and their sons Disease and Destruction went to
the Accursed Place, where the boys married women from this place, and
died.) Like Sarah, absent a miracle, Naomi is too old to build the House
of Israel. Moreover, she is remote from home, left only with two foreign,
Moabite daughters-in-law. In the biblical imagination, she is the least of
all persons in the worst of all situations. If ever someone had reason not
to get out of bed in the morning, that person is Naomi.

The question that emerges from this tragedy seems to be "now what?"
The rest of the story transforms the tragedy into comedy. Naomi, resisting
despair, decides to go home, and Ruth insists on accompanying her. By
the end of four quick chapters, Naomi, back in now-fertile Bethlehem, is
gifted with a son through Ruth. Although just a shape on his grandmother's lap, this is not just any baby. The narrator who introduced the story
with "once upon a time" offers a coda in the form of a genealogy that begins in Genesis, crosses through this baby, whose name is Obed, and ends
with King David: "This is the line of Perez: Perez begot Hezron, Hezron
begot Ram, Ram begot Amminadab, Amminadab begot Nachshon, Nachshon begot Salmon, Salmon begot Boaz, Boaz begot Obed, Obed begot
Jesse, and Jesse begot David" (Ruth 4:18–22). Unstated but nevertheless
clear to the reader within Jewish and Christian traditions is that from
this line will someday come the anointed one, the Messiah himself. In its
details, this is the story of a family from Bethlehem that takes a journey
to and back from Moab, from the worst of times to the best of times. The
frame offers, however, a much longer timeline: from "once upon a time"
to the end of time as we know it, the story stretches infinitely backward
and forward.

The book of Ruth contains the Hebrew Bible. Embedded in the narrative are allusions to the stories of Adam and Eve (using a relatively rare
biblical verb [d-b-k], Ruth "cleaves" to Naomi as Adam and Eve are said
to "cleave" to each other); Abraham and Sarah (who also "go forth,"
struggle to fulfill the promise, and are fruitful in old age); Rachel and
Leah (Ruth is blessed by Bethlehem's women to build the House of Israel
on the model of Rachel and Leah); Judah and Tamar (Boaz, Ruth's new
husband, appropriately descends from Judah and Tamar's son Perez,
who is himself both a product of Tamar's bed trick and another odd instance of Levirate marriage). Naomi is a kind of female Job, a character
who loses everything only to recover something better. The story occurs

in the mythic time of the judges, ironically, an era of failures of leadership and justice, and in this correction of earlier stories, adherence to Deuteronomic and Levitical laws—particularly to laws of gleaning and of Levirate marriage—guarantees its happy outcome. Thus, this short book connects to the fullness of Jewish scripture. A story that features women, it also culminates the two main traditions of biblical heroines: those of the barren mother and the seductress.

BOTH BARREN MOTHER AND BEDROOM VICTOR

With only a few significant exceptions, women in the Hebrew Bible are either barren mothers or seducers. Ruth—or perhaps, Naomi through Ruth—is both. When the story begins, the most significant fact about Naomi and Ruth is their childlessness. There are no more sons, and as Naomi makes clear, no likelihood that there can be more sons from her line because she is too old, and even were she able to conceive another son, his birth and maturation would require too long a wait for her daughters-in-law. Because she sees no ready way to fulfill her matriarchal obligation to give Orpah and Ruth men to marry, Naomi releases the younger women bound to her through marriage, saying that they should return to their mothers' tents and be free to marry elsewhere.

The textual details bind women together. First, it is notable that the daughters-in-law are not released to the tents of their fathers. In this story with communities of women, in which Naomi has become the mother of these daughters through marriage, the girls are sent back to their birth mothers. Second, the fact that Naomi releases her sons' wives suggests that absent this formula, they would otherwise be legally bound to remain with their mother-in-law. The legal premise is that marriage joins a woman to a new corporate body, and even though the men are all dead, the younger women remain bound to the elder one, whose obligation is to provide them with men to carry on her sons' lineage through them.[2] In a shift of biblical emphasis, the purpose of men is to do their part to give women sons.

Orpah (whose name means "Nape of the Neck") turns and tearfully chooses not to accompany Naomi; paradoxically, by staying in her home of origin, she leaves. Ruth, in an extraordinarily memorable expression of devotion and commitment ("whither you go, I will go"), joins Naomi on her journey. Ruth clings to her (*davka ba*), a "clinging" (*devaykut*) that echoes back to Adam and Eve's "clinging" and forward to Kabbalistic ideas of Israel and God clinging to each other. By clinging, Ruth is available to provide the young womb through which not only will Naomi's legacy prevail, but that of everyone to whom this text is sacred.

Naomi has two sons because in the Hebrew Bible, there are always at least two sons, both for the sake of representing sibling rivalry and so that the younger can reverse the rule of primogeniture, the rule that the firstborn inherits. In this story that features women, however, Naomi seems to have two sons so that she can have two daughters-in-law. The patriarchy goes from father to son; the matriarchy goes from mother-in-law to daughter-in-law, the most significant kinship between women in the Bible and one without rivalry, just as Rebecca replaces Sarah in Isaac's tent, "comforting him" after his mother's death. Naomi has two daughters-in-law so that one will choose to go, and one will choose to stay. It is as if the text were saying, "had Ruth made the choice that Orpah made, one freely allowed to her, then: . . . no Obed . . . no Jesse . . . no David . . . no Messiah from the Davidic line." A lot hangs on the individual choice. Ruth trusts in and abides by her contract in spite of Naomi's legal release and discouragement about a source of seed.

When Naomi arrives in Bethlehem, she is greeted by a chorus of women, what George Eliot called in *Adam Bede*, "the world's wife," that female body that speaks in the single voice of communal consensus. "Can this be Naomi?" they ask. Perhaps Naomi and Elimelech had been prominent citizens, she looks relatively well, and the people are terribly glad to see her; or possibly, as Avivah Zornberg suggests, she is so transformed by loss as to be unrecognizable, a *Muselmann*; or perhaps the famine had claimed so many lives that the mere fact of her return is astonishing.[3] This ambiguity will not resolve but deepens the identity crisis indicated when Naomi denies her name. She replies that she is no longer Naomi (Pleasant) but rather should be called Mara (Bitter) because she went away full and returns empty.

With Ruth at Naomi's side, mere verses from having delivered one of the most moving speeches in the Bible, attaching herself to Naomi ("your home shall be my home"; "where you are buried will I be buried"), readers have wondered at Naomi's apparent coldness. "Empty?" Ruth might have asked, "what am I?" Ruth says no such thing, however, because indeed, Naomi left full—that is, with sons—and returns with Ruth and no prospect of progeny. Together, Naomi and Ruth are one empty body. In Naomi's renaming herself Bitter, we hear the bitter cries of Sarah, Rachel, and Hannah, the self-defining barrenness of mothers before God intervenes.

In the Hebrew Bible, whenever a hero has a birth story, the story begins with a barren mother. Not every hero has a birth story, but when he does, his existence demands a miracle. The matriarchs Sarah, Rebecca, and Rachel, Hannah (mother of the prophet Samuel), and Samson's anonymous mother are all characterized as barren. As we have seen, this condition makes the point that at crucial moments in history, humanity's creative powers are inadequate. As if to remind us that the primary Creator of life is not human, God intervenes in history for extraordinary births, generating a pregnancy that the human father could not manage. In proportion to the significance of the hero is the extent of the barrenness, and the book of Ruth is a long birth story for a major hero, leading to, over time, the hero of heroes. The book of Ruth is David's birth story and by extension, the birth story of the Messiah.

The biblical barren mother plot, however, is conflictual and typically creates familial and gender divisiveness avoided in the book of Ruth. Ordinarily, the barren mother, who is especially beloved and beautiful, competes with a co-wife whose fertility is used to torment her. The husband cannot help, but God answers the aspiring mother's prayer and intervenes to remove the curse of barrenness in exchange for the baby's servitude as a hero, often usurping an earlier born brother and sometimes creating conflict with the father as well. Mother and God are co-conspirators, and the father and sons ultimately follow the woman's directives in propelling the story forward. As we have also seen, these stories disrupt male potency and the rule of male authority. Ruth and Naomi secure their baby, however, not by a prayer and conspiracy with God but by reverting to a different biblical paradigm, that of the seductress.

Ruth and Naomi, two women in a cooperative relationship, begin with the need of Sarah, Rebecca, and Rachel, Hannah, and Samson's anonymous mother, but because they are outside of the family model (the men are all dead), they take matters into their own hands, as in the examples of Tamar, Delilah, Jael, Esther, and Judith, who acquire political power through the other stratagem of biblical heroines: a bed trick. As types, both the barren mother and the seductress disempower the men in their stories: the former by a paramount maternal alliance with God, and the latter by asserting (sometimes fatal) authority sexually. In this text, by contrast, the women succeed without engaging in a gender battle. The law, which demands selflessness and has a homogenizing effect, is the disarming victor.

The foreigner Ruth becomes a gleaner in the fields and finds kindness from a man who turns out to be a distant kinsman, Boaz. Insofar as Naomi particularly indicated that she cannot provide a husband for her daughters-in-law, it seems odd that Naomi had not mentioned Boaz earlier as a possible "redeeming kinsman." The text implies that this possibility is so far-fetched, such a slender thread, that Naomi dared not hope for, no less mention, such an outcome. After all, the law of Levirate marriage through which Boaz could claim Ruth and further her dead husband's name and estate is a law honored chiefly in the breach; beginning with Onan, who preferred to spill his seed rather than impregnate Tamar, his brother's widow, this is a law men prefer to disobey. Yet, Boaz observes the rule to leave the corners of his field for the poor to glean, and his kindness to Ruth allows Naomi to put some faith in the possibility that he may be a willing redeemer after all.

When Boaz approaches Ruth in the field, the reader recognizes a familiar type scene with a gender reversal. Like Rebecca at the well, Boaz, approaching Ruth in a show of generosity and kindness, reads as a betrothal scene. Although Rebecca had asked Eliezer, Isaac's proxy, if she might water his thirsty camels, here the man tells the woman to "stay close to my girls," apparently to avert the implicit danger that a foreign woman risks being raped. Ironically, in a now familiar sexual reversal, it is Boaz who will be approached that night, by Ruth. Boaz gives Ruth an extra measure of grain (a betrothal gift?), and seeing it, Naomi thanks God: "Blessed be he of the Lord who has not failed in his obligation, his kindness to the living and the dead" (Ruth 2:20). This story is about divine fulfillment through human agency of our obligations to the dead.

At the center of the book of Ruth we find Naomi instructing her daughter-in-law in the intricacies of seduction. She washes and beautifies her. Keep hidden, she tells Ruth, but at nightfall take note of where Boaz lies down and when it is dark, go to him, uncover his feet, and he will tell you what to do. Surely these feet are a biblical euphemism, not unlike King Ahasuerus's "royal scepter." Naomi's instructions to Ruth function within a number of noble biblical traditions. Naomi is like Mordechai, who has his niece Esther undergo months of beauty treatments in order to compete against high odds for marriage to King Ahasuerus. Esther is also told to keep herself hidden, not to reveal her identity as a Jew, and at the critical moment, Mordechai advises her that she can choose to save the Jews or someone else will have to do it in her stead. When the situation is most dire, Esther risks her life by going to the king unbidden, touching his royal scepter, finding favor in his sight, and ultimately saving the Jews of Shushan.

Similarly, Ruth is a life-saving agent, a proxy for Naomi, the people to whom she has joined her fate, and humanity. She does as she is told, inviting Boaz to cover her with his blanket because he is a redeeming kinsman. The invited gesture, backed by the explanation, suggests another legal procedure, an informal, but legitimate, marriage. Although Boaz professes to be both flattered and grateful, instead of consummating this marriage, Boaz informs Ruth that there is a redeeming kinsman even closer than himself who must legally be allowed a first opportunity to redeem. In the field, in the night, a younger woman ready and willing, Boaz—who, like Joseph, declines to sin—answers Ruth's legal allusion with his own scrupulous appeal to law. Boaz is rightly confident, however, that this kinsman will yield his rights.

When Boaz mentions a closer redeeming kinsman, the reader, in Ruth's position, is surprised. Not only is there one kinsman, but there are two. There are two so that one, in the manner of Orpah, can decline to meet his obligations to Naomi's family. Had Boaz made the choice that the closer kinsman will make, once more: no Obed, no Jesse, no David . . . no Davidic line to the Messiah. Once more, the fate of the world is shown to hang on the free choice of a single individual.

Like Boaz's ancestor Tamar, Ruth lays claim to seed on her dead husband's behalf. As we have seen, when Judah hesitates to give Tamar his remaining son in marriage as was her legal due, Tamar disguises herself as a prostitute, seduces the recently widowed Judah, validates her decision in a legal fashion, and has twin boys, one of whom is ancestor to Boaz. This law of redemption—a version of Levirate marriage—inverts the scenario of self-promoting biblical brothers who compete to inherit the birthright and the covenant. This law requires altruism, perpetuating another man's name and estate, through his wife and your good offices. Onan prefers onanism; and Judah is tricked to correct his recalcitrance.

The final chapter of the book of Ruth begins with Boaz convening a court of ten elders at the town gate. When the closer kinsman passes by, he is invited to acquire the property of Elimelech, which he is pleased to do. Only at this point does Boaz add that the acquisition of the property comes with Ruth, a surviving spouse. Although the nameless kinsman appeared to like the will, he does not like the codicil, and stating that he cannot impair his own estate, he retreats from his agreement, and before the assembled witnesses surrenders his right to Boaz. However much the kinsman's choice affected his prosperity in his lifetime, his name is unrecorded, while Boaz achieves permanence in biblical lore, perhaps making a point to the reader about the importance of a long view.

The long view is immediately reinforced by a textual detail. When the legal ritual is formalized with one man handing a sandal to the other, the narrator explains: "as was done in those times." As the story draws toward closure, the reader is thereby reminded that these events belong to "once upon a time." The phrase pulls us into a later present, underscoring that from the story's own point of view, all of this happened long ago, a story of time was when. From that vantage point, the book of Ruth can be read as the ups and downs in the history of a law of selflessness, with the moral that long-term benefit derives from investment beyond the self. From Judah—who gives us Judaism—to Ruth—grandmother of David—the promise of messianic redemption is guaranteed by honoring an antique requirement to perpetuate the names of the dead.

The chorus of the book of Ruth reacts to the birth of Ruth's baby—given to Naomi—with a blessing for Naomi: "The Lord make the woman that is come into thine house like Rachel and like Leah, which two did build the House of Israel" (Ruth 4:11). As Ilana Pardes has eloquently argued, the book of Ruth is an "idyllic reinterpretation of the history of the founding mothers of Israel," a rereading of the story of Leah and Rachel.[4] The rivalry between the sisters in Genesis is here seen from the distance of history and with a wide angle lens: in life (or rather, in the present tense of their stories) these sisters competed for Jacob's love and for sons. The future honors them both in the same breath, however, as the mothers of the House of Israel, who together, as one, began the great family that Naomi is blessed, through Ruth, to extend.

The business of birthing heroes and advancing the estate of the Hebrews, full of contention in the Hebrew Bible, happens harmoniously in the book of Ruth. Barren mothers of the Hebrew Bible are typically desperate and controlling. The biblical seductress typically ensnares a powerful man and saves her people through her commanding authority in bed. As threatening as she is convincingly beautiful, she charms men out of all reason. As we have seen, their modern descendants are the stereotypical Jewish mother and the JAP, who seem to have little in common; the former is all self-denial, the latter all self-interest. But the one does grow up to become the other; both manipulate men, and both are represented as having unreasonable power in domestic space. In these stories, ruthlessness is a response to scarcity, and competition and gender envy are represented as conditions of family and social life.

Naomi and Ruth, however, transcend the barren mother and seductress patterns. These trajectories meet in Ruth, where the text offers a quieter, richer version of human possibility. Not confined to the tent, moving in a wider world, Naomi and Ruth struggle simply to live and evidence simple courage. They observe, and fall into the company of others who observe, the laws of gleaning and kinship and are the redemptive heirs to the last matriarchs, Rachel and Leah. Rachel and Leah, rivals in the Bible, with the distance of time, are represented as a unit in Ruth, and as friends in Midrash and later literature. As a Moabite, the exemplary foreigner, Ruth also recuperates Hagar (whose name means "the stranger"). Whereas Hagar declined surrogacy and taunted her mistress Sarah, such that her son Ishmael fathers a different nation, Ruth (the Moabite) gives her baby to Naomi at the story's end. In the book of Ruth are Sarah and Hagar, and Leah and Rachel—without rivalry—and Tamar, Yael, Judith, and Esther without death threats or deception.

STORY, MEMORY, AND THE ART OF MISREADING

Marge Piercy begins her poem, "The Book of Ruth and Naomi," with the observation that "When you pick up the Tanakh and read / the Book of

Ruth, it is a shock / how little it resembles memory. / It's concerned with inheritance/ lands, men's names." Accounting for the gap between story and memory, the poet suggests that we misremember this biblical book as the story of Ruth's friendship with Naomi because every woman "dreams / a double, heart's twin, a sister / of the mind in whose ear she can whisper." She concludes her poem by situating the book of Ruth in the holiday when Jews liturgically evoke these characters: "At the season of the first fruits we recall / these travellers / co-conspirators, scavengers, . . . whose friendship was stronger than fear, / stronger than hunger / who walked together / the road of shards, hands joined."[5]

Piercy laments that the story is not the story of women's friendship as she remembers it, but, rather, is a story of men's laws. Having acknowledged this mistake, the poet does her part to romanticize the relationship between Ruth and Naomi and perpetuate the very misreading that she identified. She indicates that women need this biblical book to be about Ruth and Naomi and adapts the title of the biblical book accordingly, calling her poem "The Book of Ruth and Naomi" and waxing eloquent about women's fantasy of another woman who can be her "heart's twin." Piercy reasons that women have kept this story dear for the rare pleasure of reading about a woman who put another woman first. By the time the reader comes to the poem's end, the book of Ruth is reconstituted as a story of women's love and friendship. The poem conspires with the co-conspirators and the reader to reinstate the misreading.

Using a similar reading strategy, Rebecca Alpert observes that Jewish lesbians choose to use language from the book of Ruth ceremonially and argues that the book of Ruth should be read, using techniques of Midrash, as a lesbian text. Alpert concludes, "[r]eading Ruth this way should be considered an obligation to our nameless ancestors, to give them, too, an opportunity to speak."[6] Foundation stories are asked, in every generation, to supply role models for contemporary identities. So it is that the book of Ruth is remembered as a love story for women even as, as Piercy recognizes, it is a book about men's laws, names, and inheritances.

Rather, sex and gender in Ruth are configured outside of familiar social hierarchies: women's bodies in this story represent both the whole body politic and the (female) land; the movement from barrenness (Naomi) to fecundity (her double, Ruth) occurs on at least three levels: first, on the personal level of the characters in the story in the conception of the significant heir; second, on the agricultural level, as a rich harvest ends the famine; and third, on a national, or even universal level, as the story augers a future of peace. The mere obedience to men's laws as represented in Ruth has a revolutionary effect because the consequences transcend the divisions of gender, time, and place.

These different planes of meaning are mirrored in the religious rationales for the festival on which the book of Ruth is read, the liturgical context in which Piercy situates her poem: "At the season of first fruits we recall these travelers." The book of Ruth is read during the holiday of Shavuot, which is the harvest festival or the season of first fruits. A pastoral romance set in the fields is seasonally appropriate. As is typical of Jewish festivals, however, the holiday's meaning is overdetermined, and superimposed on the agricultural celebration is a specifically Jewish religious commemoration, in this case, the celebration of the people-defining moment of receiving Torah, the Law, on Mount Sinai. The festival, like the book of Ruth, is at the nexus of land and law.

Shavuot, when Ruth is read, honors the climactic moment on the people's journey home and the culmination of a season that begins with Passover, which celebrates the liberation from slavery. Understood in terms of developmental psychology, as we have seen, the liberation is a birthing, through the narrow straits ("*mi'tzraim*") and the parted Red Sea waters. The Israelites then enter adolescence, the years in the desert, when, like babies, the children of Israel receive manna just for the asking. Finally, the onset of maturity is marked by the receiving of the Law, a sign of adulthood and readiness for adult responsibility, celebrated at Shavuot with the reading of Ruth.

These two mythic moments, with accompanying narratives, the stories of Exodus and Ruth, are not discrete events but are ritually associated in the annual cycle of Jewish observances. During this single long season of forty-nine days, seven weeks of seven days, between Passover and Shavuot, it is customary to count a measure or "*omer*" of barley. As if marching toward Sinai, each day, beginning at Passover, one counts the *omer* until Shavuot and Sinai are reached. One counts the days (as the psalmist writes: "*limnot yameynu*") to make them count. Counting one's days in a measure of barley reinforces yet another theme of the book of Ruth, a rabbinic dictum: "No flour; no Torah" (*ayn kemach; ayn Torah*). To get from birth to maturity requires sustenance; to live a religiously productive life, one must have food and law; or, for Ruth to conceive the grandfather of David, Boaz must provide the poor with barley. These multiple levels of meaning sustain an identification among the land, the law, and the bodies of women, with fertility of every sort the consequence of undiscriminating generosity.

Finally, the timeless quality of Ruth—a story about long ago with implications for the far future—is also mirrored in the Jewish concept of the receiving of the Torah as an event outside of time. In the Jewish imagination, receiving the Law at Sinai is not a one-time event, but occurs in perpetuity. All Jews from all times were present, and when the part of the Torah that reports receiving the Law at Sinai is read aloud in synagogues, everyone rises, dramatically enacting the return to Sinai. In this philosophic spirit, in every generation, the work of reading the Bible is the work of recovering the hidden meanings that were heard at Sinai and have been waiting for this historical moment to be discovered. From a cosmic perspective, and from a psychoanalytic perspective, time is not linear; the future changes the past. Creation is ever revisited. Within this framework, the Jewish messianic vision is similarly timeless, one of timeless peace.

INTIMATIONS OF IMMORTALITY

The story in the book of Ruth stretches far into the past before and the future beyond these episodes in the lives of a widow and her daughter-in-law. This little romance ends with Ruth and a newborn baby. Readers might freeze the frame there. But the genealogical epilogue actually invites us to glimpse this newborn as a grandfather, the grandfather of King David. Just a shape on his grandmother's lap, we will learn nothing about this baby's later life except that he has a bright genetic future. When I read the ending of the book of Ruth, I want to jump into the story and tell the mother and grand-mother the secret importance of their baby in much the same way as there are moments when I long for my own dead to be able to take pride in their future by seeing my children now. The story's characterization of faithful living, however, requires the presumption of mysterious future fulfillment.

In his beautiful poem "Among School Children," William Butler Yeats confronts the exquisitely poignant mystery of the body's relationship to itself and to others over time. The poet sees himself, "an aged public man" of sixty, through the eyes of school children, a scarecrow, and suddenly, by looking at a child, he flips the hourglass and wonders about the likeness of a beloved as she might have been, long ago, when she was a child. Thinking then of the fantasies of worshipful mothers, he asks: "What youthful mother, a shape upon her lap / Honey of generation had betrayed / . . . Would think her Son, did she but see that shape / With sixty or more winters on its head, / A compensation for the pang of his birth, / Or the uncertainty of his setting forth?"

Naomi and Ruth's baby defines the shape—the amorphous baby shape—that guarantees compensation for the pangs of birth and the many uncertainties of setting forth. Like Job, who lost one family and gained another, Naomi cannot know for certain, except as an act of faith (though the reader is given a genealogical reassurance), that the "shape upon her lap" will answer for the immense losses of her life. Yet, all of life is compromised by loss, and so Ruth begins with the most important deaths already accomplished: husband and sons are dead; home is elsewhere, and the future is cut off from the past.

Naomi's story begins with an undisclosed prehistory. The text alludes to a full, earlier life, from the hunger that led to the decision to leave home to the wedding ceremonies that bridged cultures. From the unrecorded laughter and arguments to the details of the deaths themselves, the characters of the dead men are left to our imagination, part of the plot's deep background. The book of Ruth tells a story of recovery without attempting to capture what was lost, and it is significant that Ruth's first husband is memorialized in the child she has by another man. The text demands imaginative identification with this ancestry: Perhaps the dead man remains present too in some trick of communicating tenderness that Ruth passed on through her son in a continuous chain until today. This is a text that reminds us that each of us carries genetic material in our bodies that is as old as life on the planet. How exactly the future will manage to contain the past is ultimately mysterious.

What is certain is that the future will contain (and from a Jewish view, will redeem) the past, no matter how deeply that past seems to retreat. Naomi and Ruth left behind the remains of husbands and children in order to start over, and what they carried of these men in their hearts and bodies the text declines to say. The conspiracy between the narrator and reader of Ruth is that we know what they never knew, which is that their moving on in life carried the promise of blessing for everyone. The book of Ruth triumphs over death by intimating at the widest possible perspective on life. One honors the dead by living with the convictions that one's life is infinitely promising, no matter how grim things may seem, and the promise of the future, partly owed to the dead, is knowable only as a hint, an intimation of immortality.

There is a long timeline here—a family tree with ancient roots in Bethlehem that extend through David and stretch on to eternity—and someone placed a magnifying glass on a single tiny dot on the line, a little detour in and out of Moab, in which two women who survived great personal losses befriended each other and found a way to move on, coincidentally redeeming humanity through their promising new baby. Thought of in this way, we might just as well move the magnifying glass to any other place on the line and find ourselves in another story on the way to redemption with different characters on different adventures, whose lives share the simple facts of birth and death.

CLOSURE AND CATEGORICAL IMPERATIVES

Whether we subscribe to the myth of science or of biblical narrative, each Adam, each earthling, is unified with the earth from which it came, blending with the matter of all humanity. In Jewish mystical thought, soul matter is similarly blended in a unifying cosmic cauldron from which new souls will be eternally drawn. The boundaries so carefully adhered to in life count for little in death.

God creates the world by separating this from that, and the chaos of *"tohu-vavohu"* is organized as night is separated from day and water is separated from land. The world as we know it emerges from the swirl. Adam and Eve create taxonomies of their own that humanity has been adapting ever since. How humanity has classified itself over time—ethnically, religiously, sexually, politically, geographically—is core to our reality, governing our experience of self and of others. Wars are fought over matters of identity; health, life, and death depend on them.

The main premise of this book, however, is that these all-important categories are arbitrary and not inevitable. *Tohu vavohu*—the chaos that precedes creation or culture—is what Sigmund Freud characterized as the infant's "polymorphous perversity." Before culture, still undirected, a person is capable of taking pleasure from many sources in many ways. Civilizing directs libidinal energies according to the models that civilization has endorsed. No sooner do Adam and Eve take an initiative of disobedience than they are exiled from home, weapon-toting angels guarding the borders of their birthplace. In this book, I have argued that biblical foundation stories record stories of exile simultaneously from the self and from home. Each story is fraught with anxiety and insecurity about identity, expressed through contradiction and category confusion: patriarchs masquerade as men; mothers are infertile, fathers lack authority; sexual women lack desire; all power is tenuous; all love is uncertain.

Scripture's first stories begin the process of inscribing Jewish sexual identities. The book of Ruth reiterates and repudiates these patterns of representation. Enemies are beloved; familial roles are arbitrary; rivalry is absent. All that matters is elemental fertility: bread and babies. Glimpsing the world from God's perspective, Eden re-created in a barley field, we can return to Sinai, where Law is still given and received, without question and with imperfect understanding. Outside of time and space, between once-upon-a-time, where stories invent possible worlds, and the peace at the end of time is the narrow bridge of history. It is a dangerous walk of limitless possibility.

Notes

INTRODUCTION

1. I studied what was called "humanities" with Allen Grossman at Brandeis University in the 1970s, and I have found these ideas continuously useful as a reader, though I cannot know the extent to which I have refashioned the lessons from my own critical beginnings.

2. Classic expositions on the significance of beginnings and endings in literary texts include: Edward W. Said, *Beginnings: Intention and Method* and Barbara Herrnstein Smith, *Poetic Closure: A Study of How Poems End.* Stéphane Mallarmé, as Julia Epstein reminds me, famously idealized the blank page, noting the power of writing to shrink potential.

3. Daniel Boyarin's readings of rabbinic Judaism and its construction of masculinity have been particularly influential, especially, *Unheroic Conduct: The Rise of Heterosexuality and the Invention of the Jewish Man* and *Carnal Israel: Reading Sex in Talmud.* Early explorations of the concept of Jewish masculinity include Howard Eilberg-Schwartz, *God's Phallus: And Other Problems for Men and Monotheism* and Harry Brod's early edited collection, *A Mensch Among Men: Explorations in Jewish Masculinity.*

4. Sander Gilman has written extensively on the Jewish body. His books include: *The Jew's Body* and *Jewish Frontiers: Essays on Bodies, Histories, and Identities.*

5. *Lilith* 20, No. 1, Spring 1995.

6. Karen Brodkin, *How Jews Became White Folks and What that Says about Race in America.*

7. Roland Barthes (notably in *S/Z*) and Tzvetan Todorov are among the narratologists whose work can construe humanity as a product of language, built by grammar.

8. This is the thesis of Judith Butler's *Bodies that Matter: On the Discursive Limits of Sex*. Butler's demonstrations that human bodies, sex, and sexuality are discursive formations have been the most radical and influential contribution to contemporary gender and queer theory, and I approach biblical narrative from this perspective.

9. In "Imitation and Gender Insubordination," Judith Butler argues that the terms "man" and "woman" have no "ontological status" but are, rather, "theatrical effects" or "consolidated phantasms." In Abelove, Barale, and Halperin, eds., *The Lesbian and Gay Studies Reader*, p. 313.

10. Butler, *Gender Trouble*, pp. 148–49.

CHAPTER 1

1. Anne Lapidus Lerner, in *Eternally Eve: Images of Eve in the Hebrew Bible, Midrash, and Contemporary Hebrew Poetry*, finds that to this day, Eve is everywhere. She opens her discussion: "Eve seems ubiquitous in contemporary American popular culture. She is employed to market a diverse list of products, from bathroom fixtures and fruit juices to sex toys, Colombian coffee, and hand creams—an indication of the extent to which received notions about Eve have become devalued, common coin," p. 1.

2. I deliberately use "sexual" rather than "gender" to describe "identities and roles" because these stories are about the birth of human sexuality and demonstrate that "gender" is so inseparable from "sex" as to be virtually meaningless. (For the different views on when Eve, and through her woman, becomes characterized as evil, see note 12 in this chapter.)

3. Rabbinic commentary on the command (or blessing) to multiply, beautifully synthesized by Avivah Gottlieb Zornberg in *Genesis: The Beginning of Desire*, recognizes the base, animal quality of human propagation as standing against those higher purposes that analogize humanity to a nonprocreating One God. Zornberg, borrowing imagery from Franz Kafka, illuminates a philosophic tension between the horizontal and vertical planes of human life, seeing humanity chained, as it were, simultaneously to earth and heaven. For my study, what is important is that the resistance felt by writing men, who aspire otherwise, nevertheless accept the characterization of people as first and foremost biological propagators of the species.

4. Anne Fausto-Sterling, *Myths of Gender* and *Sexing the Body: Gender Politics and the Construction of Sexuality*. See also Julia Epstein, "Either/Or, Neither/Both: Sexual Ambiguity and the Ideology of Gender."

5. Northrop Frye has called the Bible (and titled his book) *The Great Code* by which we decipher the Western tradition. William Blake referred to the Old and New Testaments as "the Great Code of Art" in his etching "The Laocoon."

6. Michel Foucault, in *The Order of Things*, demonstrates how discursive classification systems—such as zoological charts—change over time and suggests an evolving experience of the material world. Basic to their analyses of language and meaning, Ferdinand de Saussure and Charles Sanders Peirce, founding figures

in the fields of semiology, semiotics, and structural linguistics, recognize the arbitrary relationship between words and what they name and between linguistic signifiers and what they signify ("signifieds").

7. Feminist Bible critics, most notably, Mieke Bal, following the groundbreaking analyses of Phyllis Trible, convincingly argue that Adam is not first of all male, but only becomes male after the separation of (from?) Eve. Logically, there can only be male and female after woman is formed, and the text allows, in multiple ways, for the reading of an androgynous or hermaphroditic earthling who is split into two sexes. For Bal, the history of misogynistic interpretation of this story has influenced us into the retrospective fallacy. Bal further shows that we impose a characterization on Eve only in light of what we later come to "know" about her. I read differently. Since I am convinced that we can only know the text in light of what we know, the biblical Adam, like God, is necessarily male, already preinscribed into the two-sexed world for which the story accounts.

8. For a history of this idea, see Arthur O. Lovejoy, *The Great Chain of Being: A Study of the History of an Idea.*

9. I recall learning a version of this lesson from Philip Fisher's lectures on Charlotte Brontë's *Jane Eyre*, which begins with the orphaned heroine's rebellion, and therefore, the first day of her self. Jane has been called "ungrateful" by the cruel aunt who is Jane's self-identified benefactress, and Jane rejects these labels and replaces them with her own. Jane calls Aunt Reed "a tyrant," and names her aunt out of books, calling her, among other things, "Caligula." Seizing the power to name, Jane re-creates her self and her aunt. "Terrorist" or "freedom-fighter," "occupier" or "peacekeeper" exemplify how self-definition names everyone in the system.

10. From *Paradise Lost* Book 4:

> "him there they found
> Squat like a Toad, *close at the* eare of Eve;
> Assaying by his Devilish art to reach
> The Organs of her Fancie, and with them forge
> Illusions as he list, Phantasms and Dreams,
> Or if, inspiring venom, he might taint
> Th' *animal spirits* that from pure blood arise" (ll. 799–805).

11. According to the Zohar, a thirteenth-century Kabbalist commentary on the Bible: "After the serpent mounted Eve and injected filth into her, she gave birth to Cain" (Zohar 3:76b–77a).

12. Gale A. Yee writes: "In Western tradition, the symbolization of woman as evil is usually traced back to the person of Eve. In the words of the ancient sage Sirach, 'From a woman sin had its beginning, and because of her we all die' (Sir. 25:24)." *Poor Banished Children of Eve: Woman as Evil in the Hebrew Bible*, p. 59. Yee's materialist study accounts for women as evil in the Bible by analyzing women's place in forces of race, class, and ethnicity at the time of the text's production. Earlier studies, such as John A. Phillip's *Eve: The History of an Idea* or Nechama Aschkenasy, *Eve's Journey: Feminine Images in Hebraic Literary Tradition*, have traced the history of literary representation and interpretations of Eve as the source of

evil. For a rich account of a history of readings of Eve, see Anne Lapidus Lerner, *Eternally Eve*. Phyllis Trible, from a theological perspective, Carol Meyers, from an anthropological perspective, Mieke Bal, from a literary perspective all find the original story kinder to women than the interpretations of women's evil that followed from it, and feminist poets and storytellers, including, notably, Judith Plaskow and Enid Dame, have worked to recuperate womanhood by reimagining woman's story, effectively extending and countering the work of early midrashists with interpretive fantasies of their own.

13. See Freud's analysis in "The Head of the Medusa," in which he interprets the Medusa's hair of writhing snakes as a multiplication of the phallus. Seeing the terrifying woman and her beauty makes the man stiffen, in the myth, and for Freud, the stiffening in fear actually has a reassuring effect since stiffening reminds him of his own superior, penetrative, relatively powerful sexuality. Freud codifies both the mortal fear of female sexuality and man's conviction of control over it.

14. Jan Goldman reminds me that psychoanalytically, young boys may experience erections as "magic" and outside of their control.

15. Umberto Eco invents a parable about the development of language in the Garden of Eden. In "On the Possibility of Generating Aesthetic Messages in Edenic Language," the third chapter of *The Role of the Reader: Explorations in the Semiotics of Texts*, Eco imagines complexity being introduced into the simple distinctions the first creatures made when something that is apparently edible and good is characterized as forbidden food, generating the first metaphor or paradox: a phrase applied to the fruit that means edible/inedible. The critique of linguistic binaries is, by now, familiar. Words can be made to define their own opposites, and poetry may indeed be defined as the articulation of paradox. I want to extend that point to the first stories of two sexes, showing that here too—and why not?—two will not do.

16. The Exodus myth is susceptible to an analogous psychological reading: The people of Israel are birthed out of the "narrow straits" of Egypt (the Hebrew for Egypt, "*mitzraim*," may be translated as "from narrow straits") through parted waters (the Red Sea), in an event fraught with danger and miracle. In the desert, the infant people are fed manna, which comes effortlessly and which Midrash describes as having varied flavor (like mother's milk). Desert wandering, the in-between years—later invented as adolescence—leads to Sinai, where the mature people receive the gift and responsibility of the Law. A repeated pattern follows: transgression, punishment, repentance, and forgiveness, with God ever-judgmental, protective, and demanding. Ilana Pardes reads Exodus as a national biography in her *The Biography of Ancient Israel: National Narratives in the Bible*.

17. See Michelangelo's "Temptation and Fall" from the Sistine Chapel ceiling and John Collier's "Lilith" 1887, at the Atkinson Gallery, Southport, England, reproduced here, page 23 and page 28.

18. In the seventeenth-century Kabbalistic commentary, *Emek HaMelekh* by Rabbi Naftali Hertz (a.k.a., Bacharach), Lilith is identified with the serpent, as the woman of harlotry who mounts Eve (as serpent), leaving her impure when she has relations with Adam; the sin of this impurity permits Lilith to seduce Adam, to whom she bears demons (23c-d). This fantasy interchanges the sexes of the characters without compunction.

19. See for example, Mary Gendler, "The Restoration of Vashti, in *The Jewish Woman*, Elizabeth Koltun, ed., pp. 241–45; Aviva Cantor, "The Lilith Question," in *On Being a Jewish Feminist*, Susannah Heschel, ed., pp. 40–50, for the terms of the original debate about reclaiming heroines to which the tradition had been hostile. Especially influential was Judith Plaskow's 1972 Midrash (variously titled: "Epilogue: The Coming of Lilith" and "Applesource") reprinted as "The Coming of Lilith: Toward a Feminist Theology," in the comprehensive Lilith collection edited by Enid Dame, Lilly Rivlin, and Henny Wenkart, *Which Lilith: Feminist Writers Re-create the World's First Woman*; Alicia Ostriker has written "The Lilith Poems," *Women's Review of Books* 8, No. 12 (September 1991); and my favorite collection is Enid Dame's Chapbook, *Lilith and Her Demons*.

20. Yiskah Rosenfeld's feminist argument to "reclaim Eve as we have reclaimed Lilith" hints at feminist complicity in perpetuating the competition between female types. "You Take Lilith, I'll Take Eve: A Closer Look at the World's Second Feminist," in *Yentl's Revenge: The Next Wave of Jewish Feminism*, Danya Ruttenberg, ed., pp. 131–53.

21. Ginzberg, *The Legends of the Jews*, p. 66. Ginzberg cites Genesis Rabbah.

CHAPTER 2

1. Freud famously posed the unanswerable question, "*Was will das Weib?*" [What does a woman want?]. In a letter to Marie Bonaparte in 1925, he wrote: "The great question, which has never been answered, and which I have yet not been able to answer, despite my thirty years of research into the feminine soul, is 'What does a woman want?'" Jones, *Sigmund Freud: Life and Work*, Vol. 2, Part 3, chapter 16, p. 468.

2. The biblical matriarchs' stories contain details that transfer to later stereotypes of the "Jewish Mother." Again, my view is that there is nothing "natural" to motherhood that is available in biblical myths, but instead, these early articulations of cultural patterns later became normative. See Elisabeth Badinter, *Mother Love: Myth and Reality: Motherhood in Modern History*. Badinter is among historians of the family who describe historical periods of widespread maternal neglect and indifference to build a case that maternal instinct does not exist, and mother love is a cultural construct.

3. Analyses of gender and Judaism have examined Jewish law and ritual practice, the characterization of the sexes and of sex in the textual tradition from biblical narrative through the documents of rabbinism and contemporary culture, and the history of women's and men's roles, privileges, and burdens. Judith Plaskow's *Standing Again at Sinai* is exemplary in many regards and in this regard as well; as its subtitle indicates, it approaches "Judaism from a Feminist Perspective," and in doing so, it uses the categories of Jewish theology: in this instance, Torah, Israel, and God. Rachel Adler, in *Engendering Judaism*, picks up the challenge of constructing an inclusive Jewish feminist theology with consequences for Jewish practice. Adler, responding to an earlier exploration of the ideas in this chapter (in Rudavsky's *Gender and Judaism*), resists my reading of woman as "mysterious and

indefinable" because she is concerned that attention to the categories of fluids and voices risks "constructing one more world dichotomized by gender" (p. xii). (Like me, Adler does, however, attend to the meanings of Sarah's laughter.) I want to clarify here that I also resist gender dichotomies. Instead, I attempt to show that biblical heroines defy social definitions of gender.

4. Robert Alter in *The Art of Biblical Narrative* discusses the role of convention and type-scenes in making meaning in the Bible.

5. Esther Fuchs, among other feminist readers, correctly understands the barren mother's function within the narrative as an agent of patriarchal interests. By attending less to the linear narrative and its motivating interests and instead looking, perversely, at textual anomalies, I mean to suggest that these heroines nevertheless overflow the boundaries established for them. Because gender distinctions are themselves incoherent, the text fails to keep the limits on sex roles that it works so hard to inscribe. Mothers are colored outside the lines. Esther Fuchs, *Sexual Politics in the Biblical Narrative: Reading the Hebrew Bible as a Woman*, chapter 3, "The Biblical Mother: The Annunciation and Temptation Type Scenes," pp. 43 ff. See also Cheryl Exum, "Mother in Israel: A Familiar Figure Reconsidered," in Letty M. Russell, ed., *Feminist Interpretations of the Bible*, pp. 73–85.

6. Paradoxically, the ordeal of bitter waters designed to appease the husband of a suspected adulterous woman (Numbers 5) can reinforce his inadequacy. If a jealous husband suspects his wife of infidelity, she swallows a muddy mixture and submits to the priest's curses. The guilty woman either dies or is visited with devastating barrenness. The innocent woman will be fertile. A man with a barren wife is either a "cuckold" or destined to be belatedly, the father of a hero.

7. See Sigmund Freud, "The Dissolution of the Oedipal Complex," pp. 321–22.

8. See Jacques Lacan. "Au-delà du 'principe de réalité'," pp. 73–92.

9. A passage in the Babylonian Talmud (Berachot 31a) identifies Hannah as the ideal practitioner of silent devotion. Rabbi Hamnunah asks how many lessons can be derived from Hannah's prayer. He concludes that the *amidah* (a central Jewish prayer) must be prayed with a full heart; clearly as indicated by moving lips; without a raised voice, and that one who is drunken may not recite the *amidah*. The full heart and moving lips that was unfamiliar and apparently drunken behavior to Eli became codified as a norm for religious prayerfulness at a later time in Jewish history. Samuel's birth and entry into temple service is celebrated with Hannah's beautiful poem, which (like the songs of Deborah and Miriam) is another discrete unit of biblical text ascribed to a heroine and described as poetry.

10. See Shaye Cohen, *Why Aren't Jewish Women Circumcised: Gender and Covenant in Judaism*. Especially relevant here is Cohen's tracing of the history of a homology between the blood of circumcision and menstrual blood in Jewish thought.

11. *Jewish American Literature: A Norton Anthology*, edited by Jules Chametzky et al., p. 323.

12. I. L Peretz's classic story of the long-suffering Jewish hero "Bontshe Shvayg" in *The I. L. Peretz Reader*, Ruth Wisse, ed. (New Haven: Yale University Press, 2002), pp. 146–52; I. B. Singer, "Gimpel the Fool," in *Jewish American Literature: A Norton Anthology*, pp. 614–23.

13. Carol L. Meyers, *Discovering Eve: Ancient Israelite Women in Context*; Peter Pitzele, *Our Fathers' Wells: A Personal Encounter with the Myths of Genesis*. I chose these among many possible writers about Bible stories as representing extremes on the spectrum: Meyers, exemplary archaeologist and anthropologist, who ventures to reconstruct whatever is possible of male and female roles in ancient Israel, and Pitzele, among many writers who see in biblical relationships models for our own families. All variety of scholarship on Genesis takes for granted the normativity of the family itself.

14. Women are selves divided: part watchers, part actors, part human (male), and part other (female). John Berger, in *Ways of Seeing*, explains that woman "comes to consider the *surveyor* and the *surveyed* within her as two constituent yet always distinct elements of her identity as a woman" (p. 46). Further: "The surveyor of woman in herself is male; the surveyed female" (p. 47).

15. See also Adler, *Engendering Judaism*, p. 106.

16. Rashi, quoting Genesis Rabbah, 58:1.

17. Babylonian Talmud, Megillah, 14a.

18. The *Oxford Study Bible* (1992) supports this reading in a footnote that indicates that "Sarai" means "mocker," explaining that when God changes Sarai's name to Sarah, it is a change in meaning from "mocker" to "princess." The standard dictionary, Brown, Driver, and Briggs's *Lexicon*, however, has no suggestion of mockery in any variant of Sarai or Sarah, only variants of "noblewoman."

19. Note that the biblical use of the verb "to play" is written with the letter "*tzadi*," as in "laugh," where the letter "*sin*" would be in the modern Hebrew word for "play" ("*misachek*," for the biblical, "*mitzachek*").

20. Ibn Ezra interprets this "playing" as just that: "child's play." The Midrash Rabbah (53.15) offers the interpretation of usurpation: Ishmael's play represents a threat to Isaac's inheritance. Rashi and Nahmanides interpret this playing as mockery; Rashi (and Nahmanides) also cite rabbinic authorities who interpret "playing" to mean idolatry and even murder; the interpretation of "playing" as "sexual play" is attributed by Nahmanides to Rabbi Akiva, a reading consistent with most other biblical usages of this verb.

21. In the apocryphal book of Judith, the same narrative effect is achieved when the heroine's motives and piety are distrusted by the guards as she sneaks out of the city, creating an obstacle that heightens the reader's appreciation for her bravery.

22. Accordingly, Isaac Schiff and Morty Schiff actually treat this story as a "first case" of anorexia, almost as if Hannah is other than a mythic, fictional character. See their "The Biblical Diagnostician and the Anorexic Bride." I want to thank Dr. Frances Batzer for drawing this essay to my attention.

23. I am reminded of literary critic Tony Tanner's answer to an early complaint about Jane Austen's *Pride and Prejudice* that it is a story in which not much happens except that "a gentleman changes his manners, and a lady changes her mind." Tanner observes that reversing one's opinion is a significantly rarer occurrence than one might imagine. Tanner, *Jane Austen*, p. 103.

24. Mikhail Bakhtin, *Rabelais and His World*, p. 94.

25. Kathleen Norris, "A Prayer to Eve," *Paris Review* No. 15 (summer 1990), 1990; Hélène Cixous, "The Laugh of the Medusa," in *New French Feminisms: An*

Anthology, edited by Elaine Marks and Isabelle de Courtivron; Carol P. Christ, *Laughter of Aphrodite: Reflections on the Journey to the Goddess* (San Francisco: Harper and Row, 1987), p. 6.

26. Hélène Cixous and Catherine Clément, *The Newly Born Woman*, pp. 32–33. For Aristotle, laughter—even more than language—distinguishes humanity from lower creatures, a central conceit of Umberto Eco's *Name of the Rose*. Recently, scientists have begun to identify evidence of laughter in animals, from mice to monkeys.

27. Mary Douglas, *Purity and Danger: An Analysis of Concepts of Pollution and Taboo*, quoted in Cixous and Clément, *The Newly Born Woman*, p. 33.

28. Cixous and Clément, *The Newly Born Woman*, pp. 32–33.

29. Cixous, "Laugh of Medusa," in *New French Feminisms*, pp. 245–64.

30. Chava Weissler, "*Mizvot* Built into the Body: *Tkhines* for *Niddah*, Pregnancy, and Childbirth," in Howard Eilberg-Schwartz, ed., *People of the Body: Jews and Judaism from an Embodied Perspective*, p. 101.

31. Nina Auerbach's study of the images of women in Victorian literature, *Women and the Demon*, exemplifies a type of study that celebrates the power of monstrous heroines in literature and the arts without exposing the extent to which these fantasies' expression of fear of unleashed female sexuality created restrictive social policies. By contrast, Carol Gilligan's *In a Different Voice: Psychological Theory and Women's Development*, which appreciates girls' undervalued "different" moral choices, has been subject to the critique of essentialism.

32. Diana Fuss, "Reading like a feminist"; Luce Irigaray, *Speculum of the Other Woman*.

33. Patti Lather, *Getting Smart: Feminist Research and Pedagogy With/in the Postmodern*, p. 27.

34. Denise Riley, *"Am I That Name?": Feminism and the Category of Women in History*, p. 114.

35. Riley, *"Am I That Name?,"* p. 108.

36. Lewis Hyde explains: "Trickster isn't a run-of-the-mill liar and thief. When he lies and steals, it isn't so much to get away with something or get rich as to disturb the established categories of truth and property and, by so doing, open the road to possible new worlds." In *Trickster Makes the World: Mischief, Myth, and Art*, p. 13.

37. As Bakhtin defines it, "during carnival time, life is subject only to its laws, that is, the laws of its own freedom," *Rabelais and His World*, p. 7.

CHAPTER 3

1. In his 1919 essay, "The Uncanny," Freud writes: "A study of dreams, phantasies and myths has taught us that anxiety about one's eyes, the fear of going blind, is often enough a substitute for the dread of being castrated. The self-blinding of the mythical criminal, Oedipus, was simply a mitigated form of the punishment of castration—the only punishment that was adequate for him by the *lex talionis*." "The uncanny" connects blindness with guilt and shame through the concept of "the hidden." Sigmund Freud, "The Uncanny," in *The Standard Edition of the Com-*

plete Psychological Works of Sigmund Freud, James Strachey, ed. and trans., vol. XVII (London: Hogarth, 1953), pp. 219–52.

2. Although passing is more usually associated with transgressing racial boundaries and the metaphor of "the closet" belongs most often to gay identity, "passing" and "closeted identity" have been imported to describe an occasionally and partially analogous Jewish relationship to dominant culture. In such stories, passing produces anxiety that requires containment, and so, these insider/outsider plots may share details of pathology and resistance. I acknowledge the limits to this kind of comparison. When Eve Kosofsky Sedgwick, in *Epistemology of the Closet,* sees in the story of Queen Esther an example of coming out of the closet, her objective is to underline not the similarities but rather the differences between the gay and the Jewish experience of coming out (pp. 67–90). I do not mean to press the analogy or elide the complexities within identities or of overlapping identities or crossed histories. On "colonial mimicry" see Bhabha, *The Location of Culture.*

3. Judith Butler, "Imitation and Gender Insubordination," in *The Lesbian and Gay Studies Reader,* Henry Abelove, Michele Aina Barale, David M. Halperin, eds., p. 313.

4. Erich Auerbach, *Mimesis: The Representation of Reality in Western Literature,* p. 12.

5. Revealing his own psychic life, Freud records that his father (Jakob!) was diminished in the eyes of his son because of his inability to stand up to demeaning anti-Semitism. To Sigmund, Jakob's inadequacy as "man" was evidenced when he passively tolerated anti-Semitic abuse and allowed himself to be driven off the sidewalk and into the street. Freud, "Material and Sources of Dreams," A. A. Brill, ed. and trans. (New York: Modern Library, 1938), p. 260. John Murray Cuddihy argues, in *The Ordeal of Civility: Freud, Marx, Lévi-Strauss and the Jewish Struggle with Modernity,* that Freud universalizes the Jewish experience of attempting to "pass" in European society.

6. I am grateful to David Richter for this point.

7. A successful resolution to the oedipal conflict involves the son's recognition that his mother "belongs" to his father. In the Jewish/homosexual Freudian narrative of dysfunction, the mother inappropriately chooses her son (oedipal victor).

8. I am indebted to Ilana Blumberg for this observation.

9. Avivah Gottlieb Zornberg makes explicit that this would be a kind of delayed posttraumatic response, and she observes that a like response occurred in Cambodian women who observed the horrors of massacre. *Genesis: The Beginning of Desire,* p. 157.

10. Ibn Ezra interprets this "playing" as just that: "child's play." The Midrash Rabbah (53:15) offers the interpretation of usurpation: Ishmael's play represents a threat to Isaac's inheritance. Rashi and Nahmanides interpret this playing as mockery; Rashi (and Nahmanides) also cite rabbinic authorities who interpret "playing" to mean idolatry and even murder; the interpretation of "playing" as "sexual play" is attributed by Nahmanides to Rabbi Akiva, a reading consistent with most other biblical usages of this verb.

11. See Zornberg, *Genesis,* pp. 172 ff.

12. See for example Roberta Davidson's essay on medieval romance (in Lefkovitz, *Textual Bodies,* pp. 59–74) and elaborations on the work of historians of the

body, Michel Foucault and Thomas Laqueur. The essays in Epstein and Straub, *Body Guards*, also addresses the history of the gendered body. The medieval view of a flexible embodied self resembles current ideas of the material body as performed.

13. Midrash Zuta to Song of Songs (1:15): "Esau was worthy to be called Jacob, and Jacob was worthy to be called Esau." Theologically, these commentaries emphasize that the doubled characters began life the same but made different choices.

14. Zornberg, *Genesis*, p. 171.

15. Discussions of gay Camp challenge precisely the Freudian idea that homosexuality is narcissistic sexuality by interrogating the idea that gender identity is based on essential or meaningful differences. Gregory W. Bredbeck, who confers on Oscar Wilde's "almost mythical status as the origin of modern gay Camp," analyzes Oscar Wilde's "Narcissus" and campiness as a critique of the Freudian equivalence of homosexuality and narcissism (in Meyer, *The Politics and Poetics of Camp*, p. 51). Further, in Meyer, Bredbeck explains: "Narcissus in the Wilde, then, seems to display the idea of identity as difference—as subject *to* difference(s) *and* the subject *of* difference(s)—and, in the process, to display the cultural narratives that seek to legislate what this difference should or should not be" (p. 69, emphasis in the original).

16. See Charles Taylor, *Sources of the Self: The Making of the Modern Identity*.

17. For a good example: Jane Austen's heroines in *Sense and Sensibility*.

18. Sibling research shows that within families, one child may be spoken of as, for example, "the quiet one" and her sibling, "the talkative one," whereas outside of the family, people are likely to group the children from one family together: "those quiet Smith children." See the discussion by Stephen P. Bank and Michael D. Kahn in *The Sibling Bond*, pp. 23–24, and the research that they cite about "making each child different" and "fusing the children."

19. Jay Geller, "(G)nos(e)ology: The Cultural Construction of the Other," in *People of the Body: Jews and Judaism from an Embodied Perspective*, Howard Eilberg-Schwartz, ed., pp. 243–82.

20. See John L. Beusterien, "Jewish Male Menstruation in Seventeenth-Century Spain," p. 447, emphasis mine.

21. John M. Efron, *Medicine and the German Jews: A History*, pp. 105, 143, and 142. Efron introduces his chapter on "The Jewish Body Degenerate?" with this context: "In the nineteenth century, the age of empire, robustness and virility were seen as the true hallmarks of national greatness. . . . Jews represented the antithesis of European nations. Their languages were perceived as either dead (Hebrew) or bastardized (Yiddish). . . . Jews were seen as rootless, homeless, and devoid of martial values and spirit" (p. 105). Efron shows how after the Enlightenment such diverse ideologies as anti-Semitism and Zionism, which agreed on Jewish "otherness," unwittingly conspired to produce the conviction of the sickly Jew, all evidence to the contrary notwithstanding.

22. Mitchell P. Hart, *Social Science and the Politics of Modern Jewish Identity*, p. 225. I am grateful to Guy Miron for this reference as well as for pointing me to John Efron's compelling work.

23. Meyer, *The Politics and Poetics of Camp*, pp. 1–3.

24. Quoted by Pellegrini in "Interarticulations: Gender, Race, and the Jewish Woman Question," in *Judaism Since Gender*, Miriam Peskowitz and Laura Levitt, eds., p. 50.

25. Meyer, p. 2.

26. Peter Stallybrass and Allon White analyze this effect in *The Politics and Poetics of Transgression*.

27. Homi Bhabha, *The Location of Culture*, p. 86.

28. Sander Gilman, *Jewish Self-Hatred: Anti-Semitism and the Hidden Language of the Jews.*

29. Butler, "Imitation and Gender Insubordination," in *The Lesbian and Gay Studies Reader*, p. 313.

30. Joan Riviere, "Womanliness as a Masquerade."

31. Among other places, the story appears in *Eicha Rabbati*, Salomon Buber, ed., p. 28.

32. Genesis Rabbah, p. 174.

33. *Europa Europa*, set in 1939, is about a German Jewish boy's assumed identities (MGM, 1991).

34. Cohen, in *Why Aren't Jewish Women Circumcised?*, discusses something of the history of the threat posed by circumcision. A question sometimes playfully asked about George Eliot's title character in *Daniel Deronda*, who learns late in the novel that he is Jewish, is "didn't he ever look down?"

35. I had a personal insight into this identity game when, years ago, waking my then five-year-old child for school, I playfully tickled her and asked, "Who is this little girl in bed?" She laughed sleepily and answered—mischievously—"Ronya," which is her elder sister's name. I found myself playing along: "Good morning, Ronya! Did you shrink in your sleep?" I later reflected: the game was played for no stakes. Perhaps Isaac too was simply indulging an envious little brother. The younger has an ongoing fantasy of usurpation easily expressed close to sleep, when defenses are low. And finally, I thought that my younger child, Samara, was saying: "your question pretending not to know me is silly; my answer about who I am has to be silly." More specifically, "If you pretend not to know me, I will pretend to be someone else."

36. Harry Brod, "Of Mice and Supermen: Images of Jewish Masculinity," in *Gender and Judaism*, Tamar Rudavsky, ed., pp. 279–93.

CHAPTER 4

1. See Gershen Kaufman, *The Psychology of Shame: Theory and Treatment of Shame-Based Syndromes*, p. 175.

2. The complexity of sororal attachments and rivalries is addressed in Barbara Mathias, *Between Sisters: Secret Rivals, Intimate Friends.*

3. Eve Kosofsky Sedgwick, *Between Men: English Literature and Male Homosocial Desire*, pp. 25–26.

4. Sedgwick also observes that the relation between the traffic-in-women and Julia Kristeva's hypothesis (described in *The Powers of Horror*) of "a primary fear

in men and women of the power of the maternal power of women" has yet to be analyzed (Sedgwick, *Between Men*, p. 18).

5. Rosa Felsenburg Kaplan, "Sisters," in *Sarah's Daughters Sing: A Sampler of Poems by Jewish Women*, Henny Wenkart, ed., pp. 18–22. This is one of several Rachel-Leah poems in this collection.

6. From the early chronicle, Seder Olam Rabbah, 2.

7. *Tanhuma, Midrasch*, Buber, ed., *Vayetze* 20; Babylonian Talmud, Baba Batra, 21a.

8. Genesis Rabbah, 70:19 (to Genesis 29:25).

9. Babylonian Talmud, Baba Batra, 23a.

10. Babylonia Talmud, Berachot, 60a.

11. Rashi, following Genesis Rabbah.

12. Thomas Mann, *Joseph and His Brothers*, H. T. Lowe-Porter, trans., p. 316.

13. Mann, *Joseph and His Brothers*, p. 323.

14. Mann, *Joseph and His Brothers*, p. 350.

15. Mann, *Joseph and His Brothers*, p. 351.

16. For example in Norman and Jeanne MacKenzie, *Dickens: A Life*, p. 132; Fred Kaplan, *Dickens: A Biography*, p. 159; John Foster, *The Life of Charles Dickens*. 2 vols.

17. MacKenzie and MacKenzie, *Dickens: A Life*, p. 245.

18. Kaplan, *Dickens: A Biography*, p. 159.

19. MacKenzie and MacKenzie, *Dickens: A Life*, pp. 305–6.

20. Fred Kaplan, "The Real Charles Dickens, or the Old Animosity Shop."

21. Peter Gay, *Freud: A Life for Our Time*, p. 40.

22. Ernest Jones, *The Life and Work of Sigmund Freud*, abridged by Lionel Trilling and Steven Marcus (New York: Basic Books, 1961), p. 103.

23. Gay, *Freud: A Life for Our Time*, pp. 58–60.

24. Gay, *Freud: A Life for Our Time*, p. 76.

25. Gay, *Freud: A Life for Our Time*, pp. 752–53.

26. Ralph Blumenthal, "Hotel Log Hints at Illicit Desire that Dr. Freud Didn't Repress."

27. Sigmund Freud, *The Basic Writings of Sigmund Freud*, A. A. Brill, trans. and ed. (New York: Modern Library, 1958), p. 817.

28. Vincent Canby, "Woody Allen Tops Himself—Again."

29. Sedgwick, *Between Men*, p. 27.

30. Janice Doane and Devon Hodges, *Nostalgia and Sexual Difference: The Resistance to Contemporary Feminism*, p. 76.

CHAPTER 5

1. The ultimate expression of the flamboyant Joseph may be his Elvis-style incarnation in the musical extravaganza, Andrew Lloyd Weber and Tim Rice's *Joseph and the Technicolor Dream Coat* (developed between 1968 and 1972).

2. Colonized and immigrant, in their ambivalent, aspirational, cultural imitations, expose the performativity of cultural and social power. Homi Bhabha, in

The Location of Culture, conceptualizes the way the colonized mimics the colonizer, an aspirational, and never complete, performance of power. Of immigrant assimilation and language acquisition, Bhabha writes: "the immigrant's desire to 'imitate' language produces one void in the articulation of the social space." He writes further of the "racist fantasy . . . which disavows the ambivalence of its own desire" (p. 166).

3. Cf. Lord Raglan, *The Hero: A Study in Tradition, Myth, and Drama*.

4. Midrash Rabbah to 37:3. H. Freedman and Maurice Simon, eds., *Midrash Rabbah*, vol. 2, *Genesis*.

5. *Jewish Antiquities* 2:9, p. 173, Midrash Rabbah to 39:6. H. St. J. Thackeray and P. Marcus, eds., *Josephus*, vol. 4 (Cambridge, MA: Loeb Classic Library, 1926–65), p. 173.

6. E. R. Goodenough, *An Introduction to Philo Judeus* (New Haven, CT: Yale University Press, 1940), p. 77.

7. H. Colson et al., eds., *Philo* (Cambridge, MA: Loeb Classical Library, 1949–61), index.

8. *Allegorical Interpretation* 3:237–42.

9. See Freedman and Simon, *The Midrash Rabbah*, footnote to 1:xii, p. 774.

10. Genesis Rabbah to 39:25.

11. Also recorded by Ginzberg, *The Legends of the Jews*, vol. 2, pp. 52 ff.

12. Lionello Spada's painting of Joseph and Potiphar's wife, reprinted on this book's cover, captures the feeling of these late characterizations of Joseph: He is young, beautiful, and overwhelmed. See also Cignani's painting on page 92.

13. Midrash Rabbah to 39:20.

14. Quotes from Midrash Rabbah to 39:10; Midrash Rabbah, vol. 2, p. 811.

15. My translations of the Koran are taken from Mohammed Marmaduke Pickthall, trans., *The Meaning of the Glorious Koran* (New York: New American Library, n.d.).

16. Genesis Midrash to 34:1.

17. Genesis Rabbah to 34:25.

18. Just as Satan, embodied in the snake, is so engaging as to arguably become the hero in Milton's *Paradise Lost*.

19. Boyarin, *Unheroic Conduct*; Harry Brod, ed., *A Mensch Among Men*; and Harry Brod and Michael Kaufman, eds., *Theorizing Masculinities*.

CHAPTER 6

1. E. H. Gombrich, *Art and Illusion: A Study in the Psychology of Pictorial Representation*, pp. 343–44.

2. Page duBois, "Sappho's Body in Pieces," in *Textual Bodies*, Lefkovitz, ed., pp. 19–33.

3. Ilana Pardes, *Countertraditions in the Bible: A Feminist Approach*, pp. 58-59.

4. Pardes, *Countertraditions in the Bible*, p. 4.

5. For a full discussion of the debate among scholars as to chronology, authorship, and the relationship between the so-called Song of Moses and Song of Miriam,

see *On Gendering Texts: Female and Male Voices in the Hebrew Bible,* by Athalya Brenner and Fokkelien Van Dijk-Hemmes, pp. 38–42. These authors clarify that what has come to be at stake in the attributions and relative dates of the poetry in Exodus 15 is the likelihood of the biblical redactors having "muted" and subordinated the leadership of women. These authors concur with the view of Martin Noth (1965) and Annemarie Ohler (1987) that Miriam's Song is "very old indeed" (p. 40, note 17).

6. Exodus Rabbah to Exodus 15:20.

7. In his classic formalistic study of the hero, Lord Raglan, his *The Hero,* observed that a threat at birth is a common feature of hero stories. This threat encourages the reader to imagine the possibility that the hero might not have been born (the problem of barren mothers) or might have died too young to have made his impact felt in the world (Moses, Oedipus). The miracle that fertilizes the mother and/or saves the child (as Isaac is also saved at the altar) both elevates God's role and marks the child's potential for heroism.

8. Exodus Rabbah to Exodus 1:13.

9. Ellen Frankel, *The Five Books of Miriam: A Woman's Commentary on the Torah,* p. 113.

10. I have heard anecdotally that early representations of biblical stories showing women holding round objects sometimes identify what were in all likelihood intended as ritual drums as "cakes."

11. Sources for the tradition of Miriam's well include: Babylonian Talmud, Hullin 92a, which implicitly identifies Miriam with the well; more explicitly, Mishneh Avot indicates that Miriam's well was created on the eve of the Sabbath at twilight of the week of creation; Miriam's well is also depicted among the images of the ancient synagogue at Dura Europos (destroyed in the third century).

12. Babylonian Talmud, Tractate Ta'anit, p. 9a.

13. Rivkah M. Walton, "The Rock: A Midrash on Numbers 20:1–13," *Living Text: The Journal of Contemporary Midrash,* No. 1 (July 1997): 21–22.

14. See Ilana Pardes, *The Biography of Ancient Israel.*

15. Savina J. Teubal, *Sarah the Priestess: The First Matriarch of Genesis.*

16. Pardes, *Countertraditions in the Bible,* pp. 89–93.

17. Isis is also associated with Lilith (who in some stories is also the snake in Eden). Isis, like Lilith, knows the secret divine name, which gives her power over him, and causes a snake to bite the god Ra, which renders her his near equal.

18. Babylonian Talmud, Sotah 11b.

19. Avivah Gottlieb Zornberg, *The Particulars of Rapture: Reflections on Exodus,* pp. 58–59 and 223–25.

20. Pesachim 6b.

21. These poems are both in Eleanor Wilner, *Sarah's Choice.*

CHAPTER 7

1. Riviere, "Womanliness as Masquerade."

2. I am indebted to Michelle Reimer for this observation.

3. Elaine Scarry, *The Body in Pain: The Making and Unmaking of the World*, pp. 198 ff.

4. Lori Rowlett, "Violent Femmes and S/M: Queering Samson and Delilah," in *Queer Commentary and the Hebrew Bible*, Ken Stone, ed., p. 115.

5. Genesis Rabbah 34:1.

6. Nissim Gaon to B. Berakhot, 27b.

7. Ginzberg, *The Legends of the Jews*, vol. 4, p. 37.

8. Talmud B. Yebamoth 103a–103b; and Nazir 23b–24a.

9. Talmud B. Yebamoth 65b.

10. Robert Scholes, "Uncoding Mama: The Female Body as Text," in Scholes, ed., *Semiotics and Interpretation*, p. 131.

11. Mieke Bal, *Lethal Love: Feminist Literary Readings of Biblical Love Stories*, pp. 58–67.

12. These counter-effects of carnival inversion and transgression, described by Mikhail Bakhtin in *Rabelais and His World*, are analyzed by Peter Stallybrass and Allon White in *The Politics and Poetics of Transgression*.

13. Germaine Greer, *The Obstacle Race*, p. 189.

14. B. Shabbat 23a.

15. Judah Eisenstein, ed., *Midrash Maaseh Chanukah* par. 6 in *Otzar Midrashim: A Library of Minor Midrashim* (New York: 121 Canal St., 1915), pp. 185 ff.

16. *The New Oxford Annotated Bible with Apocrypha*, revised standard edition (New York: Oxford University Press, 1977).

17. Bram Dijkstra, *Idols of Perversity: Fantasies of Feminine Evil in Fin de Siècle Culture*, pp. 374–75.

18. Dijkstra, *Idols of Perversity*, p. 374.

19. Riv-Ellen Prell, "Why Jewish Princesses Don't Sweat," in Eilberg-Schwartz, ed., *People of the Body*, pp. 329–59.

20. *Haaretz*, August 18, 1998. Writing in the *Middle-East Quarterly* (March 1999, Vol. VI, No. 1), P. R. Kumaraswamy summarized: Likud-oriented Israelis, fearing the effects of presidential pressure on their government, perceived Lewinsky in positive terms, as a modern-day Queen Esther "whose intimate relationship with the nation's rulers saves her people from a horrific fate" (cited in Jonathan Broder, "Monica Lewinsky: Bibi's Queen Esther?" *The Jerusalem Report*, February 19, 1998, pp. 34–37).

21. Riviere, p. 303.

22. Stephen Heath, "Joan Riviere and the Masquerade," in *Formations of Fantasy*, Victor Burgin, James Donald, and Cora Kaplan, eds., pp. 45–61, quotes on p. 51.

23. Juliet Mitchell, *Feminine Sexuality*, p. 24.

24. Heath, "Joan Riviere and the Masquerade," p. 54.

25. Butler, "Imitation and Gender Insubordination," p. 313.

CHAPTER 8

1. On the routine use of the body as a signifier for the body politic, see Mary Douglas, *Body Symbols: Explorations in Cosmology*, especially chapter 5 "The Two

Bodies," in which she demonstrates a relationship between the perceptions of the social and physical body and "a continual exchange of meanings between the two kinds of bodily experience so that each reinforces the categories of the other" (p. 93).

2. Sheila Delany, "'This Borrowed Language': Body Politic in Judges 19." Julia Kristeva's psychoanalytic reading of abjection and impurity in biblical legislation, including discussion of women's leprosy, takes a dispassionate view of the representation of horror. Kristeva understands biblical purity legislation and other treatments of the body as effecting a "subordination of maternal power to symbolic order," or a regulating social performance. See *Powers of Horror*, pp. 90–93; see also chapter 4, "Semiotics of Biblical Abjection."

3. Adele Reinhartz explains that the daughters' anonymity emphasizes the importance of their roles as daughters and their function in characterizing Lot, especially the conflicts for a father in his role as protector. *"Why Ask my Name?": Anonymity and Identity in Biblical Narrative*, pp. 126–32.

4. Mieke Bal, in his *Death and Dissymmetry: The Politics of Coherence in the Book of Judges*, sees a different kind of narrative functionality in the murder of the women in the book of Judges, reflecting competition among men over different marriage systems. The deaths of women are consequences of larger systemic and male conflicts.

5. Tony Kushner, *Angels in America: A Gay Fantasia on National Themes*, pp. 179 and 182.

6. Moe Meyer, ed., *The Politics and Poetics of Camp*, pp. 2–3.

7. Kenneth R. R. Gros Louis, ed., *Literary Interpretations of Biblical Narrative II*, p. 142.

8. See also, Ken Stone, "Gender and Homosexuality in Judges 19: Subject— Honor, Object—Shame."

CHAPTER 9

1. Simon Rawidowicz, *Israel: The Ever-Dying People*.

2. Avivah Zornberg, "The Concealed Alternative," in *Reading Ruth: Contemporary Women Reclaim a Sacred Story*, Judith A. Kates and Gail Twersky Reimer, eds., p. 76.

3. Zornberg, "The Concealed Alternative," p. 66.

4. Pardes, *Countertraditions in the Bible*, pp. 99 ff.

5. Marge Piercy, "The Book of Ruth and Naomi," in *Reading Ruth*, Kates and Reimer, eds., p. 159.

6. Rebecca Alpert, "Finding Our Past: A Lesbian Interpretation of the Book of Ruth," in *Reading Ruth*, Kates and Reimer, eds., p. 96.

References

Abelove, Henry, Michele Aina Barale, and David M. Halperin, eds. *The Lesbian and Gay Studies Reader*. New York: Routledge, 1993.

Adler, Rachel. *Engendering Judaism: An Inclusive Theology and Ethics*. Philadelphia: Jewish Publication Society, 1998.

Alter, Robert. *The Art of Biblical Narrative*. New York: Basic Books, 1981.

Aschkenasy, Nechama. *Eve's Journey: Feminine Images in Hebraic Literary Tradition*. Detroit: Wayne State University, 1986.

Auerbach, Erich. *Mimesis: The Representation of Reality in Western Literature*. Trans. Willard Trask. Princeton, NJ: Princeton University Press, 1974.

Auerbach, Nina. *Women and the Demon*. Cambridge: Harvard University Press, 1982.

Bach, Alice, ed. *Women in the Hebrew Bible: A Reader*. New York: Routledge, 1999.

Badinter, Elisabeth. *Mother Love: Myth and Reality, Motherhood in Modern History*. New York: Macmillan, 1981.

Bal, Mieke. *Death and Dissymmetry: The Politics of Coherence in the Book of Judges*. Chicago: Chicago University Press, 1988.

———. *Lethal Love: Feminist Literary Readings of Biblical Love Stories*. Bloomington: Indiana University Press, 1987.

Bakhtin, Mikhail. *Rabelais and His World*. Cambridge: MIT Press, 1968.

Bank, Stephen P., and Michael D. Kahn. *The Sibling Bond*. New York: Basic Books, 1982.

Barthes, Roland. *Elements of Semiology*. New York: Hill and Wang, 1967.

———. *Mythologies*. New York: Hill and Wang, 1973.

———. *S/Z*. New York: Hill and Wang, 1974.

Berger, John. *Ways of Seeing*. New York: Viking Penguin, 1973.

Beusterien, John L. "Jewish Male Menstruation in Seventeenth-Century Spain." *Bulletin of the History of Medicine* 73, No. 3 (Fall 1999): 447–456.

Bhabha, Homi K. *The Location of Culture.* New York: Routledge, 1994.

Blonsky, Marshall, ed. *On Signs.* Baltimore: Johns Hopkins University Press, 1985.

Blumenthal, Ralph. "Hotel Log Hints at Illicit Desire that Freud Didn't Repress." *New York Times,* Sunday, December 24, 2006, 1: 4.

Boyarin, Daniel. *Carnal Israel: Reading Sex in Talmudic Culture.* Berkeley: University of California Press, 1995.

——. *Intertextuality and the Reading of Midrash.* Bloomington: Indiana University Press, 1994.

——. *Unheroic Conduct: The Rise of Heterosexuality and the Invention of the Jewish Man.* Berkeley: University of California Press, 1997.

Brenner, Athalya, ed. *Feminist Companion to Exodus and Deuteronomy.* Sheffield, UK: Sheffield Academic Press, 1994.

——, ed. *Feminist Companion to Genesis.* Sheffield, UK: Sheffield Academic Press, 1993.

Brenner, Athalya, and Fokkelien Van Dijk-Hemmes. *On Gendering Texts: Female and Male Voices in the Bible.* New York: Brill, 1996.

Brettler, Mark Zvi. *How to Read the Bible.* Philadelphia: Jewish Publication Society, 2005.

Brod, Harry, ed. *A Mensch among Men: Explorations in Jewish Masculinity.* Freedom, CA: Crossing Press, 1988.

Brod, Harry, and Michael Kaufman, eds. *Theorizing Masculinities.* Thousand Oaks, CA: Sage, 1994.

Brodkin, Karen. *How Jews Became White Folks and What that Says about Race in America.* New Brunswick, NJ: Rutgers University Press, 1998.

Buber, Salomon, ed. *Midrasch: Eicha Rabbati.* Wilna: Rom, 1899.

Burgin, Victor, James Donald, and Cora Kaplan, eds. *Formations of Fantasy.* New York: Routledge, 1986.

Butler, Judith. *Bodies that Matter: On the Discursive Limits of Sex.* New York, Routledge, 1993.

——. *Gender Trouble: Feminism and the Subversion of Identity.* New York: Routledge, 1990.

Canby, Vincent. Review of *Hannah and Her Sisters. New York Times,* February 7, 1986, C4.

——. "Woody Allen Tops Himself—Again." *New York Times,* February 9, 1986, "Arts and Leisure," 23: 40.

Chametzky, Jules, John Felstiner, Hilene Flanzbaum, and Kathryn Hellerstein, eds. *Jewish American Literature: A Norton Anthology.* New York: Norton, 2001.

Cixous, Hélène. "The Laugh of the Medusa." In *New French Feminisms: An Anthology.* Eds. Elaine Marks and Isabelle de Courtivron. Amherst: University of Massachusetts Press, 1980, pp. 245–264.

Cixous, Hélène, and Catherine Clément. *The Newly Born Woman.* Trans. Betsy Wing. Minneapolis: University of Minnesota Press, 1986.

Cohen, Shaye, J. D. *Why Aren't Jewish Women Circumcised? Gender and Covenant in Judaism.* Berkeley: University of California Press, 2005.

Cominos, Peter T. "Innocent Femina Sensualis in *Unconscious Conflict.*" In *Suffer and Be Still: Women in the Victorian Age.* Ed. Martha Vicinus. Bloomington: Indiana University Press, 1972, pp. 155-172.

Cuddihy, John Murray. *The Ordeal of Civility: Freud, Marx, Lévi-Strauss and the Jewish Struggle with Modernity.* New York: Basic Books, 1974.

Culler, Jonathan. *The Pursuit of Signs: Semiotics, Literature, Deconstruction.* Ithaca, NY: Cornell University Press, 1981.

Curzon, David. *Modern Poems about the Hebrew Bible: An Anthology.* Philadelphia: Jewish Publication Society, 1994.

Dijkstra, Bram. *Idols of Perversity: Fantasies of Feminine Evil in Fin de Siècle Culture.* New York: Oxford University Press, 1986.

Delany, Sheila. "'This Borrowed Language': Body Politic in Judges 19." *Shofar* 11, No. 2 (Winter 1993): 97–109.

Dame, Enid. *Lilith and Her Demons.* New York: Stanley Barkan, 1986, 1989.

Dame, Enid, Lilly Rivlin, and Henny Wenkart, eds. *Which Lilith: Feminist Writers Re-Create the World's First Woman.* New York: Jason Aronson, 1998.

Doane, Janice, and Devon Hodges. *Nostalgia and Sexual Difference: The Resistance to Contemporary Feminism.* New York: Methuen, 1987.

Douglas, Mary. *Body Symbols: Explorations in Cosmology.* New York: Routledge, 1996; Barrie and Rockliff, 1970.

———. *Purity and Danger: An Analysis of Concepts of Pollution and Taboo.* New York: Routledge and Kegan Paul, 1966.

Dupee, F. W., ed. *The Selected Letters of Charles Dickens.* New York: Farrar, Straus, and Cudahy, 1960.

Eco, Umberto. *The Role of the Reader: Explorations in the Semiotics of Texts.* Bloomington: Indiana University Press, 1979.

———. *The Theory of Semiotics.* Bloomington: Indiana University Press, 1976.

Efron, John M. *Medicine and a History of the German Jews.* New Haven: Yale University Press, 2001.

Eilberg-Schwartz, Howard. *God's Phallus: And Other Problems for Men and Monotheism.* Boston: Beacon, 1994.

———, ed. *People of the Body: Jews and Judaism from an Embodied Perspective.* Albany: SUNY Press, 1992.

Eliot, George. *Adam Bede.* New York: Penguin, 1859 [2008].

Epstein, Julia. "Either/Or—Neither/Both: Sexual Ambiguity and the Ideology of Gender. *Genders* 7 (spring 1990): 99–142.

Epstein, Julia, and Kristina Straub, eds. *Body Guards: The Cultural Politics of Gender Ambiguity.* New York: Routledge, 1991.

Fausto-Sterling, Anne. *Myths of Gender: Biological Theories about Women and Men.* New York: Basic Books, 1985.

———. *Sexing the Body: Gender Politics and the Construction of Sexuality.* New York: Basic Books, 2000.

Foster, John. *The Life of Charles Dickens.* 2 vols. New York: Dutton, 1966.

Foucault, Michel. *The History of Sexuality Volume I: An Introduction.* New York: Random House, 1978.

———. *The Order of Things: An Archeology of the Human Sciences.* New York: Routledge, 2001.

Frankel, Ellen. *The Five Books of Miriam: A Woman's Commentary on the Torah*. New York: G. P. Putnam's, 1996.

Freedman, H., and Maurice Simon, eds. *The Midrash Rabbah*. 10 vols. London: Soncino Press, 1939, 1983.

Freud, Ernst L., ed. *Letters of Sigmund Freud*. New York: Basic Books, 1960. Introduction by Steven Marcus, 1975.

Freud, Sigmund. *The Standard Edition of the Complete Psychological Works of Sigmund Freud*. 24 volumes. Edited and trans. by James Strachey. London: Hogarth, 1953.

———. "The Head of the Medusa." In *The Standard Edition of the Complete Psychological Works of Sigmund Freud*. Trans. James Strachey. London: Hogarth, 1955.

———. "The Dissolution of the Oedipal Complex," *On Sexuality*. Vol. 7 Penguin Freud Library. Trans. James Strachey. Ed. Angela Richards. New York: Penguin, 1976, pp. 313–322.

Fromm, Erich. *Sigmund Freud's Mission: An Analysis of His Personality and Influence*. New York: Harper, 1959.

Frye, Northrop. *The Great Code: The Bible and Literature*. San Diego: Harcourt Trade, 2002.

Fuchs, Esther. *Sexual Politics in the Biblical Narrative: Reading the Hebrew Bible as a Woman*. Sheffield, UK: Sheffield Academic Press, 2000.

Fuss, Diana. "Reading like a feminist," *differences* 1, No. 2 (1989), 77–92.

Gay, Peter. *Freud: A Life for Our Time*. New York: W. W. Norton, 1988.

———. "Sigmund and Minna? The Biographer as Voyeur." *New York Times Book Review*, January 29, 1989, 1: 43-45.

Gilligan, Carol. *In a Different Voice: Psychological Theory and Women's Development*. Cambridge: Harvard University Press, 1973, 1993.

Gilman, Sander. *Jewish Frontiers: Essays on Bodies, Histories, and Identities*. New York: Palgrave Macmillan, 2003.

———. *Jewish Self-Hatred: Anti-Semitism and the Hidden Language of the Jews*. Baltimore: Johns Hopkins University Press, 1986.

———. *The Jew's Body*. New York: Routledge, 1991.

Ginzberg, Louis. *The Legends of the Jews*. Philadelphia: Jewish Publication Society, 1974.

Gombrich, E. H. *Art and Illusion: A Study in the Psychology of Pictorial Representation*. Princeton, NJ: Bollingen, 1969.

Graetz, Naomi. *S/he Created Them: Feminist Retellings of Biblical Stories*. Piscataway, NJ: Gorgias Press, 2003.

Greer, Germaine. *The Obstacle Race*. New York: Farrar, Straus, and Giroux, 1979.

Hart, Mitchell B. *Social Science and the Politics of Modern Jewish Identity*. Stanford, CA: Stanford University Press, 2000.

Heschel, Susannah, ed. *On Being a Jewish Feminist*. New York: Schocken, 1983.

Hyde, Lewis. *Trickster Makes the World: Mischief, Myth, and Art*. New York: Farrar, Straus, and Giroux, 1998.

Irigaray, Luce. *Speculum of the Other Woman*. Trans. Gilian Gill. Ithaca, NY: Cornell University Press, 1985.

Johnson, Edgar. *Charles Dickens: His Tragedy and Triumph*. 2 vols. New York: Simon and Schuster, 1952.

Jones, Ernest. *Sigmund Freud: Life and Work*. London: Hogarth Press, 1955.

Josephus. Vol. 4. Edited by H. St. J. Thackeray and P. Marcus. Cambridge, MA: Loeb Classic Library, 1926–1965.

Kaplan, Fred. *Dickens: A Biography*. New York: William Morrow, 1988.

———. "The Real Charles Dickens, or the Old Animosity Shop." *New York Times Book Review*, October 9, 1988, 5-16.

Kates, Judith, and Gail Twersky Reimer. *Reading Ruth: Contemporary Women Reclaim a Sacred Story*. New York: Ballantine, 1996.

Kaufman, Gershen. *The Psychology of Shame: Theory and Treatment of Shame-Based Syndromes*. New York: Springer, 1989, 1996.

Kierkegaard, Soren. *Fear and Trembling*. New York: Penguin, 1985.

Koltun, Elizabeth, ed. *The Jewish Woman*. New York: Schocken, 1976.

Kristeva, Julia. *Desire in Language: A Semiotic Approach to Literature and Art*. New York: Columbia University Press, 1980.

———. *Powers of Horror: An Essay on Abjection*. New York: Columbia University Press, 1982.

Kushner, Tony. *Angels in America: A Gay Fantasia on National Themes*. New York: Theater Communications Group, 1995.

Lacan, Jacques. "Au-delà du 'principe de réalité.'" 1936. In *Écrits*. Paris: Seuil, 1966, 73–92.

Laqueur, Thomas. *Making Sex: Body and Gender from the Greeks to Freud*. Cambridge: Harvard University Press, 1990.

Lather, Patti. *Getting Smart: Feminist Research and Pedagogy With/in the Postmodern*. New York: Routledge, 1991.

Lefkovitz, Lori Hope. "Creating the World: Structuralism and Semiotics." *Contemporary Critical Theory*. Eds. Douglas Atkins and Laura Marrow. Amherst: University of Massachusetts Press, 1989.

———. "Coats and Tales: Joseph Stories and Myths of Jewish Masculinity." *A Mensch Among Men: Explorations in Jewish Masculinity*. Ed. Harry Brod. Freedom, CA: Crossing Press, 1988.

———. "Eavesdropping on Angels and Laughing at God: Theorizing a Subversive Matriarchy." In *Gender and Judaism: The Transformation of Tradition*. Ed. T. M. Rudavsky. New York: New York University Press, 1995.

———, ed. *Textual Bodies: Changing Boundaries of Literary Representation*. Albany: SUNY Press, 1997.

Lerner, Ann Lapidus. *Eternally Eve: Images of Eve in the Hebrew Bible, Midrash, and Modern Jewish Poetry*. Waltham, MA: Brandeis University Press, 2007.

Louis, Kenneth R. R. Gros, ed. *Literary Interpretations of Biblical Narrative II*. Nashville: Abington, 1982.

Lovejoy, Arthur O. *The Great Chain of Being: A Study of the History of an Idea*. Cambridge: Harvard University Press, 1936, 1964.

MacKenzie, Norman, and Jeanne MacKenzie. *Dickens: A Life*. New York: Oxford University Press, 1979.

Mann, Thomas. *Joseph and His Brothers*. Trans. H. T. Lowe-Porter. New York: Alfred A. Knopf, 1936.

Mathias, Barbara. *Between Sisters: Secret Rivals, Intimate Friends*. New York: Delacorte Press, 1992.

Meyer, Moe, ed. *The Politics and Poetics of Camp*. New York: Routledge, 1994.

Meyers, Carol L. *Discovering Eve: Ancient Israelite Women in Context*. New York: Oxford University Press, 1988.

Millet, Kate. *Sexual Politics*. New York: Ballantine, 1989.

Milton, John. *Complete Poems and Major Prose*. Edited by Merritt Y. Hughes. New York: Prentice Hall, 1957.

Mishima, Yukio [Kimitake Hirakoa]. *Madame de Sade*. Trans. Donald Keene. New York: Grove Press, 1967; first Japanese publication, 1965.

Mitchell, Juliet and Jacqueline Rose, eds. [trans] *Feminine Sexuality*. New York: Norton, 1966 [1985].

Ostriker, Alicia. *The Nakedness of the Fathers: Biblical Visions and Revisions*. New Brunswick: Rutgers University Press, 1994.

Pardes, Ilana. *The Biography of Ancient Israel: National Narratives in the Bible*. Los Angeles: University of California Press, 2000.

———. *Countertraditions in the Bible: A Feminist Approach*. Cambridge: Harvard University Press, 1992.

Peskowitz, Miriam, and Laura Levitt, eds. *Judaism Since Gender*. New York: Routledge, 1997.

Phillip, John A. *Eve: The History of an Idea*. San Francisco: Harper and Row, 1984.

Philo. Vol. 1. *Allegorical Interpretations of Genesis*. Cambridge, MA: Loeb Classical Library, 1991.

Pitzele, Peter. *Our Fathers' Wells: A Personal Encounter with the Myths of Genesis*. New York: HarperCollins, 1996.

Plaskow, Judith. *Standing Again at Sinai: Judaism from a Feminist Perspective*. New York: HarperCollins, 1990.

Raglan, Lord. *The Hero: A Study in Tradition, Myth, and Drama*. New York: Methuen, 1936.

Rambuss, Richard. *Spenser's Secret Career*. Cambridge: Cambridge University Press, 1993.

Rawidowicz, Simon. *Israel: The Ever-Dying People*. Rutherford, NJ: Fairleigh Dickinson University Press, 1986.

Reinhartz, Adele. *"Why Ask My Name?": Anonymity and Identity in Biblical Narrative*. New York: Oxford University Press, 1998.

Riley, Denise. *"Am I That Name"?: Feminism and the Category of Women in History*. Minneapolis: University of Minnesota Press, 1989.

Riviere, Joan. "Womanliness as a Masquerade." *International Journal of Psychoanalysis* 10 (1929): 303–313.

Roth, Philip. *Portnoy's Complaint*. New York: Random House, 1969.

Rudavsky, T. M., ed. *Gender and Judaism: The Transformation of Tradition*. New York: New York University Press, 1995.

Russell, Letty M., ed. *Feminist Interpretations of the Bible*. Philadelphia: Westminster, 1995.

Ruttenberg, Danya. *Yentl's Revenge: The Next Wave of Jewish Feminism*. Seattle: Seal Press, 2001.

Said, Edward W. *Beginnings: Intention and Method*. New York: Columbia University Press, 1975, 1985.

Scarry, Elaine. *The Body in Pain: The Making and Unmaking of the World.* New York: Oxford University Press, 1985.

Schiff, Isaac, and Morty Schiff. "The Biblical Diagnostician and the Anorexic Bride." *Fertility and Sterility* 69 No. 1 (January 1998): 8–10.

Scholes, Robert. *Semiotics and Interpretation.* New Haven, CT: Yale University Press, 1982.

Schwartz, Howard, Caren Loebel-Fried, Elliot K. Ginsburg. *Tree of Souls: The Mythology of Judaism.* New York: Oxford University Press, 2004.

Sedgwick, Eve Kosofsky. *Between Men: English Literature and Male Homosocial Desire.* New York: Columbia University Press, 1985.

———. *Epistemology of the Closet.* Berkeley: University of California Press, 1990.

Smith, Barbara Herrnstein. *Poetic Closure: A Study of How Poems End.* Chicago: University of Chicago Press, 1968.

Stallybrass, Peter, and Allon White. *The Politics and Poetics of Transgression.* Ithaca, NY: Cornell University Press, 1986.

Sternberg, Meir. *The Poetics of Biblical Narrative: Ideological Literature and the Drama of Reading.* Bloomington: Indiana University Press, 1985.

Stone, Ken. "Gender and Homosexuality in Judges 19: Subject—Honor, Object—Shame," *Journal for the Study of the Old Testament* 20, No. 67 (1995): 87–107.

———, ed. *Queer Commentary and the Hebrew Bible.* New York: Sheffield Academic Press, 2001.

Tanakh: The Holy Scriptures. The New JPS Translation. Philadelphia: Jewish Publication Society, 1985.

Tanner, Tony. *Jane Austen.* Cambridge, MA: Harvard University Press, 1986.

Taylor, Charles. *Sources of the Self: The Making of the Modern Identity.* Cambridge: Harvard University Press, 1989.

Teubal, Savina J. *Sarah the Priestess: The First Matriarch of Genesis.* Columbus, OH: Swallow Press, 1984.

Thackeray, H. St. J., and P. Marcus, eds., *Josephus,* vol. 4, Cambridge, MA: Loeb Classic Library, 1926–1965.

Trible, Phyllis. *God and the Rhetoric of Sexuality.* Philadelphia: Fortress Press, 1978.

Wander, Nathaniel. "Structure, Contradiction and 'Resolution' in Mythology: Father's Brother's Daughter Marriage and the Treatment of Women in Genesis 11-50." *JANESCU* 13 (1981): 75–99.

Weininger, Otto. *Sex and Character.* Whitefish, MT: Kessinger Publishing, LLC, 1903 [2006].

Wenkart, Henny, ed. *Sarah's Daughters Sing: A Sampler of Poems by Jewish Women.* Hoboken: KTAV, 1990.

Wilner, Eleanor. *Sarah's Choice.* Chicago: University of Chicago Press, 1989.

Yeats, William Butler. *The Collected Poems of W. B. Yeats.* New York: Simon and Schuster, 1996.

Yee, Gale A. *Poor Banished Children of Eve: Woman as Evil in the Hebrew Bible.* Minneapolis: Fortress Press, 2003.

Zones, Jane Sprague. *Taking the Fruit: Modern Women's Tales of the Bible.* San Diego: Women's Institute for Continuing Jewish Education, 1991.

Zornberg, Avivah Gottlieb. *Genesis: The Beginning of Desire*. Philadelphia: Jewish Publication Society, 1995.

———. *The Murmuring Deep: Reflections on the Biblical Unconscious*. New York: Schocken, 2009.

———. *The Particulars of Rapture: Reflections on Exodus*. New York: Random House, 2002.

Index

About the Author

Lori Hope Lefkovitz holds the Sadie Gottesman and Arlene Gottesman Reff Chair in Gender and Judaism at the Reconstructionist Rabbinical College, where she founded and directs Kolot: The Center for Jewish Women's and Gender Studies. Under Kolot's auspices, she serves as executive editor of the web resource www.ritualwell.org.

A graduate of Brandeis University with a PhD in English from Brown University, Lefkovitz has been a Fulbright Professor at Hebrew University of Jerusalem, an associate professor at Kenyon College, and a postdoctoral fellow at the Philadelphia Association for Psychoanalysis. She is author of *The Character of Beauty in the Victorian Novel*, editor of *Textual Bodies: Changing Boundaries of Literary Representation*, and coeditor (with Julia Epstein) of *Shaping Losses: Cultural Memory and the Holocaust*. She lives in Philadelphia with husband Leonard Gordon, and they have two magnificent daughters.